201 JAPANESE VERBS
FULLY DESCRIBED
IN ALL INFLECTIONS
MOODS, ASPECTS AND
FORMALITY LEVELS

by

Roland A. Lange, Ph. D.

**Assistant Professor of Japanese
Language and Linguistics
Columbia University, New York**

BARRON'S EDUCATIONAL SERIES, Inc.
Woodbury, New York • London • Toronto • Sydney

CONTENTS

INTRODUCTION

IN ORDER TO LEARN A FOREIGN LANGUAGE efficiently the student must follow a series of organized, graded lessons which cover the essential points of grammar, pronunciation, and vocabulary. He must not only *study* such material to learn new words and grammatical constructions, but also *practice* what he has already learned in drill sessions with native speakers of the language. There are a number of textbooks designed to give that sort of well rounded introduction to Japanese. (One which has especially complete notes on grammar and usage is Eleanor Jorden's *Beginning Japanese.*)

This handbook of Japanese verbs is not designed to provide the student with a complete course in Japanese. Rather it is a reference work which gives a concise, easy-to-understand description of Japanese verbal inflection and derivation together with tables showing all the necessary forms of 201 of the most important and widely used Japanese verbs.

Since there is currently no other text which specializes in the Japanese verb, *201 Japanese Verbs* should be of help to both beginning and advanced students. For the beginner it constitutes a valuable aid in learning basic inflection of the verb. Most textbooks only provide the student with a few examples to illustrate the principles of inflection. This means that the student is hampered in writing compositions or drilling with other students because he has no way in which to check a given form of an unfamiliar verb to see if he is correct. With *201 Japanese Verbs* the student will be able to quickly verify the form he is interested in. By presenting the full array of verbal inflection and derivation in tables this book also enables the beginning student to see the language as a system rather than as a haphazard collection of stems and endings.

The more advanced student will profit from this systematic view of the language too, because it will help him to organize the many inflected forms which he has learned into a systematic body of data. Such formalization of knowledge is especially necessary for anyone who plans to teach the language some day.

PRONUNCIATION

A detailed treatment of the Japanese sound system is beyond the scope of this work, but it is necessary to give some explanation of the value of the letters used in our romanization (which is similar to that employed in Bloch and Jorden's *Spoken Japanese*). In the following explanation italics represent our romanization while English sounds and words used as examples are enclosed in single quotation marks. (A more extensive description of Japanese pronunciation which includes a section on pitch accent is available on pages xxi to xiv of part 1 of *Beginning Japanese*.)

I VOWELS

Symbol	Nearest American English Equivalent		
a	'o'	in	'cot'
i	'ee'	in	'steep'
u	'u'	in	'put'
e	'e'	in	'pet'
o	'o'	in	'post'

NOTE: All *Japanese vowels* are short and tense in comparison with their *English equivalents*. In Japanese the lips are not rounded and the vowels do not glide off into dipthongs.

II CONSONANTS

Symbol		Nearest American English Equivalent			Special Remarks
k	before *k*	'ck'	in	'sick-call'	held for full beat*
g	before vowels	'k'	in	'kangaroo'	
	as word initial	'g'	in	'goat'	
	elsewhere	'g'	in	'goat' or	
		'ng'	in	'singer'	
s	before *s*	'ss'	in	'grass-skirt'	full beat*
	before *i*	'sh'	in	'sheep'	further forward in mouth than English sound
	before *a, e, o, u*	's'	in	'sip'	
z	before *i*	'j'	in	'jest'	further forward
	before *a, e, o, u*	'z'	in	'zest'	further forward

II CONSONANTS (Continued)

t	before *t*	't-'	in	'hot-toddy'	full beat*
	before *i*	'ch'	in	'cheat'	tongue touches
	before *u*	'ts'	in	'tsetse fly'	teeth
	before *a, e, o*	't'	in	'teen'	tongue touches
d		'd'	in	'deep'	teeth
n		'n'	in	'cone'	tongue touches teeth
n̄	before *k, g*	'n'	in	'angle'	full beat*
	before *p, b, m*	'm'	in	'mine'	full beat*
	elsewhere	'n'	in	'pun'	full beat*
h	before *a, e, o*	'h'	in	'holly'	
	before *i*	'h'	in	'heap'	with more friction
	before *u*	'wh'	in	'whom'	made by puffing air between lips
p	before *p*	'p-'	in	'hip-pocket'	full beat*
	elsewhere	'p'	in	'compare'	
b		'b'	in	'combine'	
m		'm'	in	'mince'	
w		'w'	in	'went'	
y		'y'	in	'yacht'	
r		no American equivalent but similar to the 'r' of 'very' in clipped British pronunciation.			made by single flip of tongue tip against ridge behind teeth.

*See description of the Japanese syllable below.

III CONSONANT CLUSTERS

Symbol	Nearest American English Equivalent		
ky	'c'	in	'curious'
gy	'g'	in	'angular'
sy	'sh'	in	'sheep'
zy	'j'	in	'jest'
ty	'ch'	in	'cheer'
ny	'n'	in	'menu'

III CONSONANTS (Continued)

hy	'H' in 'Hubert' (in those American dialects in which the 'H' is not silent)
py	'p' in 'pure'
by	'b' in 'bureau'
my	'm' in 'amuse'
ry	flapped 'r' followed by palatalization.

The Japanese equivalent of the English syllable is not really a syllable but a mora, a unit of relative meter like a beat in music. People may speak quickly or slowly, but within a given stream of speech each mora will occupy the same length of time. This is true regardless of the type or number of sounds which make up each mora. For instance, the five words

sa.ku.ra	'cherry'
a.o.i	'blue'
hi.n̄.i	'quality'
ki.p.pu	'ticket'
ryo.ka.n̄	'inn'

each consist of three mora (with the division indicated by dots) and each takes the same length of time to say. These examples serve to illustrate all the possible mora types in Japanese: a single vowel, a vowel preceded by a single consonant, a vowel preceded by a cluster of consonant plus *y*, and a single consonant. Only five consonants occur as independent mora: *k* (only before *k*), *s* (only before *s*), *t* (only before *t*), *p* (only before *p*), and *n̄* (in all occurrences).

The system of syllable division in Japanese can be summed up in two simple rules:

1. *THERE IS NEVER MORE THAN ONE VOWEL IN A SYLLABLE.* This holds true whether the vowels are of the same type or of different types. A word like *oi* 'nephew' is pronounced as *o + i*, not as the 'oy' in the English word 'boy.' A word like *yooi* 'preparation' is pronounced as *yo + o + i*. In some romanization systems two *o*, *a*, or *u* which occur in juxtaposition are treated as a single 'long vowel' and are written as *ō*, *ā*, and *ū* respectively. In this book, however, they are written as *oo*, *aa*, and *uu*.

2. *EXCEPT FOR THOSE CONSONANTS WHICH OCCUR AS INDEPENDENT MORA* (n̄ in all occurrences and *k, s, t* and *p* before themselves) *CONSONANTS ARE ALWAYS PRONOUNCED WITH THE VOWELS WHICH COME AFTER THEM.* Thus the words *ben̄kyoo* 'study', *han̄noo* 'reaction', and *hakkiri* 'clearly' are pronounced as *be·n̄·kyo·o, ha·n̄·no·o,* and *ha·k·ki·ri.*

Japanese does not have a stress accent like that of English in which some syllables of a word are given special prominence by being pronounced louder than others. Instead, Japanese has a pitch accent system. This means that syllables are all pronounced with about the same force (giving a rather monotonous impression to the stress accent oriented American) but some are pronounced on a higher pitch than others. In order to keep the romanization simple we have not indicated the pitch accent, but the pitch accent for the citation form of verbs can be found in *Kenkyusha's New Japanese-English Dictionary.* Information on the patterns of Japanese pitch accent in inflected words may be found in Appendix I of Jorden's *Beginning Japanese.*

SPEECH LEVELS

Languages are arbitrary systems used for communication within the societies which develop them. Since societies differ in their view of the world, one can expect that languages will differ not only in vocabulary and pronunciation, but also in their fundamental grammatical categories. When a native speaker of English confronts the Japanese verb this expectation is fully borne out. Instead of the familiar (to him) distinctions involving number and person, he finds distinctions between levels of formality and deference which serve to indicate the speaker's relationship to the person he is speaking to or about.

The proper use of these grammatical categories requires keen judgment as to the relative social status of speaker and listener and whether an occasion or relationship is formal or informal. These judgments must be in line with *JAPANESE* social views, and so the student's success or failure will depend upon his knowledge of Japanese social custom. Within the scope of this book we can only give some explanation as to the working of these categories as a linguistic system.

FORMALITY

The two sentences *Otya o nonda.* and *Otya o nomimasita.* both mean

'I (you, he, she, it, we, or they) drank tea,' but the second is more formal (and polite) than the first. While the more formal sentence with *nomimasita* could be used under any circumstances without giving offence, a Japanese would use the sentence with *noṅda only on informal occasions when speaking to persons of lower social status or to persons of the same status with whom he was on close terms such as members of his immediate family or close friends at school.* While informal and formal sentences are used by both men and women, in general, women's speech tends to be even more formal and polite than that of men. (Women also make greater use of the honorific and humble deference levels explained later in the text.)

The style of speech is kept uniform throughout a conversation and is determined by the form of the final verb, adjective, or copula in a sentence. It is this which expresses the general tone of the occasion and of *the relationship between the speaker and the person spoken to.* Since it is the final verb (adjective or copula) which sets the style, other verbs (adjectives or copula) which may occur earlier in the sentence are usually of the shorter informal type even in formal speech. For example, the sentence *Kare ga otya o noṅda kara, watakusi mo nomimasita.* 'He drank tea, so I drank tea too.' is in the formal style even though it contains the informal *noṅda. Students must be familiar with both forms of the verb but should use only the formal sentence style* until long residence in Japan has taught them when the informal style can be used without offending the person spoken to.

DEFERENCE

While the formality style expresses the speaker's attitude toward *the person he is speaking to,* the deference level expresses the speaker's attitude toward *the person he is speaking about.* As far as verbs are concerned the deference level shows the speaker's attitude toward the subject of the verb. There are three basic levels: honorific, plain or neutral, and humble when the subject is a person, and another 'neutral-polite' category which is used when the subject is inanimate. The plain level is the most common, with the honorific and humble levels being used when the speaker wishes to express special deference toward someone. The categories of formality and deference operate independently of each other so that each verb form can be classified according to both systems as in the following table which shows a partial paradigm of the verb *kaku* 'to write.'

	INFORMAL	FORMAL
Honorific	okaki ni naru	okaki ni narimasu
Neutral	kaku	kakimasu
Humble	okaki suru	okakisimasu
	okaki itasu	okakiitasimasu

In addition to indicating respect, the use of the humble or honorific level serves to vaguely identify the subject because one never uses the honorific to refer to oneself, nor the humble to refer to the person one is speaking to.* So while *kakimasu* could mean 'I (you, he, she, it, we, or they) write.' *okaki ni narimasu* could not mean 'I (or we) write.' nor could *okaki simasu* mean 'You write.' In the absence of other context the honorific level will refer to an action of the listener, and the humble level will refer to an action of the speaker.

As with the category of formality, the best guide to proper use of deference levels is a thorough knowledge of Japanese social custom. Until the student gains this he can follow the general principle that honorifics are used most often in reference to actions performed by the listener or members of his family, and humble forms are used most often in referring to actions performed by the speaker.

*An exception to this is the humble presumptive in which the person spoken to is sometimes covered in an inclusive 'we.' For example, *Hune de ikimasyoo ka* may mean 'Shall we (you and I) go by ship?'

INFLECTION AND DERIVATION OF JAPANESE VERBS

Japanese has two main classes of verbs: those with stems ending in *i* or *e* and those whose stems end in consonants. We shall call them Class I and II respectively. The following is a list of basic inflectional endings (informal) using *ake.ru* 'open' and *kat.u* 'win' as examples. Here the dot shows the division between stem and ending, but it will also be used at times to mark the division between the infinitive of a verb and an infinitive-based ending.

	Class I	Class II
Infinitive	ake	kat.i
Indicative	ake.ru	kat.u
Imperative I*	ake.ro	kat.e
Presumptive	ake.yoo	kat.oo
Provisional	ake.reba	kat.eba
Gerund	ake.te	kat.te
Past Indicative	ake.ta	kat.ta

Past Presumptive	ake.taroo	kat.taroo
Conditional	ake.tara	kat.tara
Alternative	ake.tari	kat.tari

*This form is used only by male speakers when speaking harshly. Otherwise it is replaced by more polite informal imperative expressions. Two common ones which we will label informal imperatives II and III are infinitive + *nasai* (imperative of *nasar.u* 'to do') and gerund + kudasai (imperative of *kudasar.u* 'give to me'). Of these the second is the more polite and is the one preferred for general use in making requests.

Comparing the endings for the two verb classes we find that in the last five categories they are the same (-*te*, -*ta*, -*taroo*, -*tara*, and -*tari*) but in the first five categories they differ as follows:

	Class I	Class II
Infinitive	-zero	-i
Indicative	-ru	-u
Imperative	-ro	-e
Presumptive	-yoo	-oo
Provisional	-reba	-eba

Except for the discrepancy between the vowels in the two imperative endings, the differences between the endings can be accounted for by a rule to the effect that the initial vowel of a suffix is lost when the stem ends in a vowel (Class I), and the initial consonant of a suffix is lost when the stem ends in a consonant (Class II). For example, *kat-* + -*i* = *kat.i*, but *ake-* + -*i* = *ake*; while *ake-* + -*ru* = *ake.ru*, but *kat-* + -*ru* = *kat.u*.

Turning now to the verb stems we find that both Class I *ake-* and Class II *kat-* remain constant throughout the ten categories. This behavior is typical of Class I verb stems, but not of Class II verb stems. *All Class II verb stems which do not end in -t- undergo a change when attached directly to one of the five suffixes which begin with -t- (-te, -ta, -taroo, -tara, and -tari).*

These changes differ according to the final consonant of the stem, but all Class II stems which end in the same consonant undergo the same change. All of the possible changes are illustrated in the following list of examples. (-*te* is used as an example, but the change would be the same before any of the other four -*t*- endings.)

kas- + -te	becomes kasi.te	(kas.u 'lend')
kak- + -te	becomes kai.te	(kak.u 'write')
kag- + -te	becomes kai.de	(kag.u 'sniff')
yob- + -te	becomes yoñ.de	(yob.u 'call')
yom- + -te	becomes yoñ.de	(yom.u 'read')
sin- + -te	becomes siñ.de	(sin.u 'die')
kar- + -te	becomes kat.te	(kar.u 'cut')
kaw- + -te	becomes kat.te	(ka(w).u 'buy')*

*Since in Japanese *w* only occurs before *a*, Class II verbs whose stems end in this sound do not show it in all forms of the verb, but only when the suffix begins with *a*.

This concludes our outline of inflection, but Japanese verbs have many more forms which are the result of derivation or the addition of various auxiliary endings. Up until now we have considered only informal affirmative forms. Our next step is to cover the formal affirmative which in both verb classes is derived by ending the auxiliary verb *-mas.u* to the infinitive of the original verb. *-mas-u* occurs only as an ending for other verbs and has no substantive meaning of its own, serving only to raise the level of formality of the verb to which it is attached.

In general *-mas.u* behaves like a Class II verb, but it lacks an infinitive, has dual forms in the provisional, and has a Class I-type ending *-yoo* in the presumptive.

Indicative	-mas.u
Imperative	-mas.e
Presumptive	-mas.yoo
Provisional	-mas.eba / -mas.ureba
Gerund	-masi.te
Past Indicative	-masi.ta
Past Presumptive	-masi.taroo
Conditional	-masi.tara
Alternative	-masi.tari

All of these forms except the presumptive and the past and non-past indicative indicate a higher than normal level of formality or politeness. As a rule the imperative *-mas.e* is only used with honorific verbs such as *nasar.u* 'to do,' and *kudasar.u* 'give to me.' In the past presumptive the infinitive + *masi.taroo* is usually replaced by a combination of the informal past indicative + *des.yoo* (the formal presumptive form of the copula). A similar construction using *des.yoo* is also used in the non-past presumptive category. This differs from the -*mas.yoo* form not in degree of formality, but in the identity of the subject and other modal content. Consequently the -*mas.yoo* form and the informal indicative + *des.yoo* form will be labeled presumptive I and II respectively. The two forms using *des.yoo* are paralleled by informal ones using *dar.oo* the informal presumptive form of the copula.

We are now ready to move to the informal negative category. Here we find that, except for the imperative and presumptive, the "verb" is really an adjective derived by adding the adjectival ending -*ana.i* 'negative' to the stem of the verb. The resulting negative adjective then inflects like any other adjective. It will be noted that our earlier juncture rule works for -*ana.i* too because the initial vowel -*a*- is lost when it is joined to a Class I stem ending in a vowel.

		Class I	Class II
Indicative		ake.nai	kat.anai
Imperative	I	ake.ru na	kat.u na
	II	ake.nasaru na	kati.nasaru na
	III	ake.nai de kudasai	kat.anai de kudasai
Presumptive	I	ake.mai	kat.umai
	II	ake.nai daroo	kat.anai daroo
Provisional		ake.nakereba	kat.anakereba
Gerund	I	ake.nai de	kat.anai de
	*II	ake.nakute	kat.anakute
Past Indicative		ake.nakatta	kat.anakatta
Past Presumptive		ake.nakattaroo	kat.anakattaroo
		ake.nakatta daroo	kat.anakatta daroo
Conditional		ake.nakattara	kat.anakattara
Alternative		ake.nakattari	kat.anakattari

Here we find three informal imperative constructions corresponding to those mentioned in connection with the informal affirmative imperative. The *'na'* used to form the negative imperative I is a negative command particle.

In the formal negative category we find the -*mas.u* ending again as well as various compounds using the copula.

*While gerund I has the same range of uses as the affirmative gerund, the negative gerund II is more limited. It is not used with auxilliary 'giving' verbs to form polite request or polite command constructions such as negative imperative III.

	Class I	Class II
Indicative	ake.masen̄	kati.masen̄
Imperative	oake nasaimasu na	okati nasaimasu na
Presumptive I	ake.masumai	kati.masumai
II	ake.nai desyoo	kat.anai desyoo
Provisional*	ake-masen̄ nara(ba)	kati.masen̄ nara(ba)
Gerund	ake.masen̄ de	kati.masen̄ de
Past Indicative	ake.masen̄ desita	kati.masen̄ desita
Past Presumptive	ake.masen̄ desitaroo	kati.masen̄ desitaroo
	ake.nakatta desyoo	kat.anakatta desyoo
Conditional	ake.masen̄ desitara	kati.masen̄ desitara
Alternative	ake.masen̄ desitari	kati.masen̄ desitari

The semantic difference between the presumptive I and II is the same as that between the two forms of the affirmative formal presumptive. The imperative, gerund, and alternative forms given here occur only in conjunction with honorifics or when using a very formal style.

Up till now we have dealt with derivational endings such as -mas.u and -ana.i which have a range of inflection only within a given category such as 'formal' or 'informal negative.' *The remaining derivations are different in that they result in new verbs which can themselves take the entire range of inflectional and derivational endings which we have described up to this point.* (See pages 149 and 187 for examples.)

First we will consider the derivation of the passive, potential, causative, and causative passive forms. Since the inflectional endings for these newly derived verbs will be the same as those we have already given for Class I verbs we will show only their informal affirmative indicative (citation) form in the tables which follow.

	(Original) Class I	(Original) Class II
Passive	ake.rareru	kat.areru
Potential	ake.rareru	kat.eru
Causative	ake.saseru	kat.aseru
Causative Passive	ake.saserareru	kat.aserareru

*Of the two possible provisional forms of the copula: *nara* and *naraba*, the shorter version is used more often in colloquial conversation and is the one we shall use hereinafter in our tables.

Since the newly formed verbs belong to Class I the division between stem and ending of the passive would be *akerare.ru* and *katare.ru* and so forth. It will be noted that the chief difference between the derivation in original Class I and Class II verbs is that original Class II verbs end up with a separate form for the passive and potential while original Class I verbs use the same derived form for both of these categories. In addition to the causative passive endings shown above (*-saserareru* and *-aserareru*) there are non-standard shorter endings *-sasareru* and *-asareru* which have the same meaning. We will not include these in the tables in the main body of the text, but they would be used with any verb which takes the longer forms.

The last two categories are the honorific and humble. Two forms are given for each, the second being that which shows the higher level of deference on the part of the speaker. Here, once again, we are dealing with completely new verbs so we present only their citation forms.

		Class I	Class II
Honorific	I	oake ni naru	okati ni naru
	II	oake nasaru	okati nasaru
Humble	I	oake suru	okati suru
	II	oake itasu	okati itasu

This table shows the typical derivation of honorific and humble forms wherein the infinitive of the original verb becomes a noun by the addition of the prefix *o-* and the inflectional endings are provided by the verbs *nar.u* ('to become'), *nasar.u*, *su.ru* and *itas.u* (all 'to do'). Of these *nar.u* and *itas.u* are Class II verbs but *su.ru* and *nasar.u* are irregular. The student should consult the appropriate tables in the main body of the text to find out the inflectional forms of these two verbs as well as those of the seven other irregular verbs *ar.u*, *gozar.u*, *ik.u*, *irassyar.u*, *kudasar.u*, *ku.ru*, and *ossyar.u*.

In the honorific and humble categories a number of common verbs do not follow the typical pattern, but instead use suppletive forms which are not derived from the original verb. For instance, the verbs *nasar.u* and *itas.u* encountered above are, respectively, honorific and humble equivalents of the verb *su.ru*. Normally in such a case there will be only one form each for the honorific and humble categories.

Next we will present tables for the verbs *ake.ru* and *kat.u* showing all of the inflectional and derivational categories which we have discussed. The form of these tables is the same as that which will be used throughout the main body of our text. (There is no standard arrangement or list of categories in use for teaching Japanese. The names for the ten basic inflectional categories have been taken from Bloch's study on inflection, but the content and arrangement of the tables in this book represent the author's opinion as to the most important forms of the Japanese verb and the most convenient arrangement for their presentation.) In order to assist the student in learning the distinctions between these verb forms the Japanese tables are followed by a chart containing English translations of each form of *ake.ru*. But before we proceed to these tables two forms of the verb — the infinitive and the informal affirmative gerund — demand some additional comment.

THE INFINITIVE

The infinitive is the form of the verb which is used in making compound words. We have already seen how the addition of the prefix *o-* 'deference' changes an infinitive into a noun. There are, in addition, a number of nouns which are added to the end of infinitives to form compound nouns. For instance *kata* 'method' and *te* 'hand, doer,' when added to the infinitive of *kak.u* 'to write' give *kakikata* 'way of writing,' and *kakite* 'one who writes.'

To form an adjective from the infinitive one simply adds one of a number of adjectival endings. The most important endings of this type are *-ta.i* 'desiderative', *-yasu.i* 'easy', and *-niku.i* 'difficult.' By attaching these endings to *kaki* one gets *kakitai, kakiyasui, and kakinikui* which mean respectively 'want to write,' 'easy to write,' and 'difficult to write.' There are also many verbs which are attached to the infinitives of other verbs to make compound verbs. We have already encountered *-mas.u* which is by far the most common. Three other of the more important ones are *-tagar.u* 'desiderative' (which like *-mas.u* occurs only as an ending for compounds), *-hazime.ru* 'to begin,' and *-naos.u* 'to repair or fix.' If we add these to *kaki* we get three new verbs: *kakitagaru* 'to wish to write,' *kakihazimeru* 'to begin to write,' and *kakinaosu* 'to rewrite.'

INFORMAL AFFIRMATIVE GERUND

This is the form which is used when a verb occurs before another verb to indicate two actions taking place in chronological sequence as in *akete kimasu*. 'I (or someone else) will open it and come back.' While any two verbs may be used in sequence if their combined meanings make sense, certain combinations which occur frequently have taken on special fixed meanings. The most important of these is the combination of (informal affirmative) gerund plus *i.ru* 'existence verb.' Generally speaking, when the gerund of a transitive verb is used with *i.ru* the combination shows continuing action as in the English progressive, but when the gerund of an intransitive verb is used the combination shows the existence of a continuing state. A good example of this contrast is seen in comparing combinations using the gerunds of two verbs which mean 'to open.' *Ake.ru* is transitive and would be used to convey such information as 'I opened the door,' *ak.u* is intransitive and is used to convey such information as 'The door opened.' The transitive gerund *akete* plus *i.ru* means 'I (or someone else) am opening it.' On the other hand, *aite iru* from *ak.u* means 'It is (in the state of being) open,' NOT 'It is opening.'

Other productive gerund-verb combinations are those in which the gerund precedes *sima.u* 'to finish,' *ok.u* 'to put or place,' and the various verbs for giving and receiving. That with *sima.u* means 'to do something completely, to finish doing something,' or 'to end up by doing something.' That with *ok.u* means 'to do something in advance or for future benefit,' while those with verbs for giving and receiving mean 'to perform an action for the benefit of another or to have another perform an action for one's own benefit.' The informal imperative III (both affirmative and negative) which uses the gerund plus the appropriate form of *kudasar.u* 'give to me' falls into this last group.

We are now ready for our final verb tables and English equivalent chart.

			AFFIRMATIVE	NEGATIVE
Indicative	**INFORMAL**		akeru	akenai
	FORMAL		akemasu	akemaseñ
Imperative	**INFORMAL**	I	akero	akeru na
		II	akenasai	akenasaru na
		III	akete kudasai	akenai de kudasai
	FORMAL		oake nasaimase	oake nasaimasu na
Presumptive	**INFORMAL**	I	akeyoo	akemai
		II	akeru daroo	akenai daroo
	FORMAL	I	akemasyoo	akemasumai
		II	akeru desyoo	akenai desyoo
Provisional	**INFORMAL**		akereba	akenakereba
	FORMAL		akemaseba	akemaseñ nara
			akemasureba	
Gerund	**INFORMAL**	I	akete	akenai de
		II		akenakute
	FORMAL		akemasite	akemaseñ de
Past Ind.	**INFORMAL**		aketa	akenakatta
	FORMAL		akemasita	akemaseñ desita
Past Presump.	**INFORMAL**		aketaroo	akenakattaroo
			aketa daroo	akenakatta daroo
	FORMAL		akemasitaroo	akemaseñ desitaroo
			aketa desyoo	akenakatta desyoo
Conditional	**INFORMAL**		aketara	akenakattara
	FORMAL		akemasitara	akemaseñ desitara
Alternative	**INFORMAL**		aketari	akenakattari
	FORMAL		akemasitari	akemaseñ desitari

	INFORMAL AFFIRMATIVE INDICATIVE
Passive	akerareru
Potential	akerareru
Causative	akesaseru
Causative Pass.	akesaserareru

Honorific	I	oake ni naru
	II	oake nasaru
Humble	I	oake suru
	II	oake itasu

			AFFIRMATIVE	NEGATIVE
Indicative	INFORMAL		katu	katanai
	FORMAL		katimasu	katimaseñ
Imperative	INFORMAL	I	kate	katu na
		II	katinasai	katinasaru na
		III	katte kudasai	katanai de kudasai
	FORMAL		okati nasaimase	okati nasaimasu na
Presumptive	INFORMAL	I	katoo	katumai
		II	katu daroo	katanai daroo
	FORMAL	I	katimasyoo	katimasumai
		II	katu desyoo	katanai desyoo
Provisional	INFORMAL		kateba	katanakereba
	FORMAL		katimaseba	katimaseñ nara
			katimasureba	
Gerund	INFORMAL	I	katte	katanai de
		II		katanakute
	FORMAL		katimasite	katimaseñ de
Past Ind.	INFORMAL		katta	katanakatta
	FORMAL		katimasita	katimaseñ desita
Past Presump.	INFORMAL		kattaroo	katanakattaroo
			katta daroo	katanakatta daroo
	FORMAL		katimasitaroo	katimaseñ desitaroo
			katta desyoo	katanakatta desyoo
Conditional	INFORMAL		kattara	katanakattara
	FORMAL		katimasitara	katimaseñ desitara
Alternative	INFORMAL		kattari	katanakattari
	FORMAL		katimasitari	katimaseñ desitari

	INFORMAL AFFIRMATIVE INDICATIVE
Passive	katareru
Potential	kateru
Causative	kataseru
Causative Pass	kataserareru

Honorific	I	okati ni naru
	II	okati nasaru
Humble		

SAMPLE TABLE OF ENGLISH EQUIVALENTS

In the following table of English equivalents two conventions have been adopted in order to avoid undue redundancy.

1. The same English translation is used to represent both the formal and informal verb forms, with the understanding that the formal will be more polite in tone.

2. Only affirmative translations are given because except where noted the student can easily deduce the meaning of the corresponding negative form.

Needless to say the translations offered here cannot hope to cover all possible cases because meaning is influenced by context. Nevertheless, they should serve to delineate the main semantic boundaries between the various forms.

Infinitive		opening (This form is non-commital as to level of formality, tense, aspect, affirmative or negative. It merely serves as a base for many endings, and sometimes to end a phrase.)
Indicative		I open (it), you open (it), he (she, it) opens (it), we (you, they) open (it)
	or:	I (you, he, she, it, we, you, they) will open (it)
Imperative		open (it)! (The Informal Imperative III and the Formal Imperative are closer to 'please open it.')
Presumptive	**I:**	I am going to open (it), we are going to open (it) or: Let's open (it) * (There is no negative form which corresponds to this second meaning of presumptive I.)
	II:	I (you, he, she, it, we, they) probably open (it) or: I am probably going to open (it), you are probably going to open (it), he (she, it) is probably going to open (it), we (you, they) are probably going to open (it)
Provisional		if I (you, she, he, it, we, they) open (it)
Gerund		opening (it) (Non-commital as to tense and aspect which are established by the final verb in a clause or sentence.)

*NOTE: In this book and in Japanese dictionaries the informal affirmative indicative is used as the citation form for verbs.

Past Indicative	I (you, he, she, it, we, they) opened (it)
or:	I (you, he, she, it, we, they) have opened (it)
or:	I (you, he, she, it, we, they) had opened (it) (*Indicates completed action.*)
Past Presumptive	I (you, he, she, it, we, they) probably opened (it)
or:	I (you, he, she, it, we, they) probably have opened (it)
or:	I (you, he, she, it, we, they) probably had opened (it)
Conditional	if I (you, he, she, it, we, they) should open (it)
or:	if I (you, he, she, it, we, they) were to open (it)
or:	when I (you, he, she, it, we, they) open (it)
or:	when I (you, he, she, it, we, they) opened (it)
Alternative	opening (it) and — (Non-commital as to tense and aspect. It merely indicates that two or more actions were, are, or will be performed alternately.)
Passive	is opened (by someone or something)
or:	will be opened (by someone or something)
or:	is opened (by someone) with bad result (for someone else)
or:	will be opened (by someone) with bad result (for someone else) (*This form is sometimes also used as a sort of honorific to show deference for the person who performs the action.*)
Potential	can be opened
or:	can open (it)
Causative	I make (someone) open (it), you make (someone) open (it), he (she, it) makes (someone) open (it), we (you, they) make (someone) open (it)
or:	I (you, he, she, it, we, they) will make (someone) open (it)
or:	I allow (someone) to open (it), you allow (someone) to open (it), he (she, it) allows (someone) to open (it), we (you, they) allow (someone) to open (it)
or:	I (you, he, she, it, we, they) will allow (someone) to open (it)
Causative Pass.	I am made to open (it), you are made to open (it), he (she, it) is made to open (it), we (you, they) are made to open (it)
or:	I (you, he, she, it, we, they) will be made to open (it)

Honorific	you open (it), he (she) opens (it) they open (it)
or:	you (he, she, they) will open (it) (all showing deference to the subject of the verb.)
Humble	I (we, or a member of my 'in group') open (it)
or:	I (we, or a member of my 'in group') will open (it) *(The speaker shows deference by lowering his own position.)*

TABLES OF 201 JAPANESE VERBS

We are now ready to enter the main body of the text which consists of tables of 201 common Japanese verbs showing all of the forms which we presented in our sample tables. The verbs shown are intransitive unless designated as transitive.

It is likely that students will approach this book looking for two basic types of information. Some will be seeking the inflection and derivation of a Japanese verb whose citation form they already know, while others will be trying to find a Japanese verb which fits a particular meaning in English. To provide for the first case, our verb tables are arranged alphabetically according to the citation form of the verb. Thus a student who wants to find out a particular form of the verb *taberu* can find it easily on page 154 between *suwaru* and *-tagaru*. For the convenience of students who are seeking a verb with a given meaning in English, an English to Japanese index of all 201 verb tables is provided beginning on page 202. Here a student can look up 'begin' and find listed the intransitive verb *hazimaru* and the transitive verb *hazimeru* on pages 25 and 26 respectively. Thus, within the narrow limits of 201 verbs this text also serves as a sort of Japanese-English, English-Japanese dictionary.

			AFFIRMATIVE	NEGATIVE
Indicative	INFORMAL		agaru	agaranai
	FORMAL		agarimasu	agarimaseñ
Imperative	INFORMAL	I	agare	agaru na
		II	agarinasai	agarinasaru na
		III	agatte kudasai	agaranai de kudasai
	FORMAL		oagari nasaimase	oagari nasaimasu na
Presumptive	INFORMAL	I	agaroo	agarumai
		II	agaru daroo	agaranai daroo
	FORMAL	I	agarimasyoo	agarimasumai
		II	agaru desyoo	agaranai desyoo
Provisional	INFORMAL		agareba	agaranakereba
	FORMAL		agarimaseba	agarimaseñ nara
			agarimasureba	
Gerund	INFORMAL	I	agatte	agaranai de
		II		agaranakute
	FORMAL		agarimasite	agarimaseñ de
Past Ind.	INFORMAL		agatta	agaranakatta
	FORMAL		agarimasita	agarimaseñ desita
Past Presump.	INFORMAL		agattaroo	agaranakattaroo
			agatta daroo	agaranakatta daroo
	FORMAL		agarimasitaroo	agarimaseñ desitaroo
			agatta desyoo	agaranakatta desyoo
Conditional	INFORMAL		agattara	agaranakattara
	FORMAL		agarimasitara	agarimaseñ desitara
Alternative	INFORMAL		agattari	agaranakattari
	FORMAL		agarimasitari	agarimaseñ desitari

	INFORMAL AFFIRMATIVE INDICATIVE
Passive	agarareru
Potential	agareru
Causative	agaraseru
Causative Pass.	agaraserareru

Honorific	I	oagari ni naru
	II	oagari nasaru

Humble

		AFFIRMATIVE	NEGATIVE
Indicative	**INFORMAL**	ageru	agenai
	FORMAL	agemasu	agemaseñ
Imperative	**INFORMAL I**	agero	ageru na
	II	agenasai	agenasaru na
	III	agete kudasai	agenai de kudasai
	FORMAL	oage nasaimase	oage nasaimasu na
Presumptive	**INFORMAL I**	ageyoo	agemai
	II	ageru daroo	agenai daroo
	FORMAL I	agemasyoo	agemasumai
	II	ageru desyoo	agenai desyoo
Provisional	**INFORMAL**	agereba	agenakereba
	FORMAL	agemaseba	agemaseñ nara
		agemasureba	
Gerund	**INFORMAL I**	agete	agenai de
	II		agenakute
	FORMAL	agemasite	agemaseñ de
Past Ind.	**INFORMAL**	ageta	agenakatta
	FORMAL	agemasita	agemaseñ desita
Past Presump.	**INFORMAL**	agetaroo	agenakattaroo
		ageta daroo	agenakatta daroo
	FORMAL	agemasitaroo	agemaseñ desitaroo
		ageta desyoo	agenakatta desyoo
Conditional	**INFORMAL**	agetara	agenakattara
	FORMAL	agemasitara	agemaseñ desitara
Alternative	**INFORMAL**	agetari	agenakattari
	FORMAL	agemasitari	agemaseñ desitari

	INFORMAL AFFIRMATIVE INDICATIVE
Passive	agerareru
Potential	agerareru
Causative	agesaseru
Causative Pass.	agesaserareru

Honorific	**I**	oage ni naru
	II	oage nasaru
Humble		sasiageru

TRANSITIVE   *to open*

		AFFIRMATIVE	NEGATIVE
Indicative	**INFORMAL**	akeru	akenai
	FORMAL	akemasu	akemaseñ
Imperative	**INFORMAL I**	akero	akeru na
	II	akenasai	akenasaru na
	III	akete kudasai	akenai de kudasai
	FORMAL	oake nasaimase	oake nasaimasu na
Presumptive	**INFORMAL I**	akeyoo	akemai
	II	akeru daroo	akenai daroo
	FORMAL I	akemasyoo	akemasumai
	II	akeru desyoo	akenai desyoo
Provisional	**INFORMAL**	akereba	akenakereba
	FORMAL	akemaseba	akemaseñ nara
		akemasureba	
Gerund	**INFORMAL I**	akete	akenai de
	II		akenakute
	FORMAL	akemasite	akemaseñ de
Past Ind.	**INFORMAL**	aketa	akenakatta
	FORMAL	akemasita	akemaseñ desita
Past Presump.	**INFORMAL**	aketaroo	akenakattaroo
		aketa daroo	akenakatta daroo
	FORMAL	akemasitaroo	akemaseñ desitaroo
		aketa desyoo	akenakatta desyoo
Conditional	**INFORMAL**	aketara	akenakattara
	FORMAL	akemasitara	akemaseñ desitara
Alternative	**INFORMAL**	aketari	akenakattari
	FORMAL	akemasitari	akemaseñ desitari

	INFORMAL AFFIRMATIVE INDICATIVE
Passive	akerareru
Potential	akerareru
Causative	akesaseru
Causative Pass.	akesaserareru

Honorific	**I**	oake ni naru
	II	oake nasaru
Humble	**I**	oake suru
	II	oake itasu

3

			AFFIRMATIVE	NEGATIVE
Indicative	INFORMAL		arau	arawanai
	FORMAL		araimasu	araimaseñ
Imperative	INFORMAL	I	arae	arau na
		II	arainasai	arainasaru na
		III	aratte kudasai	arawanai de kudasai
	FORMAL		oarai nasaimase	oarai nasaimasu na
Presumptive	INFORMAL	I	araoo	araumai
		II	arau daroo	arawanai daroo
	FORMAL	I	araimasyoo	araimasumai
		II	arau desyoo	arawanai desyoo
Provisional	INFORMAL		araeba	arawanakereba
	FORMAL		araimaseba	araimaseñ nara
			araimasureba	
Gerund	INFORMAL	I	aratte	arawanai de
		II		arawanakute
	FORMAL		araimasite	araimaseñ de
Past Ind.	INFORMAL		aratta	arawanakatta
	FORMAL		araimasita	araimaseñ desita
Past Presump.	INFORMAL		arattaroo	arawanakattaroo
			aratta daroo	arawanakatta daroo
	FORMAL		araimasitaroo	araimaseñ desitaroo
			aratta desyoo	arawanakatta desyoo
Conditional	INFORMAL		arattara	arawanakattara
	FORMAL		araimasitara	araimaseñ desitara
Alternative	INFORMAL		arattari	arawanakattari
	FORMAL		araimasitari	araimaseñ desitari

	INFORMAL AFFIRMATIVE INDICATIVE
Passive	arawareru
Potential	araeru
Causative	arawaseru
Causative Pass.	arawaserareru

Honorific	I	oarai ni naru
	II	oarai nasaru
Humble	I	oarai surú
	II	oarai itasu

4

		AFFIRMATIVE	NEGATIVE
Indicative	**INFORMAL**	arawareru	arawarenai
	FORMAL	arawaremasu	arawaremaseñ
Imperative	**INFORMAL** I	arawarero	arawareru na
	II	arawarenasai	arawarenasaru na
	III	arawarete kudasai	arawarenai de kudasai
	FORMAL		
Presumptive	**INFORMAL** I	arawareyoo	arawaremai
	II	arawareru daroo	arawarenai daroo
	FORMAL I	arawaremasyoo	arawaremasumai
	II	arawareru desyoo	arawarenai desyoo
Provisional	**INFORMAL**	arawarereba	arawarenakereba
	FORMAL	arawaremaseba	arawaremaseñ nara
		arawaremasureba	
Gerund	**INFORMAL** I	arawarete	arawarenai de
	II		arawarenakute
	FORMAL	arawaremasite	arawaremaseñ de
Past Ind.	**INFORMAL**	arawareta	arawarenakatta
	FORMAL	arawaremasita	arawaremaseñ desita
Past Presump.	**INFORMAL**	arawaretaroo	arawarenakattaroo
		arawareta daroo	arawarenakatta daroo
	FORMAL	arawaremasitaroo	arawaremaseñ desitaroo
		arawareta desyoo	arawarenakatta desyoo
Conditional	**INFORMAL**	arawaretara	arawarenakattara
	FORMAL	arawaremasitara	arawaremaseñ desitara
Alternative	**INFORMAL**	arawaretari	arawarenakattari
	FORMAL	arawaremasitari	arawaremaseñ desitari

	INFORMAL AFFIRMATIVE INDICATIVE
Passive	
Potential	arawarerareru
Causative	arawaresaseru
Causative Pass.	arawaresaserareru

Honorific

Humble

			AFFIRMATIVE	NEGATIVE
Indicative	**INFORMAL**		arawasu	arawasanai
	FORMAL		arawasimasu	arawasimaseñ
Imperative	**INFORMAL**	I	arawase	arawasu na
		II	arawasinasai	arawasinasaru na
		III	arawasite kudasai	arawasanai de kudasai
	FORMAL		oarawasi nasaimase	oarawasi nasaimasu na
Presumptive	**INFORMAL**	I	arawasoo	arawasumai
		II	arawasu daroo	arawasanai daroo
	FORMAL	I	arawasimasyoo	arawasimasumai
		II	arawasu desyoo	arawasanai desyoo
Provisional	**INFORMAL**		arawaseba	arawasanakereba
	FORMAL		arawasimaseba	arawasimaseñ nara
			arawasimasureba	
Gerund	**INFORMAL**	I	arawasite	arawasanai de
		II		arawasanakute
	FORMAL		arawasimasite	arawasimaseñ de
Past Ind.	**INFORMAL**		arawasita	arawasanakatta
	FORMAL		arawasimasita	arawasimaseñ desita
Past Presump.	**INFORMAL**		arawasitaroo	arawasanakattaroo
			arawasita daroo	arawasanakatta daroo
	FORMAL		arawasimasitaroo	arawasimaseñ desitaroo
			arawasita desyoo	arawasanakatta desyoo
Conditional	**INFORMAL**		arawasitara	arawasanakattara
	FORMAL		arawasimasitara	arawasimaseñ desitara
Alternative	**INFORMAL**		arawasitari	arawasanakattari
	FORMAL		arawasimasitari	arawasimaseñ desitari

	INFORMAL AFFIRMATIVE INDICATIVE
Passive	arawasareru
Potential	arawaseru
Causative	arawasaseru
Causative Pass.	arawasaserareru

Honorific	I	oarawasi ni naru
	II	oarawasi nasaru

Humble

6

ar.u
to have, to exist (inanimate)

		AFFIRMATIVE	NEGATIVE
Indicative	**INFORMAL**	aru	nai
	FORMAL	arimasu	arimaseñ
Imperative	**INFORMAL I**		
	II		
	III		
	FORMAL		
Presumptive	**INFORMAL I**	aroo	arumai
	II	aru daroo	nai daroo
	FORMAL I	arimasyoo	arimasumai
	II	aru desyoo	nai desyoo
Provisional	**INFORMAL**	areba	nakereba
	FORMAL	arimaseba	arimaseñ nara
		arimasureba	
Gerund	**INFORMAL I**	atte	
	II		nakute
	FORMAL	arimasite	arimaseñ de
Past Ind.	**INFORMAL**	atta	nakatta
	FORMAL	arimasita	arimaseñ desita
Past Presump.	**INFORMAL**	attaroo	nakattaroo
		atta daroo	nakatta daroo
	FORMAL	arimasitaroo	arimaseñ desitaroo
		atta desyoo	nakatta desyoo
Conditional	**INFORMAL**	attara	nakattara
	FORMAL	arimasitara	arimaseñ desitara
Alternative	**INFORMAL**	attari	nakattari
	FORMAL	arimasitari	arimaseñ desitari

INFORMAL AFFIRMATIVE INDICATIVE

Passive

Potential

Causative

Causative Pass.

Polite*   gozaru

*This is neither honorific nor humble (because the subject is inanimate), but rather neutral polite.

			AFFIRMATIVE	NEGATIVE
Indicative	**INFORMAL**		aruku	arukanai
	FORMAL		arukimasu	arukimaseñ
Imperative	**INFORMAL**	I	aruke	aruku na
		II	arukinasai	arukinasaru na
		III	aruite kudasai	arukanai de kudasai
	FORMAL		oaruki nasaimase	oaruki nasaimasu na
Presumptive	**INFORMAL**	I	arukoo	arukumai
		II	aruku daroo	arukanai daroo
	FORMAL	I	arukimasyoo	arukimasumai
		II	aruku desyoo	arukanai desyoo
Provisional	**INFORMAL**		arukeba	arukanakereba
	FORMAL		arukimaseba	arukimaseñ nara
			arukimasureba	
Gerund	**INFORMAL**	I	aruite	arukanai de
		II		arukanakute
	FORMAL		arukimasite	arukimaseñ de
Past Ind.	**INFORMAL**		aruita	arukanakatta
	FORMAL		arukimasita	arukimaseñ desita
Past Presump.	**INFORMAL**		aruitaroo	arukanattaroo
			aruita daroo	arukanakatta daroo
	FORMAL		arukimasitaroo	arukimaseñ desitaroo
			aruita desyoo	arukanakatta desyoo
Conditional	**INFORMAL**		aruitara	arukanakattara
	FORMAL		arukimasitara	arukimaseñ desitara
Alternative	**INFORMAL**		aruitari	arukanakattari
	FORMAL		arukimasitari	arukimaseñ desitari

	INFORMAL AFFIRMATIVE INDICATIVE
Passive	arukareru
Potential	arukeru
Causative	arukaseru
Causative Pass.	arukaserareru

Honorific	I	oaruki ni naru
	II	oaruki nasaru
Humble		

		AFFIRMATIVE	**NEGATIVE**
Indicative	**INFORMAL**	asobu	asobanai
	FORMAL	asobimasu	asobimaseñ
Imperative	**INFORMAL I**	asobe	asobu na
	II	asobinasai	asobinasaru na
	III	asoñde kudasai	asobanai de kudasai
	FORMAL	oasobi nasaimase	oasobi nasaimasu na
Presumptive	**INFORMAL I**	asoboo	asobumai
	II	asobu daroo	asobanai daroo
	FORMAL I	asobimasyoo	asobimasumai
	II	asobu desyoo	asobanai desyoo
Provisional	**INFORMAL**	asobeba	asobanakereba
	FORMAL	asobimaseba	asobimaseñ nara
		asobimasureba	
Gerund	**INFORMAL I**	asoñde	asobanai de
	II		asobanakute
	FORMAL	asobimasite	asobimaseñ de
Past Ind.	**INFORMAL**	asoñda	asobanakatta
	FORMAL	asobimasita	asobimaseñ desita
Past Presump.	**INFORMAL**	asoñdaroo	asobanakattaroo
		asoñda daroo	asobanakatta daroo
	FORMAL	asobimasitaroo	asobimaseñ desitaroo
		asoñda desyoo	asobanakatta desyoo
Conditional	**INFORMAL**	asoñdara	asobanakattara
	FORMAL	asobimasitara	asobimaseñ desitara
Alternative	**INFORMAL**	asoñdari	asobanakattari
	FORMAL	asobimasitari	asobimaseñ desitari

	INFORMAL AFFIRMATIVE INDICATIVE
Passive	asobareru
Potential	asoberu
Causative	asobaseru
Causative Pass.	asobaserareru

Honorific	**I**	oasobi ni naru
	II	oasobi nasaru
Humble		

		AFFIRMATIVE	NEGATIVE
Indicative	**INFORMAL**	au	awanai
	FORMAL	aimasu	aimaseñ
Imperative	**INFORMAL** I	ae	au na
	II	ainasai	ainasaru na
	III	atte kudasai	awanai de kudasai
	FORMAL	oai nasaimase	oai nasaimasu na
Presumptive	**INFORMAL** I	aoo	aumai
	II	au daroo	awanai daroo
	FORMAL I	aimasyoo	aimasumai
	II	au desyoo	awanai desyoo
Provisional	**INFORMAL**	aeba	awanakereba
	FORMAL	aimaseba	aimaseñ nara
		aimasureba	
Gerund	**INFORMAL** I	atte	awanai de
	II		awanakute
	FORMAL	aimasite	aimaseñ de
Past Ind.	**INFORMAL**	atta	awanakatta
	FORMAL	aimasita	aimaseñ desita
Past Presump.	**INFORMAL**	attaroo	awanakattaroo
		atta daroo	awanakatta daroo
	FORMAL	aimasitaroo	aimaseñ desitaroo
		atta desyoo	awanakatta desyoo
Conditional	**INFORMAL**	attara	awanakattara
	FORMAL	aimasitara	aimaseñ desitara
Alternative	**INFORMAL**	attari	awanakattari
	FORMAL	aimasitari	aimaseñ desitari

	INFORMAL AFFIRMATIVE INDICATIVE
Passive	awareru
Potential	aeru
Causative	awaseru
Causative Pass.	awaserareru

Honorific	I	oai ni naru
	II	oai nasaru
Humble		ome ni kakaru

		AFFIRMATIVE	NEGATIVE
Indicative	**INFORMAL**	azukeru	azukenai
	FORMAL	azukemasu	azukemaseñ
Imperative	**INFORMAL** I	azukero	azukeru na
	II	azukenasai	azukenasaru na
	III	azukete kudasai	azukenai de kudasai
	FORMAL	oazuke nasaimase	oazuke nasaimasu na
Presumptive	**INFORMAL** I	azukeyoo	azukemai
	II	azukeru daroo	azukenai daroo
	FORMAL I	azukemasyoo	azukemasumai
	II	azukeru desyoo	azukenai desyoo
Provisional	**INFORMAL**	azukereba	azukenakereba
	FORMAL	azukemaseba	azukemaseñ nara
		azukemasureba	
Gerund	**INFORMAL** I	azukete	azukenai de
	II		azukenakute
	FORMAL	azukemasite	azukemaseñ de
Past Ind.	**INFORMAL**	azuketa	azukenakatta
	FORMAL	azukemasita	azukemaseñ desita
Past Presump.	**INFORMAL**	azuketaroo	azukenakattaroo
		azuketa daroo	azukenakatta daroo
	FORMAL	azukemasitaroo	azukemaseñ desitaroo
		azuketa desyoo	azukenakatta desyoo
Conditional	**INFORMAL**	azuketara	azukenakattara
	FORMAL	azukemasitara	azukemaseñ desitara
Alternative	**INFORMAL**	azuketari	azukenakattari
	FORMAL	azukemasitari	azukemaseñ desitari

	INFORMAL AFFIRMATIVE INDICATIVE
Passive	azukerareru
Potential	azukerareru
Causative	azukesaseru
Causative Pass.	azukesaserareru

Honorific	I	oazuke ni naru
	II	oazuke nasaru
Humble	I	oazuke suru
	II	oazuke itasu

			AFFIRMATIVE	NEGATIVE
Indicative	INFORMAL		damasu	damasanai
	FORMAL		damasimasu	damasimaseñ
Imperative	INFORMAL	I	damase	damasu na
		II	damasinasai	damasinasaru na
		III	damasite kudasai	damasanai de kudasai
	FORMAL		odamasi nasaimase	odamasi nasaimasu na
Presumptive	INFORMAL	I	damasoo	damasumai
		II	damasu daroo	damasanai daroo
	FORMAL	I	damasimasyoo	damasimasumai
		II	damasu desyoo	damasanai desyoo
Provisional	INFORMAL		damaseba	damasanakereba
	FORMAL		damasimaseba	damasimaseñ nara
			damasimasureba	
Gerund	INFORMAL	I	damasite	damasanai de
		II		damasanakute
	FORMAL		damasimasite	damasimaseñ de
Past Ind.	INFORMAL		damasita	damasanakatta
	FORMAL		damasimasita	damasimaseñ desita
Past Presump.	INFORMAL		damasitaroo	damasanakattaroo
			damasita daroo	damasanakatta daroo
	FORMAL		damasimasitaroo	damasimaseñ desitaroo
			damasita desyoo	damasanakatta desyoo
Conditional	INFORMAL		damasitara	damasanakattara
	FORMAL		damasimasitara	damasimaseñ desitara
Alternative	INFORMAL		damasitari	damasanakattari
	FORMAL		damasimasitari	damasimaseñ desitari

		INFORMAL AFFIRMATIVE INDICATIVE
Passive		damasareru
Potential		damaseru
Causative		damasaseru
Causative Pass.		damasaserareru
Honorific	I	odamasi ni naru
	II	odamasi nasaru
Humble		

			AFFIRMATIVE	NEGATIVE
Indicative	**INFORMAL**		dasu	dasanai
	FORMAL		dasimasu	dasimaseñ
Imperative	**INFORMAL**	**I**	dase	dasu na
		II	dasinasai	dasinasaru na
		III	dasite kudasai	dasanai de kudasai
	FORMAL		odasi nasaimase	odasi nasaimasu na
Presumptive	**INFORMAL**	**I**	dasoo	dasumai
		II	dasu daroo	dasanai daroo
	FORMAL	**I**	dasimasyoo	dasimasumai
		II	dasu desyoo	dasanai desyoo
Provisional	**INFORMAL**		daseba	dasanakereba
	FORMAL		dasimaseba	dasimaseñ nara
			dasimasureba	
Gerund	**INFORMAL**	**I**	dasite	dasanai de
		II		dasanakute
	FORMAL		dasimasite	dasimaseñ de
Past Ind.	**INFORMAL**		dasita	dasanakatta
	FORMAL		dasimasita	dasimaseñ desita
Past Presump.	**INFORMAL**		dasitaroo	dasanakattaroo
			dasita daroo	dasanakatta daroo
	FORMAL		dasimasitaroo	dasimaseñ desitaroo
			dasita desyoo	dasanakatta desyoo
Conditional	**INFORMAL**		dasitara	dasanakattara
	FORMAL		dasimasitara	dasimaseñ desitara
Alternative	**INFORMAL**		dasitari	dasanakattari
	FORMAL		dasimasitari	dasimaseñ desitari

	INFORMAL AFFIRMATIVE INDICATIVE
Passive	dasareru
Potential	daseru
Causative	dasaseru
Causative Pass.	dasaserareru

Honorific	**I**	odasi ni naru
	II	odasi nasaru
Humble	**I**	odasi suru
	II	odasi itasu

13

		AFFIRMATIVE	NEGATIVE
Indicative	**INFORMAL**	dekiru	dekinai
	FORMAL	dekimasu	dekimaseñ
Imperative	**INFORMAL I**	dekiro	dekiru na
	II	dekinasai	dekinasaru na
	III		
	FORMAL		
Presumptive	**INFORMAL I**	dekiyoo	dekimai
	II	dekiru daroo	dekinai daroo
	FORMAL I	dekimasyoo	dekimasumai
	II	dekiru desyoo	dekinai desyoo
Provisional	**INFORMAL**	dekireba	dekinakereba
	FORMAL	dekimaseba	dekimaseñ nara
		dekimasureba	
Gerund	**INFORMAL I**	dekite	dekinai de
	II		dekinakute
	FORMAL	dekimasite	dekimaseñ de
Past Ind.	**INFORMAL**	dekita	dekinakatta
	FORMAL	dekimasita	dekimaseñ desita
Past Presump.	**INFORMAL**	dekitaroo	dekinakattaroo
		dekita daroo	dekinakatta daroo
	FORMAL	dekimasitaroo	dekimaseñ desitaroo
		dekita desyoo	dekinakatta desyoo
Conditional	**INFORMAL**	dekitara	dekinakattara
	FORMAL	dekimasitara	dekimaseñ desitara
Alternative	**INFORMAL**	dekitari	dekinakattari
	FORMAL	dekimasitari	dekimaseñ desitari

INFORMAL AFFIRMATIVE INDICATIVE

Passive

Potential

Causative

Causative Pass.

Honorific	**I**	odeki ni naru
	II	odeki nasaru

Humble

		AFFIRMATIVE	NEGATIVE
Indicative	**INFORMAL**	deru	denai
	FORMAL	demasu	demaseñ
Imperative	**INFORMAL I**	dero	deru na
	II	denasai	denasaru na
	III	dete kudasai	denai de kudasai
	FORMAL	ode nasaimase	ode nasaimasu na
Presumptive	**INFORMAL I**	deyoo	demai
	II	deru daroo	denai daroo
	FORMAL I	demasyoo	demasumai
	II	deru desyoo	denai desyoo
Provisional	**INFORMAL**	dereba	denakereba
	FORMAL	demaseba	demaseñ nara
		demasureba	
Gerund	**INFORMAL I**	dete	denai de
	II		denakute
	FORMAL	demasite	demaseñ de
Past Ind.	**INFORMAL**	deta	denakatta
	FORMAL	demasita	demaseñ desita
Past Presump.	**INFORMAL**	detaroo	denakattaroo
		deta daroo	denakatta daroo
	FORMAL	demasitaroo	demaseñ desitaroo
		deta desyoo	denakatta desyoo
Conditional	**INFORMAL**	detara	denakattara
	FORMAL	demasitara	demaseñ desitara
Alternative	**INFORMAL**	detari	denakattari
	FORMAL	demasitari	demaseñ desitari

INFORMAL AFFIRMATIVE INDICATIVE

Passive	derareru
Potential	derareru
Causative	desaseru
Causative Pass.	desaserareru

Honorific	**I**	ode ni naru
	II	ode nasaru
Humble		

gozar.u   gozai
to exist (inanimate neutral polite)*

		AFFIRMATIVE	NEGATIVE
Indicative INFORMAL		gozaru	
FORMAL		gozaimasu	gozaimaseñ
Imperative INFORMAL I			
II			
III			
FORMAL			
Presumptive INFORMAL I		gozaroo	gozarumai
II			
FORMAL I		gozaimasyoo	gozaimasumai
II			
Provisional INFORMAL			
FORMAL		gozaimaseba	gozaimaseñ nara
		gozaimasureba	
Gerund INFORMAL I			
II			
FORMAL		gozaimasite	gozaimaseñ de
Past Ind. INFORMAL			
FORMAL		gozaimasita	gozaimaseñ desita
Past Presump. INFORMAL			
FORMAL		gozaimasitaroo	gozaimaseñ desitaroo
Conditional INFORMAL			
FORMAL		gozaimasitara	gozaimaseñ desitara
Alternative INFORMAL			
FORMAL		gozaimasitari	gozaimaseñ desitari

INFORMAL AFFIRMATIVE INDICATIVE

Passive

Potential

Causative

Causative Pass.

Honorific

Humble

*The forms *gozaru*, *gozaroo*, and *gozarumai* are rarely used in standard conversation, being replaced by their formal equivalents.

16

			AFFIRMATIVE	NEGATIVE
Indicative	**INFORMAL**		hairu	hairanai
	FORMAL		hairimasu	hairimaseñ
Imperative	**INFORMAL**	I	haire	hairu na
		II	hairinasai	hairinasaru na
		III	haitte kudasai	hairanai de kudasai
	FORMAL		ohairi nasaimase	ohairi nasaimasu na
Presumptive	**INFORMAL**	I	hairoo	hairumai
		II	hairu daroo	hairanai daroo
	FORMAL	I	hairimasyoo	hairimasumai
		II	hairu desyoo	hairanai desyoo
Provisional	**INFORMAL**		haireba	hairanakereba
	FORMAL		hairimaseba	hairimaseñ nara
			hairimasureba	
Gerund	**INFORMAL**	I	haitte	hairanai de
		II		hairanakute
	FORMAL		hairimasite	hairimaseñ de
Past Ind.	**INFORMAL**		haitta	hairanakatta
	FORMAL		hairimasita	hairimaseñ desita
Past Presump.	**INFORMAL**		haittaroo	hairanakattaroo
			haitta daroo	hairanakatta daroo
	FORMAL		hairimasitaroo	hairimaseñ desitaroo
			haitta desyoo	hairanakatta desyoo
Conditional	**INFORMAL**		haittara	hairanakattara
	FORMAL		hairimasitara	hairimaseñ desitara
Alternative	**INFORMAL**		haittari	hairanakattari
	FORMAL		hairimasitari	hairimasen desitari

	INFORMAL AFFIRMATIVE INDICATIVE
Passive	hairareru
Potential	haireru
Causative	hairaseru
Causative Pass.	hairaserareru

Honorific	I	ohairi ni naru
	II	ohairi nasaru
Humble		

hakar.u
to measure   TRANSITIVE

hakari

			AFFIRMATIVE	NEGATIVE
Indicative	INFORMAL		hakaru	hakaranai
	FORMAL		hakarimasu	hakarimaseñ
Imperative	INFORMAL	I	hakare	hakaru na
		II	hakarinasai	hakarinasaru na
		III	hakatte kudasai	hakaranai de kudasai
	FORMAL		ohakari nasaimase	ohakari nasaimasu na
Presumptive	INFORMAL	I	hakaroo	hakarumai
		II	hakaru daroo	hakaranai daroo
	FORMAL	I	hakarimasyoo	hakarimasumai
		II	hakaru desyoo	hakaranai desyoo
Provisional	INFORMAL		hakareba	hakaranakereba
	FORMAL		hakarimaseba	hakarimaseñ nara
			hakarimasureba	
Gerund	INFORMAL	I	hakatte	hakaranai de
		II		hakaranakute
	FORMAL		hakarimasite	hakarimaseñ de
Past Ind.	INFORMAL		hakatta	hakaranakatta
	FORMAL		hakarimasita	hakarimaseñ desita
Past Presump.	INFORMAL		hakattaroo	hakaranakattaroo
			hakatta daroo	hakaranakatta daroo
	FORMAL		hakarimasitaroo	hakarimaseñ desitaroo
			hakatta desyoo	hakaranakatta desyoo
Conditional	INFORMAL		hakattara	hakaranakattara
	FORMAL		hakarimasitara	hakarimaseñ desitara
Alternative	INFORMAL		hakattari	hakaranakattari
	FORMAL		hakarimasitari	hakarimaseñ desitari

		INFORMAL AFFIRMATIVE INDICATIVE
Passive		hakarareru
Potential		hakareru
Causative		hakaraseru
Causative Pass.		hakaraserareru

Honorific	I	ohakari ni naru
	II	ohakari nasaru
Humble	I	ohakari suru
	II	ohakari itasu

haki

hak.u

TRANSITIVE   *to put on or wear on the feet or legs* (as with shoes, trousers, etc.)

			AFFIRMATIVE	NEGATIVE
Indicative	**INFORMAL**		haku	hakanai
	FORMAL		hakimasu	hakimaseñ
Imperative	**INFORMAL**	I	hake	haku na
		II	hakinasai	hakinasaru na
		III	haite kudasai	hakanai de kudasai
	FORMAL		ohaki nasaimase	ohaki nasimasu na
Presumptive	**INFORMAL**	I	hakoo	hakumai
		II	haku daroo	hakanai daroo
	FORMAL	I	hakimasyoo	hakimasumai
		II	haku desyoo	hakanai desyoo
Provisional	**INFORMAL**		hakeba	hakanakereba
	FORMAL		hakimaseba	hakimaseñ nara
			hakimasureba	
Gerund	**INFORMAL**	I	haite	hakanai de
		II		hakanakute
	FORMAL		hakimasite	hakimaseñ de
Past Ind.	**INFORMAL**		haita	hakanakatta
	FORMAL		hakimasita	hakimaseñ desita
Past Presump.	**INFORMAL**		haitaroo	hakanakattaroo
			haita daroo	hakanakatta daroo
	FORMAL		hakimasitaroo	hakimaseñ desitaroo
			haita desyoo	hakanakatta desyoo
Conditional	**INFORMAL**		haitara	hakanakattara
	FORMAL		hakimasitara	hakimaseñ desitara
Alternative	**INFORMAL**		haitari	hakanakattari
	FORMAL		hakimasitari	hakimaseñ desitari

INFORMAL AFFIRMATIVE INDICATIVE

Passive		hakareru
Potential		hakeru
Causative		hakaseru
Causative Pass.		hakaserareru

Honorific	I	ohaki ni naru
	II	ohaki nasaru
Humble		

19

		AFFIRMATIVE	NEGATIVE
Indicative	INFORMAL	hanasu	hanasanai
	FORMAL	hanasimasu	hanasimaseñ
Imperative	INFORMAL I	hanase	hanasu na
	II	hanasinasai	hanasinasaru na
	III	hanasite kudasai	hanasanai de kudasai
	FORMAL	ohanasi nasaimase	ohanasi nasaimasu na
Presumptive	INFORMAL I	hanasoo	hanasumai
	II	hanasu daroo	hanasanai daroo
	FORMAL I	hanasimasyoo	hanasimasumai
	II	hanasu desyoo	hanasanai desyoo
Provisional	INFORMAL	hanaseba	hanasanakereba
	FORMAL	hanasimaseba	hanasimaseñ nara
		hanasimasureba	
Gerund	INFORMAL I	hanasite	hanasanai de
	II		hanasanakute
	FORMAL	hanasimasite	hanasimaseñ de
Past Ind.	INFORMAL	hanasita	hanasanakatta
	FORMAL	hanasimasita	hanasimaseñ desita
Past Presump.	INFORMAL	hanasitaroo	hanasanakattaroo
		hanasita daroo	hanasanakatta daroo
	FORMAL	hanasimasitaroo	hanasimaseñ desitaroo
		hanasita desyoo	hanasanakatta desyoo
Conditional	INFORMAL	hanasitara	hanasanakattara
	FORMAL	hanasimasitara	hanasimaseñ desitara
Alternative	INFORMAL	hanasitari	hanasanakattari
	FORMAL	hanasimasitari	hanasimaseñ desitari

INFORMAL AFFIRMATIVE INDICATIVE

Passive	hanasareru
Potential	hanaseru
Causative	hanasaseru
Causative Pass.	hanasaserareru

Honorific	I	ohanasi ni naru
	II	ohanasi nasaru
Humble	I	ohanasi suru
	II	ohanasi itasu

		AFFIRMATIVE	NEGATIVE
Indicative	**INFORMAL**	harau	harawanai
	FORMAL	haraimasu	haraimaseñ
Imperative	**INFORMAL I**	harae	harau na
	II	harainasai	harainasaru na
	III	haratte kudasai	harawanai de kudasai
	FORMAL	oharai nasaimase	oharai nasaimasu na
Presumptive	**INFORMAL I**	haraoo	haraumai
	II	harau daroo	harawanai daroo
	FORMAL I	haraimasyoo	haraimasumai
	II	harau desyoo	harawanai desyoo
Provisional	**INFORMAL**	haraeba	harawanakereba
	FORMAL	haraimaseba	haraimaseñ nara
		haraimasureba	
Gerund	**INFORMAL I**	haratte	harawanai de
	II		harawanakute
	FORMAL	haraimasite	haraimaseñ de
Past Ind.	**INFORMAL**	haratta	harawanakatta
	FORMAL	haraimasita	haraimaseñ desita
Past Presump.	**INFORMAL**	harattaroo	harawanakattaroo
		haratta daroo	harawanakatta daroo
	FORMAL	haraimasitaroo	haraimaseñ desitaroo
		haratta desyoo	harawanakatta desyoo
Conditional	**INFORMAL**	harattara	harawanakattara
	FORMAL	haraimasitara	haraimaseñ desitara
Alternative	**INFORMAL**	harattari	harawanakattari
	FORMAL	haraimasitari	haraimaseñ desitari

INFORMAL AFFIRMATIVE INDICATIVE

Passive	harawareru
Potential	haraeru
Causative	harawaseru
Causative Pass.	harawaserareru

Honorific	I	oharai ni naru
	II	oharai nasaru
Humble	I	oharai suru
	II	oharai itasu

21

		AFFIRMATIVE	NEGATIVE
Indicative	INFORMAL	hareru	harenai
	FORMAL	haremasu	haremaseñ
Imperative	INFORMAL I	harero	hareru na
	II	harenasai	harenasaru na
	III		
	FORMAL		
Presumptive	INFORMAL I	hareyoo	haremai
	II	hareru daroo	harenai daroo
	FORMAL I	haremasyoo	haremasumai
	II	hareru desyoo	harenai desyoo
Provisional	INFORMAL	harereba	harenakereba
	FORMAL	haremaseba	haremaseñ nara
		haremasureba	
Gerund	INFORMAL I	harete	harenai de
	II		harenakute
	FORMAL	haremasite	haremaseñ de
Past Ind.	INFORMAL	hareta	harenakatta
	FORMAL	haremasita	haremaseñ desita
Past Presump.	INFORMAL	haretaroo	harenakattaroo
		hareta daroo	harenakatta daroo
	FORMAL	haremasitaroo	haremaseñ desitaroo
		hareta desyoo	harenakatta desyoo
Conditional	INFORMAL	haretara	harenakattara
	FORMAL	haremasitara	haremaseñ desitara
Alternative	INFORMAL	haretari	harenakattari
	FORMAL	haremasitari	haremaseñ desitari

INFORMAL AFFIRMATIVE INDICATIVE

Passive	
Potential	harerareru
Causative	haresaseru
Causative Pass.	

Honorific	
Humble	

		AFFIRMATIVE	**NEGATIVE**
Indicative	**INFORMAL**	hataraku	hatarakanai
	FORMAL	hatarakimasu	hatarakimaseñ
Imperative	**INFORMAL I**	hatarake	hataraku na
	II	hatarakinasai	hatarakinasaru na
	III	hataraite kudasai	hatarakanai de kudasai
	FORMAL	ohataraki nasaimase	ohataraki nasaimasu na
Presumptive	**INFORMAL I**	hatarakoo	hatarakumai
	II	hataraku daroo	hatarakanai daroo
	FORMAL I	hatarakimasyoo	hatarakimasumai
	II	hataraku desyoo	hatarakanai desyoo
Provisional	**INFORMAL**	hatarakeba	hatarakanakereba
	FORMAL	hatarakimaseba	hatarakimaseñ nara
		hatarakimasureba	
Gerund	**INFORMAL I**	hataraite	hatarakanai de
	II		hatarakanakute
	FORMAL	hatarakimasite	hatarakimaseñ de
Past Ind.	**INFORMAL**	hataraita	hatarakanakatta
	FORMAL	hatarakimasita	hatarakimaseñ desita
Past Presump.	**INFORMAL**	hataraitaroo	hatarakanakattaroo
		hataraita daroo	hatarakanakatta daroo
	FORMAL	hatarakimasitaroo	hatarakimaseñ desitaroo
		hataraita desyoo	hatarakanakatta desyoo
Conditional	**INFORMAL**	hataraitara	hatarakanakattara
	FORMAL	hatarakimasitara	hatarakimaseñ desitara
Alternative	**INFORMAL**	hataraitari	hatarakanakattari
	FORMAL	hatarakimasitari	hatarakimaseñ desitari

INFORMAL AFFIRMATIVE INDICATIVE

Passive	
Potential	hatarakeru
Causative	hatarakaseru
Causative Pass.	hatarakaserareru

Honorific	**I**	ohataraki ni naru
	II	ohataraki nasaru
Humble		

		AFFIRMATIVE	NEGATIVE
Indicative	**INFORMAL**	hayaru	hayaranai
	FORMAL	hayarimasu	hayarimaseñ
Imperative	**INFORMAL I**	hayare	hayaru na
	II		
	III		
	FORMAL		
Presumptive	**INFORMAL I**	hayaroo	hayarumai
	II	hayaru daroo	hayaranai daroo
	FORMAL I	hayarimasyoo	hayarimasumai
	II	hayaru desyoo	hayaranai desyoo
Provisional	**INFORMAL**	hayareba	hayaranakereba
	FORMAL	hayarimaseba	hayarimaseñ nara
		hayarimasureba	
Gerund	**INFORMAL I**	hayatte	hayaranai de
	II		hayaranakute
	FORMAL	hayarimasite	hayarimaseñ de
Past Ind.	**INFORMAL**	hayatta	hayaranakatta
	FORMAL	hayarimasita	hayarimaseñ desita
Past Presump.	**INFORMAL**	hayattaroo	hayaranakattaroo
		hayatta daroo	hayaranakatta daroo
	FORMAL	hayarimasitaroo	hayarimaseñ desitaroo
		hayatta desyoo	hayaranakatta desyoo
Conditional	**INFORMAL**	hayattara	hayaranakattara
	FORMAL	hayarimasitara	hayarimaseñ desitara
Alternative	**INFORMAL**	hayattari	hayaranakattari
	FORMAL	hayarimasitari	hayarimaseñ desitari

INFORMAL AFFIRMATIVE INDICATIVE

Passive	
Potential	
Causative	hayaraseru
Causative Pass.	hayaraserareru

Honorific	
Humble	

		AFFIRMATIVE	NEGATIVE
Indicative	INFORMAL	hazimaru	hazimaranai
	FORMAL	hazimarimasu	hazimarimaseñ
Imperative	INFORMAL I	hazimare	hazimaru na
	II		
	III		
	FORMAL		
Presumptive	INFORMAL I	hazimaroo	hazimarumai
	II	hazimaru daroo	hazimaranai daroo
	FORMAL I	hazimarimasyoo	hazimarimasumai
	II	hazimaru desyoo	hazimaranai desyoo
Provisional	INFORMAL	hazimareba	hazimaranakereba
	FORMAL	hazimarimaseba	hazimarimaseñ nara
		hazimarimasureba	
Gerund	INFORMAL I	hazimatte	hazimaranai de
	II		hazimaranakute
	FORMAL	hazimarimasite	hazimarimaseñ de
Past Ind.	INFORMAL	hazimatta	hazimaranakatta
	FORMAL	hazimarimasita	hazimarimaseñ desita
Past Presump.	INFORMAL	hazimattaroo	hazimaranakattaroo
		hazimatta daroo	hazimaranakatta daroo
	FORMAL	hazimarimasitaroo	hazimarimaseñ desitaroo
		hazimatta desyoo	hazimaranakatta desyoo
Conditional	INFORMAL	hazimattara	hazimaranakattara
	FORMAL	hazimarimasitara	hazimarimaseñ desitara
Alternative	INFORMAL	hazimattari	hazimaranakattari
	FORMAL	hazimarimasitari	hazimarimaseñ desitari

INFORMAL AFFIRMATIVE INDICATIVE

Passive	
Potential	
Causative	hazimaraseru
Causative Pass.	
Honorific	
Humble	

to begin   TRANSITIVE

		AFFIRMATIVE	NEGATIVE
Indicative	**INFORMAL**	hazimeru	hazimenai
	FORMAL	hazimemasu	hazimemaseñ
Imperative	**INFORMAL I**	hazimero	hazimeru na
	II	hazimenasai	hazimenasaru na
	III	hazimete kudasai	hazimenai de kudasai
	FORMAL	ohazime nasaimase	ohazime nasaimasu na
Presumptive	**INFORMAL I**	hazimeyoo	hazimemai
	II	hazimeru daroo	hazimenai daroo
	FORMAL I	hazimemasyoo	hazimemasumai
	II	hazimeru desyoo	hazimenai desyoo
Provisional	**INFORMAL**	hazimereba	hazimerakereba
	FORMAL	hazimemaseba	hazimemaseñ nara
		hazimemasureba	
Gerund	**INFORMAL I**	hazimete	hazimenai de
	II		hazimenakute
	FORMAL	hazimemasite	hazimemaseñ de
Past Ind.	**INFORMAL**	hazimeta	hazimenakatta
	FORMAL	hazimemasita	hazimemaseñ desita
Past Presump.	**INFORMAL**	hazimetaroo	hazimenakattaroo
		hazimeta daroo	hazimenakatta daroo
	FORMAL	hazimemasitaroo	hazimemaseñ desitaroo
		hazimeta desyoo	hazimenakatta desyoo
Conditional	**INFORMAL**	hazimetara	hazimenakattara
	FORMAL	hazimemasitara	hazimemaseñ desitara
Alternative	**INFORMAL**	hazimetari	hazimenakattari
	FORMAL	hazimemasitari	hazimemaseñ desitari

INFORMAL AFFIRMATIVE INDICATIVE

Passive	hazimerareru
Potential	hazimerareru
Causative	hazimesaseru
Causative Pass.	hazimesaserareru

Honorific	**I**	ohazime ni naru
	II	ohazime nasaru

Humble

		AFFIRMATIVE	NEGATIVE
Indicative	**INFORMAL**	hiku	hikanai
	FORMAL	hikimasu	hikimaseñ
Imperative	**INFORMAL I**	hike	hiku na
	II	hikinasai	hikinasaru na
	III	hiite kudasai	hikanai de kudasai
	FORMAL	ohiki nasaimase	ohiki nasaimasu na
Presumptive	**INFORMAL I**	hikoo	hikumai
	II	hiku daroo	hikanai daroo
	FORMAL I	hikimasyoo	hikimasumai
	II	hiku desyoo	hikanai desyoo
Provisional	**INFORMAL**	hikeba	hikanakereba
	FORMAL	hikimaseba	hikimaseñ nara
		hikimasureba	
Gerund	**INFORMAL I**	hiite	hikanai de
	II		hikanakute
	FORMAL	hikimasite	hikimaseñ de
Past Ind.	**INFORMAL**	hiita	hikanakatta
	FORMAL	hikimasita	hikimaseñ desita
Past Presump.	**INFORMAL**	hiitaroo	hikanakattaroo
		hiita daroo	hikanakatta daroo
	FORMAL	hikimasitaroo	hikimaseñ desitaroo
		hiita desyoo	hikanakatta desyoo
Conditional	**INFORMAL**	hittara	hikanakattara
	FORMAL	hikimasitara	hikimaseñ desitara
Alternative	**INFORMAL**	hiitari	hikanakattari
	FORMAL	hikimasitari	hikimaseñ desitari

INFORMAL AFFIRMATIVE INDICATIVE

Passive	hikareru
Potential	hikeru
Causative	hikaseru
Causative Pass.	hikaserareru

Honorific	**I**	ohiki ni naru
	II	ohiki nasaru
Humble	**I**	ohiki suru
	II	ohiki itasu

to pick up (from ground etc.) *to find* (by accident)   TRANSITIVE

		AFFIRMATIVE	NEGATIVE
Indicative	**INFORMAL**	hirou	hirowanai
	FORMAL	hiroimasu	hiroimaseñ
Imperative	**INFORMAL I**	hiroe	hirou na
	II	hiroinasai	hiroinasaru na
	III	hirotte kudasai	hirowanai de kudasai
	FORMAL	ohiroi nasaimase	ohiroi nasaimasu na
Presumptive	**INFORMAL I**	hirooo	hiroumai
	II	hirou daroo	hirowanai daroo
	FORMAL I	hiroimasyoo	hiroimasumai
	II	hirou desyoo	hirowanai desyoo
Provisional	**INFORMAL**	hiroeba	hirowanakereba
	FORMAL	hiroimaseba	hiroimaseñ nara
		hiroimasureba	
Gerund	**INFORMAL I**	hirotte	hirowanai de
	II		hirowanakute
	FORMAL	hiroimasite	hiroimaseñ de
Past Ind.	**INFORMAL**	hirotta	hirowanakatta
	FORMAL	hiroimasita	hiroimaseñ desita
Past Presump.	**INFORMAL**	hirottaroo	hirowanakattaroo
		hirotta daroo	hirowanakatta daroo
	FORMAL	hiroimasitaroo	hiroimaseñ desitaroo
		hirotta desyoo	hirowanakatta desyoo
Conditional	**INFORMAL**	hirottara	hirowanakattara
	FORMAL	hiroimasitara	hiroimaseñ desitara
Alternative	**INFORMAL**	hirottari	hirowanakattari
	FORMAL	hiroimasitari	hiroimaseñ desitari

	INFORMAL AFFIRMATIVE INDICATIVE
Passive	hirowareru
Potential	hiroeru
Causative	hirowaseru
Causative Pass.	hirowaserareru

Honorific	**I**	ohiroi ni naru
	II	ohiroi nasaru
Humble	**I**	ohiroi suru
	II	ohiroi itasu

			AFFIRMATIVE	NEGATIVE
Indicative	**INFORMAL**		huku	hukanai
	FORMAL		hukimasu	hukimaseñ
Imperative	**INFORMAL**	**I**	huke	huku na
		II	hukinasai	hukinasaru na
		III	huite kudasai	hukanai de kudasai
	FORMAL		ohuki nasaimase	ohuki nasaimasu na
Presumptive	**INFORMAL**	**I**	hukoo	hukumai
		II	huku daroo	hukanai daroo
	FORMAL	**I**	hukimasyoo	hukimasumai
		II	huku desyoo	hukanai desyoo
Provisional	**INFORMAL**		hukeba	hukanakereba
	FORMAL		hukimaseba	hukimaseñ nara
			hukimasureba	
Gerund	**INFORMAL**	**I**	huite	hukanai de
		II		hukanakute
	FORMAL		hukimasite	hukimaseñ de
Past Ind.	**INFORMAL**		huita	hukanakatta
	FORMAL		hukimasita	hukimaseñ desita
Past Presump.	**INFORMAL**		huitaroo	hukanakattaroo
			huita daroo	hukanakatta daroo
	FORMAL		hukimasitaroo	hukimaseñ desitaroo
			huita desyoo	hukanakatta desyoo
Conditional	**INFORMAL**		huitara	hukanakattara
	FORMAL		hukimasitara	hukimaseñ desitara
Alternative	**INFORMAL**		huitari	hukanakattari
	FORMAL		hukimasitari	hukimaseñ desitari

INFORMAL AFFIRMATIVE INDICATIVE

Passive		hukareru
Potential		hukeru
Causative		hukaseru
Causative Pass.		hukaserareru

Honorific	**I**	ohuki ni naru
	II	ohuki nasaru
Humble	**I**	ohuki suru
	II	ohuki itasu

		AFFIRMATIVE	NEGATIVE
Indicative	INFORMAL	huru	huranai
	FORMAL	hurimasu	hurimaseñ
Imperative	INFORMAL I	hure	huru na
	II	hurinasai	hurinasaru na
	III	hutte kudasai	huranai de kudasai
	FORMAL		
Presumptive	INFORMAL I	huroo	hurumai
	II	huru daroo	huranai daroo
	FORMAL I	hurimasyoo	hurimasumai
	II	huru desyoo	huranai desyoo
Provisional	INFORMAL	hureba	huranakereba
	FORMAL	hurimaseba	hurimaseñ nara
		hurimasureba	
Gerund	INFORMAL I	hutte	huranai de
	II		huranakute
	FORMAL	hurimasite	hurimaseñ de
Past Ind.	INFORMAL	hutta	huranakatta
	FORMAL	hurimasita	hurimaseñ desita
Past Presump.	INFORMAL	huttaroo	huranakattaroo
		hutta daroo	huranakatta daroo
	FORMAL	hurimasitaroo	hurimaseñ desitaroo
		hutta desyoo	huranakatta desyoo
Conditional	INFORMAL	huttara	huranakattara
	FORMAL	hurimasitara	hurimaseñ desitara
Alternative	INFORMAL	huttari	huranakattari
	FORMAL	hurimasitari	hurimaseñ desitari

INFORMAL AFFIRMATIVE INDICATIVE

Passive	hurareru
Potential	hureru
Causative	huraseru
Causative Pass.	huraserareru

Honorific

Humble

		AFFIRMATIVE	NEGATIVE
Indicative	**INFORMAL**	hutoru	hutoranai
	FORMAL	hutorimasu	hutorimaseñ
Imperative	**INFORMAL I**	hutore	hutoru na
	II	hutorinasai	hutorinasaru na
	III	hutotte kudasai	hutoranai de kudasai
	FORMAL	ohutori nasaimase	ohutori nasaimasu na
Presumptive	**INFORMAL I**	hutoroo	hutorumai
	II	hutoru daroo	hutoranai daroo
	FORMAL I	hutorimasyoo	hutorimasumai
	II	hutoru desyoo	hutoranai desyoo
Provisional	**INFORMAL**	hutoreba	hutoranakereba
	FORMAL	hutorimaseba	hutorimaseñ nara
		hutorimasureba	
Gerund	**INFORMAL I**	hutotte	hutoranai de
	II		hutoranakute
	FORMAL	hutorimasite	hutorimaseñ de
Past Ind.	**INFORMAL**	hutotta	hutoranakatta
	FORMAL	hutorimasita	hutorimaseñ desita
Past Presump.	**INFORMAL**	hutottaroo	hutoranakattaroo
		hutotta daroo	hutoranakatta daroo
	FORMAL	hutorimasitaroo	hutorimaseñ desitaroo
		hutotta desyoo	hutoranakatta desyoo
Conditional	**INFORMAL**	hutottara	hutoranakattara
	FORMAL	hutorimasitara	hutorimaseñ desitara
Alternative	**INFORMAL**	hutottari	hutoranakattari
	FORMAL	hutorimasitari	hutorimaseñ desitari

	INFORMAL AFFIRMATIVE INDICATIVE
Passive	hutorareru
Potential	hutoreru
Causative	hutoraseru
Causative Pass.	hutoraserareru

Honorific	**I**	ohutori ni naru
	II	ohutori nasaru
Humble		

ik.u
to go

		AFFIRMATIVE	NEGATIVE
Indicative	INFORMAL	iku	ikanai
	FORMAL	ikimasu	ikimaseñ
Imperative	INFORMAL I	ike	iku na
	II	ikinasai	ikinasaru na
	III	itte kudasai	ikanai de kudasai
	FORMAL	oide nasaimase	oide nasaimasu na
Presumptive	INFORMAL I	ikoo	ikumai
	II	iku daroo	ikanai daroo
	FORMAL I	ikimasyoo	ikimasumai
	II	iku desyoo	ikanai desyoo
Provisional	INFORMAL	ikeba	ikanakereba
	FORMAL	ikimaseba	ikimaseñ nara
		ikimasureba	
Gerund	INFORMAL I	itte	ikanai de
	II		ikanakute
	FORMAL	ikimasite	ikimaseñ de
Past Ind.	INFORMAL	itta	ikanakatta
	FORMAL	ikimasita	ikimaseñ desita
Past Presump.	INFORMAL	ittaroo	ikanakattaroo
		itta daroo	ikanakatta daroo
	FORMAL	ikimasitaroo	ikimaseñ desitaroo
		itta desyoo	ikanakatta desyoo
Conditional	INFORMAL	ittara	ikanakattara
	FORMAL	ikimasitara	ikimaseñ desitara
Alternative	INFORMAL	ittari	ikanakattari
	FORMAL	ikimasitari	ikimaseñ desitari

	INFORMAL AFFIRMATIVE INDICATIVE	
Passive	ikareru	
Potential	ikareru	ikeru
Causative	ikaseru	
Causative Pass.	ikaserareru	

Honorific	irassyaru	{ oide ni naru (I) oide nasaru (II)
Humble	mairu	

		AFFIRMATIVE	NEGATIVE
Indicative	INFORMAL	irassyaru	irassyaranai
	FORMAL	irassyaimasu	irassyaimaseñ
Imperative	INFORMAL I	irassyai	irassyaru na
	II		
	III	irassyatte kudasai	irassyaranai de kudasai
	FORMAL	irassyaimase	irassyaimasu na
Presumptive	INFORMAL I	irassyaroo	irassyarumai
	II	irassyaru daroo	irassyaranai daroo
	FORMAL I	irassyaimasyoo	irassyaimasumai
	II	irassyaru desyoo	irassyaranai desyoo
Provisional	INFORMAL	irassyareba	irassyaranakereba
	FORMAL	irassyaimaseba	irassyaimaseñ nara
		irassyaimasureba	
Gerund	INFORMAL I	irassyatte*	irassyaranai de
	II		irassyaranakute
	FORMAL	irassyaimasite	irassyaimaseñ de
Past Ind.	INFORMAL	irassyatta*	irassyaranakatta
	FORMAL	irassyaimasita	irassyaimaseñ desita
Past Presump.	INFORMAL	irassyattaroo*	irassyaranakattaroo
		irassyatta daroo	irassyaranakatta daroo
	FORMAL	irassyaimasitaroo	irassyaimaseñ desitaroo
		irassyatta desyoo	irassyaranakatta desyoo
Conditional	INFORMAL	irassyattara*	irassyaranakattara
	FORMAL	irassyaimasitara	irassyaimaseñ desitara
Alternative	INFORMAL	irassyattari*	irassyaranakattari
	FORMAL	irassyaimasitari	irassyaimaseñ desitari

INFORMAL AFFIRMATIVE INDICATIVE

Passive

Potential

Causative

Causative Pass.

Honorific

Humble

*Shorter forms: *irasite, irasita, irasitaroo, irasitara,* and *irasitari* also occur in the same environments as the longer forms given above.

		AFFIRMATIVE	NEGATIVE
Indicative	INFORMAL	ireru	irenai
	FORMAL	iremasu	iremaseñ
Imperative	INFORMAL I	irero	ireru na
	II	irenasai	irenasaru na
	III	irete kudasai	irenai de kudasai
	FORMAL	oire nasaimase	oire nasaimasu na
Presumptive	INFORMAL I	ireyoo	iremai
	II	ireru daroo	irenai daroo
	FORMAL I	iremasyoo	iremasumai
	II	ireru desyoo	irenai desyoo
Provisional	INFORMAL	irereba	irenakereba
	FORMAL	iremaseba	iremaseñ nara
		iremasureba	
Gerund	INFORMAL I	irete	irenai de
	II		irenakute
	FORMAL	iremasite	iremaseñ de
Past Ind.	INFORMAL	ireta	irenakatta
	FORMAL	iremasita	iremaseñ desita
Past Presump.	INFORMAL	iretaroo	irenakattaroo
		ireta daroo	irenakatta daroo
	FORMAL	iremasitaroo	iremaseñ desitaroo
		ireta desyoo	irenakatta desyoo
Conditional	INFORMAL	iretara	irenakattara
	FORMAL	iremasitara	iremaseñ desitara
Alternative	INFORMAL	iretari	irenakattari
	FORMAL	iremasitari	iremaseñ desitari

	INFORMAL AFFIRMATIVE INDICATIVE
Passive	irerareru
Potential	irerareru
Causative	iresaseru
Causative Pass.	iresaserareru

Honorific	I	oire ni naru
	II	oire nasaru
Humble	I	oire suru
	II	oire itasu

34

			AFFIRMATIVE	NEGATIVE
Indicative	INFORMAL		iru	inai
	FORMAL		imasu	imaseñ
Imperative	INFORMAL	I	iro	iru na
		II	inasai	inasaru na
		III	ite kudasai	inai de kudasai
	FORMAL		oide nasaimase	oide nasaimasu na
Presumptive	INFORMAL	I	iyoo	imai
		II	iru daroo	inai daroo
	FORMAL	I	imasyoo	imasumai
		II	iru desyoo	inai desyoo
Provisional	INFORMAL		ireba	inakereba
	FORMAL		imaseba	imaseñ nara
			imasureba	
Gerund	INFORMAL	I	ite	inai de
		II		inakute
	FORMAL		imasite	imaseñ de
Past Ind.	INFORMAL		ita	inakatta
	FORMAL		imasita	imaseñ desita
Past Presump.	INFORMAL		itaroo	inakattaroo
			ita daroo	inakatta daroo
	FORMAL		imasitaroo	imaseñ desitaroo
			ita desyoo	inakatta desyoo
Conditional	INFORMAL		itara	inakattara
	FORMAL		imasitara	imaseñ desitara
Alternative	INFORMAL		itari	inakattari
	FORMAL		imasitari	imaseñ desitari

	INFORMAL AFFIRMATIVE INDICATIVE	
Passive	irareru	
Potential	irareru	
Causative	isaseru	
Causative Pass.	isaserareru	

Honorific	irassyaru	oide ni naru
Humble	oru	

		AFFIRMATIVE	NEGATIVE
Indicative	**INFORMAL**	iru	iranai
	FORMAL	irimasu	irimaseñ
Imperative	**INFORMAL I**		
	II		
	III		
	FORMAL		
Presumptive	**INFORMAL I**	iroo	irumai
	II	iru daroo	iranai daroo
	FORMAL I	irimasyoo	irimasumai
	II	iru desyoo	iranai desyoo
Provisional	**INFORMAL**	ireba	iranakereba
	FORMAL	irimaseba	irimaseñ nara
		irimasureba	
Gerund	**INFORMAL I**	itte	iranai de
	II		iranakute
	FORMAL	irimasite	irimaseñ de
Past Ind.	**INFORMAL**	itta	iranakatta
	FORMAL	irimasita	irimaseñ desita
Past Presump.	**INFORMAL**	ittaroo	iranakattaroo
		itta daroo	iranakatta daroo
	FORMAL	irimasitaroo	irimaseñ desitaroo
		itta desyoo	iranakatta desyoo
Conditional	**INFORMAL**	ittara	iranakattara
	FORMAL	irimasitara	irimaseñ desitara
Alternative	**INFORMAL**	ittari	iranakattari
	FORMAL	irimasitari	irimaseñ desitari

INFORMAL AFFIRMATIVE INDICATIVE

Passive

Potential

Causative

Causative Pass.

Honorific

Humble

TRANSITIVE *to hurry*

			AFFIRMATIVE	NEGATIVE
Indicative	**INFORMAL**		isogu	isoganai
	FORMAL		isogimasu	isogimaseñ
Imperative	**INFORMAL**	I	isoge	isogu na
		II	isoginasai	isoginasaru na
		III	isoide kudasai	isoganai de kudasai
	FORMAL		oisogi nasaimase	oisogi nasaimasu na
Presumptive	**INFORMAL**	I	isogoo	isogumai
		II	isogu daroo	isoganai daroo
	FORMAL	I	isogimasyoo	isogimasumai
		II	isogu desyoo	isoganai desyoo
Provisional	**INFORMAL**		isogeba	isoganakereba
	FORMAL		isogimaseba	isogimaseñ nara
			isogimasureba	
Gerund	**INFORMAL**	I	isoide	isoganai de
		II		isoganakute
	FORMAL		isogimasite	isogimaseñ de
Past Ind.	**INFORMAL**		isoida	isoganakatta
	FORMAL		isogimasita	isogimaseñ desita
Past Presump.	**INFORMAL**		isoidaroo	isoganakattaroo
			isoida daroo	isoganakatta daroo
	FORMAL		isogimasitaroo	isogimaseñ desitaroo
			isoida desyoo	isoganakatta desyoo
Conditional	**INFORMAL**		isoidara	isoganakattara
	FORMAL		isogimasitara	isogimaseñ desitara
Alternative	**INFORMAL**		isoidari	isoganakattari
	FORMAL		isogimasitari	isogimaseñ desitari

	INFORMAL AFFIRMATIVE INDICATIVE
Passive	isogareru
Potential	isogeru
Causative	isogaseru
Causative Pass.	isogaserareru

Honorific	I	oisogi ni naru
	II	oisogi nasaru
Humble		

itadak.u   **itadaki**
to receive, to take food or drink (humble)   TRANSITIVE

			AFFIRMATIVE	**NEGATIVE**
Indicative	INFORMAL		itadaku	itadakanai
	FORMAL		itadakimasu	itadakimaseñ
Imperative	INFORMAL	I		
		II		
		III		
	FORMAL			
Presumptive	INFORMAL	I	itadakoo	itadakumai
		II	itadaku daroo	itadakanai daroo
	FORMAL	I	itadakimasyoo	itadakimasumai
		II	itadaku desyoo	itadakanai desyoo
Provisional	INFORMAL		itadakeba	itadakanakereba
	FORMAL		itadakimaseba	itadakimaseñ nara
			itadakimasureba	
Gerund	INFORMAL	I	itadaite	itadakanai de
		II		itadakanakute
	FORMAL		itadakimasite	itadakimaseñ de
Past Ind.	INFORMAL		itadaita	itadakanakatta
	FORMAL		itadakimasita	itadakimaseñ desita
Past Presump.	INFORMAL		itadaitaroo	itadakanakattaroo
			itadaita daroo	itadakanakatta daroo
	FORMAL		itadakimasitaroo	itadakimaseñ desitaroo
			itadaita desyoo	itadakanakatta desyoo
Conditional	INFORMAL		itadaitara	itadakanakattara
	FORMAL		itadakimasitara	itadakimaseñ desitara
Alternative	INFORMAL		itadaitari	itadakanakattari
	FORMAL		itadakimasitari	itadakimaseñ desitari

INFORMAL AFFIRMATIVE INDICATIVE

Passive	
Potential	itadakeru
Causative	itadakaseru
Causative Pass.	itadakaserareru

Honorific	
Humble	

38

to become hurt, spoiled, or damaged

		AFFIRMATIVE	NEGATIVE
Indicative	**INFORMAL**	itamu	itamanai
	FORMAL	itamimasu	itamimaseñ
Imperative	**INFORMAL** I		
	II		
	III		
	FORMAL		
Presumptive	**INFORMAL** I	itamoo	itamumai
	II	itamu daroo	itamanai daroo
	FORMAL I	itamimasyoo	itamimasumai
	II	itamu desyoo	itamanai desyoo
Provisional	**INFORMAL**	itameba	itamanakereba
	FORMAL	itamimaseba	itamimaseñ nara
		itamimasureba	
Gerund	**INFORMAL** I	itañde	itamanai de
	II		itamanakute
	FORMAL	itamimasite	itamimaseñ de
Past Ind.	**INFORMAL**	itañda	itamanakatta
	FORMAL	itamimasita	itamimaseñ desita
Past Presump.	**INFORMAL**	itañdaroo	itamanakattaroo
		itañda daroo	itamanakatta daroo
	FORMAL	itamimasitaroo	itamimaseñ desitaroo
		itañda desyoo	itamanakatta desyoo
Conditional	**INFORMAL**	itañdara	itamanakattara
	FORMAL	itamimasitara	itamimaseñ desitara
Alternative	**INFORMAL**	itañdari	itamanakattari
	FORMAL	itamimasitari	itamimaseñ desitari

	INFORMAL AFFIRMATIVE INDICATIVE
Passive	itamareru
Potential	itameru
Causative	itamaseru
Causative Pass.	itamaserareru

Honorific	I	oitami ni naru
	II	oitami nasaru
Humble		

			AFFIRMATIVE	NEGATIVE
Indicative	**INFORMAL**		itasu	itasanai
	FORMAL		itasimasu	itasimaseñ
Imperative	**INFORMAL**	**I**	itase	itasu na
		II		
		III		
	FORMAL			
Presumptive	**INFORMAL**	**I**	itasoo	itasumai
		II	itasu daroo	itasanai daroo
	FORMAL	**I**	itasimasyoo	itasimasumai
		II	itasu desyoo	itasanai desyoo
Provisional	**INFORMAL**		itaseba	itasanakereba
	FORMAL		itasimaseba	itasimaseñ nara
			itasimasureba	
Gerund	**INFORMAL**	**I**	itasite	itasanai de
		II		itasanakute
	FORMAL		itasimasite	itasimaseñ de
Past Ind.	**INFORMAL**		itasita	itasanakatta
	FORMAL		itasimasita	itasimaseñ desita
Past Presump.	**INFORMAL**		itasitaroo	itasanakattaroo
			itasita daroo	itasanakatta daroo
	FORMAL		itasimasitaroo	itasimaseñ desitaroo
			itasita desyoo	itasanakatta desyoo
Conditional	**INFORMAL**		itasitara	itasanakattara
	FORMAL		itasimasitara	itasimaseñ desitara
Alternative	**INFORMAL**		itasitari	itasanakattari
	FORMAL		itasimasitari	itasimaseñ desitari

INFORMAL AFFIRMATIVE INDICATIVE

Passive

Potential

Causative

Causative Pass.

Honorific

Humble

TRANSITIVE   *to say, to tell*

			AFFIRMATIVE	NEGATIVE
Indicative	**INFORMAL**		iu	iwanai
	FORMAL		iimasu	iimaseñ
Imperative	**INFORMAL**	I	ie	iu na
		II	iinasai	iinasaru na
		III	itte kudasai	iwanai de kudasai
	FORMAL		ossyaimase	ossyaimasu na
Presumptive	**INFORMAL**	I	ioo	iumai
		II	iu daroo	iwanai daroo
	FORMAL	I	iimasyoo	iimasumai
		II	iu desyoo	iwanai desyoo
Provisional	**INFORMAL**		ieba	iwanakereba
	FORMAL		iimaseba	iimaseñ nara
			iimasureba	
Gerund	**INFORMAL**	I	itte	iwanai de
		II		iwanakute
	FORMAL		iimasite	iimaseñ de
Past Ind.	**INFORMAL**		itta	iwanakatta
	FORMAL		iimasita	iimaseñ desita
Past Presump.	**INFORMAL**		ittaroo	iwanakattaroo
			itta daroo	iwanakatta daroo
	FORMAL		iimasitaroo	iimaseñ desitaroo
			itta desyoo	iwanakatta desyoo
Conditional	**INFORMAL**		ittara	iwanakattara
	FORMAL		iimasitara	iimaseñ desitara
Alternative	**INFORMAL**		ittari	iwanakattari
	FORMAL		iimasitari	iimaseñ desitari

	INFORMAL AFFIRMATIVE INDICATIVE
Passive	iwareru
Potential	ieru
Causative	iwaseru
Causative Pass.	iwaserareru

Honorific	ossyaru
Humble	moosu

			AFFIRMATIVE	NEGATIVE
Indicative	INFORMAL		kaeru	kaenai
	FORMAL		kaemasu	kaemaseñ
Imperative	INFORMAL	I	kaero	kaeru na
		II	kaenasai	kaenasaru na
		III	kaete kudasai	kaenai de kudasai
	FORMAL		okae nasaimase	okae nasaimasu na
Presumptive	INFORMAL	I	kaeyoo	kaemai
		II	kaeru daroo	kaenai daroo
	FORMAL	I	kaemasyoo	kaemasumai
		II	kaeru desyoo	kaenai desyoo
Provisional	INFORMAL		kaereba	kaenakereba
	FORMAL		kaemaseba	kaemaseñ nara
			kaemasureba	
Gerund	INFORMAL	I	kaete	kaenai de
		II		kaenakute
	FORMAL		kaemasite	kaemaseñ de
Past Ind.	INFORMAL		kaeta	kaenakatta
	FORMAL		kaemasita	kaemaseñ desita
Past Presump.	INFORMAL		kaetaroo	kaenakattaroo
			kaeta daroo	kaenakatta daroo
	FORMAL		kaemasitaroo	kaemaseñ desitaroo
			kaeta desyoo	kaenakatta desyoo
Conditional	INFORMAL		kaetara	kaenakattara
	FORMAL		kaemasitara	kaemaseñ desitara
Alternative	INFORMAL		kaetari	kaenakattari
	FORMAL		kaemasitari	kaemaseñ desitari

		INFORMAL AFFIRMATIVE INDICATIVE
Passive		kaerareru
Potential		kaerareru
Causative		kaesaseru
Causative Pass.		kaesaserareru

Honorific	I	okae ni naru
	II	okae nasaru
Humble	I	okae suru
	II	okae itasu

to return (to a place)

		AFFIRMATIVE	NEGATIVE
Indicative	**INFORMAL**	kaeru	kaeranai
	FORMAL	kaerimasu	kaerimaseñ
Imperative	**INFORMAL I**	kaere	kaeru na
	II	kaerinasai	kaerinasaru na
	III	kaette kudasai	kaeranai de kudasai
	FORMAL	okaeri nasaimase	okaeri nasaimasu na
Presumptive	**INFORMAL I**	kaeroo	kaerumai
	II	kaeru daroo	kaeranai daroo
	FORMAL I	kaerimasyoo	kaerimasumai
	II	kaeru desyoo	kaeranai desyoo
Provisional	**INFORMAL**	kaereba	kaeranakereba
	FORMAL	kaerimaseba	kaerimaseñ nara
		kaerimasureba	
Gerund	**INFORMAL I**	kaette	kaeranai de
	II		kaeranakute
	FORMAL	kaerimasite	kaerimaseñ de
Past Ind.	**INFORMAL**	kaetta	kaeranakatta
	FORMAL	kaerimasita	kaerimaseñ desita
Past Presump.	**INFORMAL**	kaettaroo	kaeranakattaroo
		kaetta daroo	kaeranakatta daroo
	FORMAL	kaerimasitaroo	kaerimaseñ desitaroo
		kaetta desyoo	kaeranakatta desyoo
Conditional	**INFORMAL**	kaettara	kaeranakattara
	FORMAL	kaerimasitara	kaerimaseñ desitara
Alternative	**INFORMAL**	kaettari	kaeranakattari
	FORMAL	kaerimasitari	kaerimaseñ desitari

	INFORMAL AFFIRMATIVE INDICATIVE
Passive	kaerareru
Potential	kaereru
Causative	kaeraseru
Causative Pass.	kaeraserareru

Honorific	**I**	okaeri ni naru
	II	okaeri nasaru
Humble		

to return (something to someone)   TRANSITIVE

			AFFIRMATIVE	**NEGATIVE**
Indicative	**INFORMAL**		kaesu	kaesanai
	FORMAL		kaesimasu	kaesimaseñ
Imperative	**INFORMAL**	**I**	kaese	kaesu na
		II	kaesinasai	kaesinasaru na
		III	kaesite kudasai	kaesanai de kudasai
	FORMAL		okaesi nasaimase	okaesi nasaimasu na
Presumptive	**INFORMAL**	**I**	kaesoo	kaesumai
		II	kaesu daroo	kaesanai daroo
	FORMAL	**I**	kaesimasyoo	kaesimasumai
		II	kaesu desyoo	kaesanai desyoo
Provisional	**INFORMAL**		kaeseba	kaesanakereba
	FORMAL		kaesimaseba	kaesimaseñ nara
			kaesimasureba	
Gerund	**INFORMAL**	**I**	kaesite	kaesanai de
		II		kaesanakute
	FORMAL		kaesimasite	kaesimaseñ de
Past Ind.	**INFORMAL**		kaesita	kaesanakatta
	FORMAL		kaesimasita	kaesimaseñ desita
Past Presump.	**INFORMAL**		kaesitaroo	kaesanakattaroo
			kaesita daroo	kaesanakatta daroo
	FORMAL		kaesimasitaroo	kaesimaseñ desitaroo
			kaesita desyoo	kaesanakatta desyoo
Conditional	**INFORMAL**		kaesitara	kaesanakattara
	FORMAL		kaesimasitara	kaesimaseñ desitara
Alternative	**INFORMAL**		kaesitari	kaesanakattari
	FORMAL		kaesimasitari	kaesimaseñ desitari

		INFORMAL AFFIRMATIVE INDICATIVE
Passive		kaesareru
Potential		kaeseru
Causative		kaesaseru
Causative Pass.		kaesaserareru

Honorific	**I**	okaesi ni naru
	II	okaesi nasaru
Humble	**I**	okaesi suru
	II	okaesi itasu

kake

kake.ru
TRANSITIVE · *to hang up*

		AFFIRMATIVE	**NEGATIVE**
Indicative	**INFORMAL**	kakeru	kakenai
	FORMAL	kakemasu	kakemaseñ
Imperative	**INFORMAL I**	kakero	kakeru na
	II	kakenasai	kakenasaru na
	III	kakete kudasai	kakenai de kudasai
	FORMAL	okake nasaimase	okake nasaimasu na
Presumptive	**INFORMAL I**	kakeyoo	kakemai
	II	kakeru daroo	kakenai daroo
	FORMAL I	kakemasyoo	kakemasumai
	II	kakeru desyoo	kakenai desyoo
Provisional	**INFORMAL**	kakereba	kakenakereba
	FORMAL	kakemaseba	kakemaseñ nara
		kakemasureba	
Gerund	**INFORMAL I**	kakete	kakenai de
	II		kakenakute
	FORMAL	kakemasite	kakemaseñ de
Past Ind.	**INFORMAL**	kaketa	kakenakatta
	FORMAL	kakemasita	kakemaseñ desita
Past Presump.	**INFORMAL**	kaketaroo	kakenakattaroo
		kaketa daroo	kakenakatta daroo
	FORMAL	kakemasitaroo	kakemaseñ desitaroo
		kaketa desyoo	kakenakatta desyoo
Conditional	**INFORMAL**	kaketara	kakenakattara
	FORMAL	kakemasitara	kakemaseñ desitara
Alternative	**INFORMAL**	kaketari	kakenakattari
	FORMAL	kakemasitari	kakemaseñ desitari

	INFORMAL AFFIRMATIVE INDICATIVE
Passive	kakerareru
Potential	kakerareru
Causative	kakesaseru
Causative Pass.	kakesaserareru

Honorific	**I**	okake ni naru
	II	okake nasaru
Humble	**I**	okake suru
	II	okake itasu

		AFFIRMATIVE	**NEGATIVE**
Indicative	INFORMAL	kaku	kakanai
	FORMAL	kakimasu	kakimaseñ
Imperative	INFORMAL I	kake	kaku na
	II	kakinasai	kakinasaru na
	III	kaite kudasai	kakanai de kudasai
	FORMAL	okaki nasaimase	okaki nasaimasu na
Presumptive	INFORMAL I	kakoo	kakumai
	II	kaku daroo	kakanai daroo
	FORMAL I	kakimasyoo	kakimasumai
	II	kaku desyoo	kakanai desyoo
Provisional	INFORMAL	kakeba	kakanakereba
	FORMAL	kakimaseba	kakimaseñ nara
		kakimasureba	
Gerund	INFORMAL I	kaite	kakanai de
	II		kakanakute
	FORMAL	kakimasite	kakimaseñ de
Past Ind.	INFORMAL	kaita	kakanakatta
	FORMAL	kakimasita	kakimaseñ desita
Past Presump.	INFORMAL	kaitaroo	kakanakattaroo
		kaita daroo	kakanakatta daroo
	FORMAL	kakimasitaroo	kakimaseñ desitaroo
		kaita desyoo	kakanakatta desyoo
Conditional	INFORMAL	kaitara	kakanakattara
	FORMAL	kakimasitara	kakimaseñ desitara
Alternative	INFORMAL	kaitari	kakanakattari
	FORMAL	kakimasitari	kakimaseñ desitari

	INFORMAL AFFIRMATIVE INDICATIVE
Passive	kakareru
Potential	kakeru
Causative	kakaseru
Causative Pass.	kakaserareru

Honorific	I	okaki ni naru
	II	okaki nasaru
Humble	I	okaki suru
	II	okaki itasu

TRANSITIVE   *to mind, to care about*

		AFFIRMATIVE	NEGATIVE
Indicative	INFORMAL	kamau	kamawanai
	FORMAL	kamaimasu	kamaimaseñ
Imperative	INFORMAL I	kamae	kamau na
	II	kamainasai	kamainasaru na
	III	kamatte kudasai	kamawanai de kudasai
	FORMAL	okamai nasaimase	okamai nasaimasu na
Presumptive	INFORMAL I	kamaoo	kamaumai
	II	kamau daroo	kamawanai daroo
	FORMAL I	kamaimasyoo	kamaimasumai
	II	kamau desyoo	kamawanai desyoo
Provisional	INFORMAL	kamaeba	kamawanakereba
	FORMAL	kamaimaseba	kamaimaseñ nara
		kamaimasureba	
Gerund	INFORMAL I	kamatte	kamawanai de
	II		kamawanakute
	FORMAL	kamaimasite	kamaimaseñ de
Past Ind.	INFORMAL	kamatta	kamawanakatta
	FORMAL	kamaimasita	kamaimaseñ desita
Past Presump.	INFORMAL	kamattaroo	kamawanakattaroo
		kamatta daroo	kamawanakatta daroo
	FORMAL	kamaimasitaroo	kamaimaseñ desitaroo
		kamatta desyoo	kamawanakatta desyoo
Conditional	INFORMAL	kamattara	kamawanakattara
	FORMAL	kamaimasitara	kamaimaseñ desitara
Alternative	INFORMAL	kamattari	kamawanakattari
	FORMAL	kamaimasitari	kamaimaseñ desitari

INFORMAL AFFIRMATIVE INDICATIVE

Passive	
Potential	kamaeru
Causative	kamawaseru
Causative Pass.	kamawaserareru

Honorific	I	okamai ni naru
	II	okamai nasaru
Humble	I	okamai suru
	II	okamai itasu

47

			AFFIRMATIVE	NEGATIVE
Indicative	INFORMAL		kaṅgaeru	kaṅgaenai
	FORMAL		kaṅgaemasu	kaṅgaemaseñ
Imperative	INFORMAL	I	kaṅgaero	kaṅgaeru na
		II	kaṅgaenasai	kaṅgaenasaru na
		III	kaṅgaete kudasai	kaṅgaenai de kudasai
	FORMAL		okaṅgae nasaimase	okaṅgae nasaimasu na
Presumptive	INFORMAL	I	kaṅgaeyoo	kaṅgaemai
		II	kaṅgaeru daroo	kaṅgaenai daroo
	FORMAL	I	kaṅgaemasyoo	kaṅgaemasumai
		II	kaṅgaeru desyoo	kaṅgaenai desyoo
Provisional	INFORMAL		kaṅgaereba	kaṅgaenakereba
	FORMAL		kaṅgaemaseba	kaṅgaemaseñ nara
			kaṅgaemasureba	
Gerund	INFORMAL	I	kaṅgaete	kaṅgaenai de
		II		kaṅgaenakute
	FORMAL		kaṅgaemasite	kaṅgaemaseñ de
Past Ind.	INFORMAL		kaṅgaeta	kaṅgaenakatta
	FORMAL		kaṅgaemasita	kaṅgaemaseñ desita
Past Presump.	INFORMAL		kaṅgaetaroo	kaṅgaenakattaroo
			kaṅgaeta daroo	kaṅgaenakatta daroo
	FORMAL		kaṅgaemasitaroo	kaṅgaemaseñ desitaroo
			kaṅgaeta desyoo	kaṅgaenakatta desyoo
Conditional	INFORMAL		kaṅgaetara	kaṅgaenakattara
	FORMAL		kaṅgaemasitara	kaṅgaemaseñ desitara
Alternative	INFORMAL		kaṅgaetari	kaṅgaenakattari
	FORMAL		kaṅgaemasitari	kaṅgaemaseñ desitari

		INFORMAL AFFIRMATIVE INDICATIVE
Passive		kaṅgaerareru
Potential		kaṅgaerareru
Causative		kaṅgaesaseru
Causative Pass.		kaṅgaesaserareru

Honorific	I	okaṅgae ni naru
	II	okaṅgae nasaru
Humble		

TRANSITIVE   *to borrow, to rent*

			AFFIRMATIVE	NEGATIVE
Indicative	**INFORMAL**		kariru	karinai
	FORMAL		karimasu	karimaseñ
Imperative	**INFORMAL**	I	kariro	kariru na
		II	karinasai	karinasaru na
		III	karite kudasai	karinai de kudasai
	FORMAL		okari nasaimase	okari nasaimasu na
Presumptive	**INFORMAL**	I	kariyoo	karimai
		II	kariru daroo	karinai daroo
	FORMAL	I	karimasyoo	karimasumai
		II	kariru desyoo	karinai desyoo
Provisional	**INFORMAL**		karireba	karinakereba
	FORMAL		karimaseba	karimaseñ nara
			karimasureba	
Gerund	**INFORMAL**	I	karite	karinai de
		II		karinakute
	FORMAL		karimasite	karimaseñ de
Past Ind.	**INFORMAL**		karita	karinakatta
	FORMAL		karimasita	karimaseñ desita
Past Presump.	**INFORMAL**		karitaroo	karinakattaroo
			karita daroo	karinakatta daroo
	FORMAL		karimasitaroo	karimaseñ desitaroo
			karita desyoo	karinakatta desyoo
Conditional	**INFORMAL**		karitara	karinakattara
	FORMAL		karimasitara	karimaseñ desitara
Alternative	**INFORMAL**		karitari	karinakattari
	FORMAL		karimasitari	karimaseñ desitari

	INFORMAL AFFIRMATIVE INDICATIVE
Passive	karirareru
Potential	karirareru
Causative	karisaseru
Causative Pass.	karisaserareru

Honorific	I	okari ni naru
	II	okari nasaru
Humble	I	okari suru
	II	okari itasu

			AFFIRMATIVE	NEGATIVE
Indicative	**INFORMAL**		kasu	kasanai
	FORMAL		kasimasu	kasimaseñ
Imperative	**INFORMAL**	**I**	kase	kasu na
		II	kasinasai	kasinasaru na
		III	kasite kudasai	kasanai de kudasai
	FORMAL		okasi nasaimase	okasi nasaimasu na
Presumptive	**INFORMAL**	**I**	kasoo	kasumai
		II	kasu daroo	kasanai daroo
	FORMAL	**I**	kasimasyoo	kasimasumai
		II	kasu desyoo	kasanai desyoo
Provisional	**INFORMAL**		kaseba	kasanakereba
	FORMAL		kasimaseba	kasimaseñ nara
			kasimasureba	
Gerund	**INFORMAL**	**I**	kasite	kasanai de
		II		kasanakute
	FORMAL		kasimasite	kasimaseñ de
Past Ind.	**INFORMAL**		kasita	kasanakatta
	FORMAL		kasimasita	kasimaseñ desita
Past Presump.	**INFORMAL**		kasitaroo	kasanakattaroo
			kasita daroo	kasanakatta daroo
	FORMAL		kasimasitaroo	kasimaseñ desitaroo
			kasita desyoo	kasanakatta desyoo
Conditional	**INFORMAL**		kasitara	kasanakattara
	FORMAL		kasimasitara	kasimaseñ desitara
Alternative	**INFORMAL**		kasitari	kasanakattari
	FORMAL		kasimasitari	kasimaseñ desitari

INFORMAL AFFIRMATIVE INDICATIVE

Passive	kasareru
Potential	kaseru
Causative	kasaseru
Causative Pass.	kasaserareru

Honorific	**I**	okasi ni naru
	II	okasi nasaru
Humble	**I**	okasi suru
	II	okasi itasu

TRANSITIVE   *to straighten up things*

		AFFIRMATIVE	NEGATIVE
Indicative	**INFORMAL**	katazukeru	katazukenai
	FORMAL	katazukemasu	katazukemaseñ
Imperative	**INFORMAL I**	katazukero	katazukeru na
	II	katazukenasai	katazukenasaru na
	III	katazukete kudasai	katazukenai de kudasai
	FORMAL	okatazuke nasaimase	okatazuke nasaimasu na
Presumptive	**INFORMAL I**	katazukeyoo	katazukemai
	II	katazukeru daroo	katazukenai daroo
	FORMAL I	katazukemasyoo	katazukemasumai
	II	katazukeru desyoo	katazukenai desyoo
Provisional	**INFORMAL**	katazukereba	katazukenakereba
	FORMAL	katazukemaseba	katazukemaseñ nara
		katazukemasureba	
Gerund	**INFORMAL I**	katazukete	katazukenai de
	II		katazukenakute
	FORMAL	katazukemasite	katazukemaseñ de
Past Ind.	**INFORMAL**	katazuketa	katazukenakatta
	FORMAL	katazukemasita	katazukemaseñ desita
Past Presump.	**INFORMAL**	katazuketaroo	katazukenakattaroo
		katazuketa daroo	katazukenakatta daroo
	FORMAL	katazukemasitaroo	katazukemaseñ desitaroo
		katazuketa desyoo	katazukenakatta desyoo
Conditional	**INFORMAL**	katazuketara	katazukenakattara
	FORMAL	katazukemasitara	katazukemaseñ desitara
Alternative	**INFORMAL**	katazuketari	katazukenakattari
	FORMAL	katazukemasitari	katazukemaseñ desitari

	INFORMAL AFFIRMATIVE INDICATIVE
Passive	katazukerareru
Potential	katazukerareru
Causative	katazukesaseru
Causative Pass.	katazukesaserareru

Honorific	**I**	okatazuke ni naru
	II	okatazuke nasaru
Humble	**I**	okatazuke suru
	II	okatazuke itasu

		AFFIRMATIVE	NEGATIVE
Indicative	**INFORMAL**	katu	katanai
	FORMAL	katimasu	katimaseñ
Imperative	**INFORMAL** I	kate	katu na
	II	katinasai	katinasaru na
	III	katte kudasai	katanai de kudasai
	FORMAL	okati nasaimase	okati nasaimasu na
Presumptive	**INFORMAL** I	katoo	katumai
	II	katu daroo	katanai daroo
	FORMAL I	katimasyoo	katimasumai
	II	katu desyoo	katanai desyoo
Provisional	**INFORMAL**	kateba	katanakereba
	FORMAL	katimaseba	katimaseñ nara
		katimasureba	
Gerund	**INFORMAL** I	katte	katanai de
	II		katanakute
	FORMAL	katimasite	katimaseñ de
Past Ind.	**INFORMAL**	katta	katanakatta
	FORMAL	katimasita	katimaseñ desita
Past Presump.	**INFORMAL**	kattaroo	katanakattaroo
		katta daroo	katanakatta daroo
	FORMAL	katimasitaroo	katimaseñ desitaroo
		katta desyoo	katanakatta desyoo
Conditional	**INFORMAL**	kattara	katanakattara
	FORMAL	katimasitara	katimaseñ desitara
Alternative	**INFORMAL**	kattari	katanakattari
	FORMAL	katimasitari	katimaseñ desitari

	INFORMAL AFFIRMATIVE INDICATIVE
Passive	katareru
Potential	kateru
Causative	kataseru
Causative Pass.	kataserareru

Honorific	I	okati ni naru
	II	okati nasaru
Humble		

		AFFIRMATIVE	NEGATIVE
Indicative	**INFORMAL**	kau	kawanai
	FORMAL	kaimasu	kaimaseñ
Imperative	**INFORMAL I**	kae	kau na
	II	kainasai	kainasaru na
	III	katte kudasai	kawanai de kudasai
	FORMAL	okai nasaimase	okai nasaimasu na
Presumptive	**INFORMAL I**	kaoo	kaumai
	II	kau daroo	kawanai daroo
	FORMAL I	kaimasyoo	kaimasumai
	II	kau desyoo	kawanai desyoo
Provisional	**INFORMAL**	kaeba	kawanakereba
	FORMAL	kaimaseba	kaimaseñ nara
		kaimasureba	
Gerund	**INFORMAL I**	katte	kawanai de
	II		kawanakute
	FORMAL	kaimasite	kaimaseñ de
Past Ind.	**INFORMAL**	katta	kawanakatta
	FORMAL	kaimasita	kaimaseñ desita
Past Presump.	**INFORMAL**	kattaroo	kawanakattaroo
		katta daroo	kawanakatta daroo
	FORMAL	kaimasitaroo	kaimaseñ desitaroo
		katta desyoo	kawanakatta desyoo
Conditional	**INFORMAL**	kattara	kawanakattara
	FORMAL	kaimasitara	kaimaseñ desitara
Alternative	**INFORMAL**	kattari	kawanakattari
	FORMAL	kaimasitari	kaimaseñ desitari

	INFORMAL AFFIRMATIVE INDICATIVE
Passive	kawareru
Potential	kaeru
Causative	kawaseru
Causative Pass.	kawaserareru

Honorific	**I**	okai ni naru
	II	okai nasaru
Humble	**I**	okai suru
	II	okai itasu

kawak.u
to become dry

kawaki

		AFFIRMATIVE	NEGATIVE
Indicative	INFORMAL	kawaku	kawakanai
	FORMAL	kawakimasu	kawakimaseñ
Imperative	INFORMAL I	kawake	kawaku na
	II		
	III		
	FORMAL		
Presumptive	INFORMAL I	kawakoo	kawakumai
	II	kawaku daroo	kawakanai daroo
	FORMAL I	kawakimasyoo	kawakimasumai
	II	kawaku desyoo	kawakanai desyoo
Provisional	INFORMAL	kawakeba	kawakanakereba
	FORMAL	kawakimaseba	kawakimaseñ nara
		kawakimasureba	
Gerund	INFORMAL I	kawaite	kawakanai de
	II		kawakanakute
	FORMAL	kawakimasite	kawakimaseñ de
Past Ind.	INFORMAL	kawaita	kawakanakatta
	FORMAL	kawakimasita	kawakimaseñ desita
Past Presump.	INFORMAL	kawaitaroo	kawakanakattaroo
		kawaita daroo	kawakanakatta daroo
	FORMAL	kawakimasitaroo	kawakimaseñ desitaroo
		kawaita desyoo	kawakanakatta desyoo
Conditional	INFORMAL	kawaitara	kawakanakattara
	FORMAL	kawakimasitara	kawakimaseñ desitara
Alternative	INFORMAL	kawaitari	kawakanakattari
	FORMAL	kawakimasitari	kawakimaseñ desitari

INFORMAL AFFIRMATIVE INDICATIVE

Passive	
Potential	
Causative	kawakaseru
Causative Pass.	
Honorific	
Humble	

54

		AFFIRMATIVE	NEGATIVE
Indicative	INFORMAL	kawaru	kawaranai
	FORMAL	kawarimasu	kawarimaseñ
Imperative	INFORMAL I	kaware	kawaru na
	II	kawarinasai	kawarinasaru na
	III	kawatte kudasai	kawaranai de kudasai
	FORMAL	okawari nasaimase	okawari nasaimasu na
Presumptive	INFORMAL I	kawaroo	kawarumai
	II	kawaru daroo	kawaranai daroo
	FORMAL I	kawarimasyoo	kawarimasumai
	II	kawaru desyoo	kawaranai desyoo
Provisional	INFORMAL	kawareba	kawaranakereba
	FORMAL	kawarimaseba	kawarimaseñ nara
		kawarimasureba	
Gerund	INFORMAL I	kawatte	kawaranai de
	II		kawaranakute
	FORMAL	kawarimasite	kawarimaseñ de
Past Ind.	INFORMAL	kawatta	kawaranakatta
	FORMAL	kawarimasita	kawarimaseñ desita
Past Presump.	INFORMAL	kawattaroo	kawaranakattaroo
		kawatta daroo	kawaranakatta daroo
	FORMAL	kawarimasitaroo	kawarimaseñ desitaroo
		kawatta desyoo	kawaranakatta desyoo
Conditional	INFORMAL	kawattara	kawaranakattara
	FORMAL	kawarimasitara	kawarimaseñ desitara
Alternative	INFORMAL	kawattari	kawaranakattari
	FORMAL	kawarimasitari	kawarimaseñ desitari

INFORMAL AFFIRMATIVE INDICATIVE	
Passive	kawarareru
Potential	kawareru
Causative	kawaraseru
Causative Pass.	kawaraserareru

Honorific	I	okawari ni naru
	II	okawari nasaru
Humble		

			AFFIRMATIVE	NEGATIVE
Indicative	INFORMAL		kayou	kayowanai
	FORMAL		kayoimasu	kayoimaseñ
Imperative	INFORMAL	I	kayoe	kayou na
		II	kayoinasai	kayoinasaru na
		III	kayotte kudasai	kayowanai de kudasai
	FORMAL		okayoi nasaimase	okayoi nasaimasu na
Presumptive	INFORMAL	I	kayooo	kayoumai
		II	kayou daroo	kayowanai daroo
	FORMAL	I	kayoimasyoo	kayoimasumai
		II	kayou desyoo	kayowanai desyoo
Provisional	INFORMAL		kayoeba	kayowanakereba
	FORMAL		kayoimaseba	kayoimaseñ nara
			kayoimasureba	
Gerund	INFORMAL	I	kayotte	kayowanai de
		II		kayowanakute
	FORMAL		kayoimasite	kayoimaseñ de
Past Ind.	INFORMAL		kayotta	kayowanakatta
	FORMAL		kayoimasita	kayoimaseñ desita
Past Presump.	INFORMAL		kayottaroo	kayowanakattaroo
			kayotta daroo	kayowanakatta daroo
	FORMAL		kayoimasitaroo	kayoimaseñ desitaroo
			kayotta desyoo	kayowanakatta desyoo
Conditional	INFORMAL		kayottara	kayowanakattara
	FORMAL		kayoimasitara	kayoimaseñ desitara
Alternative	INFORMAL		kayottari	kayowanakattari
	FORMAL		kayoimasitari	kayoimaseñ desitari

INFORMAL AFFIRMATIVE INDICATIVE

Passive	kayowareru
Potential	kayoeru
Causative	kayowaseru
Causative Pass	kayowaserareru

Honorific	I	okayoi ni naru
	II	okayoi nasaru
Humble		

		AFFIRMATIVE	NEGATIVE
Indicative	**INFORMAL**	kazoeru	kazoenai
	FORMAL	kazoemasu	kazoemaseñ
Imperative	**INFORMAL I**	kazoero	kazoeru na
	II	kazoenasai	kazoenasaru na
	III	kazoete kudasai	kazoenai de kudasai
	FORMAL	okazoe nasaimase	okazoe nasaimasu na
Presumptive	**INFORMAL I**	kazoeyoo	kazoemai
	II	kazoeru daroo	kazoenai daroo
	FORMAL I	kazoemasyoo	kazoemasumai
	II	kazoeru desyoo	kazoenai desyoo
Provisional	**INFORMAL**	kazoereba	kazoenakereba
	FORMAL	kazoemaseba	kazoemaseñ nara
		kazoemasureba	
Gerund	**INFORMAL I**	kazoete	kazoenai de
	II		kazoenakute
	FORMAL	kazoemasite	kazoemaseñ de
Past Ind.	**INFORMAL**	kazoeta	kazoenakatta
	FORMAL	kazoemasita	kazoemaseñ desita
Past Presump.	**INFORMAL**	kazoetaroo	kazoenakattaroo
		kazoeta daroo	kazoenakatta daroo
	FORMAL	kazoemasitaroo	kazoemaseñ desitaroo
		kazoeta desyoo	kazoenakatta desyoo
Conditional	**INFORMAL**	kazoetara	kazoenakattara
	FORMAL	kazoemasitara	kazoemaseñ desitara
Alternative	**INFORMAL**	kazoetari	kazoenakattari
	FORMAL	kazoemasitari	kazoemaseñ desitari

	INFORMAL AFFIRMATIVE INDICATIVE
Passive	kazoerareru
Potential	kazoerareru
Causative	kazoesaseru
Causative Pass.	kasoesaserareru

Honorific	**I**	okazoe ni naru
	II	okazoe nasaru
Humble	**I**	okazoe suru
	II	okazoe itasu

		AFFIRMATIVE	NEGATIVE
Indicative	**INFORMAL**	kesu	kesanai
	FORMAL	kesimasu	kesimaseñ
Imperative	**INFORMAL I**	kese	kesu na
	II	kesinasai	kesinasaru na
	III	kesite kudasai	kesanai de kudasai
	FORMAL	okesi nasaimase	okesi nasaimasu na
Presumptive	**INFORMAL I**	kesoo	kesumai
	II	kesu daroo	kesanai daroo
	FORMAL I	kesimasyoo	kesimasumai
	II	kesu desyoo	kesanai desyoo
Provisional	**INFORMAL**	keseba	kesanakereba
	FORMAL	kesimaseba	kesimaseñ nara
		kesimasureba	
Gerund	**INFORMAL I**	kesite	kesanai de
	II		kesanakute
	FORMAL	kesimasite	kesimaseñ de
Past Ind.	**INFORMAL**	kesita	kesanakatta
	FORMAL	kesimasita	kesimaseñ desita
Past Presump.	**INFORMAL**	kesitaroo	kesanakattaroo
		kesita daroo	kesanakatta daroo
	FORMAL	kesimasitaroo	kesimaseñ desitaroo
		kesita desyoo	kesanakatta desyoo
Conditional	**INFORMAL**	kesitara	kesanakattara
	FORMAL	kesimasitara	kesimaseñ desitara
Alternative	**INFORMAL**	kesitari	kesanakattari
	FORMAL	kesimasitari	kesimaseñ desitari

	INFORMAL AFFIRMATIVE INDICATIVE
Passive	kesareru
Potential	keseru
Causative	kesaseru
Causative Pass.	kesaserareru

Honorific	**I**	okesi ni naru
	II	okesi nasaru
Humble	**I**	okesi suru
	II	okesi itasu

		AFFIRMATIVE	**NEGATIVE**
Indicative	**INFORMAL**	kieru	kienai
	FORMAL	kiemasu	kiemaseñ
Imperative	**INFORMAL I**	kiero	kieru na
	II		
	III		
	FORMAL		
Presumptive	**INFORMAL I**	kieyoo	kiemai
	II	kieru daroo	kienai daroo
	FORMAL I	kiemasyoo	kiemasumai
	II	kieru desyoo	kienai desyoo
Provisional	**INFORMAL**	kiereba	kienakereba
	FORMAL	kiemaseba	kiemaseñ nara
		kiemasureba	
Gerund	**INFORMAL I**	kiete	kienai de
	II		kienakute
	FORMAL	kiemasite	kiemaseñ de
Past Ind.	**INFORMAL**	kieta	kienakatta
	FORMAL	kiemasita	kiemaseñ desita
Past Presump.	**INFORMAL**	kietaroo	kienakattaroo
		kieta daroo	kienakatta daroo
	FORMAL	kiemasitaroo	kiemaseñ desitaroo
		kieta desyoo	kienakatta desyoo
Conditional	**INFORMAL**	kietara	kienakattara
	FORMAL	kiemasitara	kiemaseñ desitara
Alternative	**INFORMAL**	kietari	kienakattari
	FORMAL	kiemasitari	kiemaseñ desitari

	INFORMAL AFFIRMATIVE INDICATIVE
Passive	kierareru
Potential	kierareru
Causative	kiesaseru
Causative Pass.	kiesaserareru
Honorific	
Humble	

kikae.ru   **kikae**
to change clothes   TRANSITIVE

		AFFIRMATIVE	NEGATIVE
Indicative	INFORMAL	kikaeru	kikaenai
	FORMAL	kikaemasu	kikaemaseñ
Imperative	INFORMAL I	kikaero	kikaeru na
	II	kikaenasai	kikaenasaru na
	III	kikaete kudasai	kikaenai de kudasai
	FORMAL	okikae nasaimase	okikae nasaimasu na
Presumptive	INFORMAL I	kikaeyoo	kikaemai
	II	kikaeru daroo	kikaenai daroo
	FORMAL I	kikaemasyoo	kikaemasumai
	II	kikaeru desyoo	kikaemasen desyoo
Provisional	INFORMAL	kikaereba	kikaenakereba
	FORMAL	kikaemaseba	kikaemaseñ nara
		kikaemasureba	
Gerund	INFORMAL I	kikaete	kikaenai de
	II		kikaenakute
	FORMAL	kikaemasite	kikaemaseñ de
Past Ind.	INFORMAL	kikaeta	kikaenakatta
	FORMAL	kikaemasita	kikaemaseñ desita
Past Presump.	INFORMAL	kikaetaroo	kikaenakattaroo
		kikaeta daroo	kikaenakatta daroo
	FORMAL	kikaemasitaroo	kikaemaseñ desitaroo
		kikaeta desyoo	kikaenakatta desyoo
Conditional	INFORMAL	kikaetara	kikaenakattara
	FORMAL	kikaemasitara	kikaemaseñ desitara
Alternative	INFORMAL	kikaetari	kikaenakattari
	FORMAL	kikaemasitari	kikaemaseñ desitari

	INFORMAL AFFIRMATIVE INDICATIVE
Passive	kikaerareru
Potential	kikaerareru
Causative	kikaesaseru
Causative Pass.	kikaesaserareru

Honorific	I	okikae ni naru
	II	okikae nasaru
Humble		

kikoe

kikoe.ru
to be audible, to be able to hear

			AFFIRMATIVE	NEGATIVE
Indicative	**INFORMAL**		kikoeru	kikoenai
	FORMAL		kikoemasu	kikoemaseñ
Imperative	**INFORMAL**	**I**		
		II		
		III		
	FORMAL			
Presumptive	**INFORMAL**	**I**	kikoeyoo	kikoemai
		II	kikoeru daroo	kikoenai daroo
	FORMAL	**I**	kikoemasyoo	kikoemasumai
		II	kikoeru desyoo	kikoenai desyoo
Provisional	**INFORMAL**		kikoereba	kikoenakereba
	FORMAL		kikoemaseba	kikoemaseñ nara
			kikoemasureba	
Gerund	**INFORMAL**	**I**	kikoete	kikoenai de
		II		kikoenakute
	FORMAL		kikoemasite	kikoemaseñ de
Past Ind.	**INFORMAL**		kikoeta	kikoenakatta
	FORMAL		kikoemasita	kikoemaseñ desita
Past Presump.	**INFORMAL**		kikoetaroo	kikoenakattaroo
			kikoeta daroo	kikoenakatta daroo
	FORMAL		kikoemasitaroo	kikoemaseñ desitaroo
			kikoeta desyoo	kikoenakatta desyoo
Conditional	**INFORMAL**		kikoetara	kikoenakattara
	FORMAL		kikoemasitara	kikoemaseñ desitara
Alternative	**INFORMAL**		kikoetari	kikoenakattari
	FORMAL		kikoemasitari	kikoemaseñ desitari

INFORMAL AFFIRMATIVE INDICATIVE

Passive

Potential

Causative

Causative Pass.

Honorific

Humble

to ask, to listen, to hear   TRANSITIVE

			AFFIRMATIVE	NEGATIVE
Indicative	**INFORMAL**		kiku	kikanai
	FORMAL		kikimasu	kikimaseñ
Imperative	**INFORMAL**	I	kike	kiku na
		II	kikinasai	kikinasaru na
		III	kiite kudasai	kikanai de kudasai
	FORMAL		okiki nasaimase	okiki nasaimasu na
Presumptive	**INFORMAL**	I	kikoo	kikumai
		II	kiku daroo	kikanai daroo
	FORMAL	I	kikimasyoo	kikimasumai
		II	kiku desyoo	kikanai desyoo
Provisional	**INFORMAL**		kikeba	kikanakereba
	FORMAL		kikimaseba	kikimaseñ nara
			kikimasureba	
Gerund	**INFORMAL**	I	kiite	kikanai de
		II		kikanakute
	FORMAL		kikimasite	kikimaseñ de
Past Ind.	**INFORMAL**		kiita	kikanakatta
	FORMAL		kikimasita	kikimaseñ desita
Past Presump.	**INFORMAL**		kiitaroo	kikanakattaroo
			kiita daroo	kikanakatta daroo
	FORMAL		kikimasitaroo	kikimaseñ desitaroo
			kiita desyoo	kikanakatta desyoo
Conditional	**INFORMAL**		kiitara	kikanakattara
	FORMAL		kikimasitara	kikimaseñ desitara
Alternative	**INFORMAL**		kiitari	kikanakattari
	FORMAL		kikimasitari	kikimaseñ desitari

	INFORMAL AFFIRMATIVE INDICATIVE	
Passive	kikareru	
Potential	kikeru*	
Causative	kikaseru	
Causative Pass.	kikaserareru	

Honorific	I	okiki ni naru
	II	okiki nasaru

*Humble***	ukagau	uketamawaru

*Only in the sense of 'can ask or listen,' 'to be audible' is a separate verb *kikoeru*.
**Ukagau* means 'to ask,' while *uketamawaru* means 'to hear or listen.'

TRANSITIVE   *to decide upon*

			AFFIRMATIVE	NEGATIVE
Indicative	INFORMAL		kimeru	kimenai
	FORMAL		kimemasu	kimemaseñ
Imperative	INFORMAL	I	kimero	kimeru na
		II	kimenasai	kimenasaru na
		III	kimete kudasai	kimenai de kudasai
	FORMAL		okime nasaimase	okime nasaimasu na
Presumptive	INFORMAL	I	kimeyoo	kimemai
		II	kimeru daroo	kimenai daroo
	FORMAL	I	kimemasyoo	kimemasumai
		II	kimeru desyoo	kimenai desyoo
Provisional	INFORMAL		kimereba	kimenakereba
	FORMAL		kimemaseba	kimemaseñ nara
			kimemasureba	
Gerund	INFORMAL	I	kimete	kimenai de
		II		kimenakute
	FORMAL		kimemasite	kimemaseñ de
Past Ind.	INFORMAL		kimeta	kimenakatta
	FORMAL		kimemasita	kimemaseñ desita
Past Presump.	INFORMAL		kimetaroo	kimenakattaroo
			kimeta daroo	kimenakatta daroo
	FORMAL		kimemasitaroo	kimemaseñ desitaroo
			kimeta desyoo	kimenakatta desyoo
Conditional	INFORMAL		kimetara	kimenakattara
	FORMAL		kimemasitara	kimemaseñ desitara
Alternative	INFORMAL		kimetari	kimenakattari
	FORMAL		kimemasitari	kimemaseñ desitari

	INFORMAL AFFIRMATIVE INDICATIVE
Passive	kimerareru
Potential	kimerareru
Causative	kimesaseru
Causative Pass.	kimesaserareru

Honorific	I	okime ni naru
	II	okime nasaru
Humble	I	okime suru
	II	okime itasu

63

ki.ru
to put on, to wear (on the body as with a coat, suit, or dress)　　TRANSITIVE

			AFFIRMATIVE	NEGATIVE
Indicative	INFORMAL		kiru	kinai
	FORMAL		kimasu	kimaseñ
Imperative	INFORMAL	I	kiro	kiru na
		II	kinasai	kinasaru na
		III	kite kudasai	kinai de kudasai
	FORMAL		omesi nasaimase	omesi nasaimasu na
Presumptive	INFORMAL	I	kiyoo	kimai
		II	kiru daroo	kinai daroo
	FORMAL	I	kimasyoo	kimasumai
		II	kiru desyoo	kinai desyoo
Provisional	INFORMAL		kireba	kinakereba
	FORMAL		kimaseba	kimaseñ nara
			kimasureba	
Gerund	INFORMAL	I	kite	kinai de
		II		kinakute
	FORMAL		kimasite	kimaseñ de
Past Ind.	INFORMAL		kita	kinakatta
	FORMAL		kimasita	kimaseñ desita
Past Presump.	INFORMAL		kitaroo	kinakattaroo
			kita daroo	kinakatta daroo
	FORMAL		kimasitaroo	kimaseñ desitaroo
			kita desyoo	kinakatta desyoo
Conditional	INFORMAL		kitara	kinakattara
	FORMAL		kimasitara	kimaseñ desitara
Alternative	INFORMAL		kitari	kinakattari
	FORMAL		kimasitari	kimaseñ desitari

	INFORMAL AFFIRMATIVE INDICATIVE
Passive	kirareru
Potential	kirareru
Causative	kisaseru
Causative Pass.	kisaserareru

Honorific	I	omesi ni naru
	II	omesi nasaru
Humble		

		AFFIRMATIVE	NEGATIVE
Indicative	INFORMAL	kiru	kiranai
	FORMAL	kirimasu	kirimaseñ
Imperative	INFORMAL I	kire	kiru na
	II	kirinasai	kirinasaru na
	III	kitte kudasai	kiranai de kudasai
	FORMAL	okiri nasaimase	okiri nasaimasu na
Presumptive	INFORMAL I	kiroo	kirumai
	II	kiru daroo	kiranai daroo
	FORMAL I	kirimasyoo	kirimasumai
	II	kiru desyoo	kiranai desyoo
Provisional	INFORMAL	kireba	kiranakereba
	FORMAL	kirimaseba	kirimaseñ nara
		kirimasureba	
Gerund	INFORMAL I	kitte	kiranai de
	II		kiranakute
	FORMAL	kirimasite	kirimaseñ de
Past Ind.	INFORMAL	kitta	kiranakatta
	FORMAL	kirimasita	kirimaseñ desita
Past Presump.	INFORMAL	kittaroo	kiranakattaroo
		kitta daroo	kiranakatta daroo
	FORMAL	kirimasitaroo	kirimaseñ desitaroo
		kitta desyoo	kiranakatta desyoo
Conditional	INFORMAL	kittara	kiranakattara
	FORMAL	kirimasitara	kirimaseñ desitara
Alternative	INFORMAL	kittari	kiranakattari
	FORMAL	kirimasitari	kirimaseñ desitari

	INFORMAL AFFIRMATIVE INDICATIVE
Passive	kirareru
Potential	kireru
Causative	kiraseru
Causative Pass.	kiraserareru

Honorific	I	okiri ni naru
	II	okiri nasaru
Humble	I	okiri suru
	II	okiri itasu

65

		AFFIRMATIVE	NEGATIVE
Indicative	**INFORMAL**	ķoboreru	koborenai
	FORMAL	koboremasu	koboremaseñ
Imperative	**INFORMAL I**	koborero	koboreru na
	II		
	III		
	FORMAL		
Presumptive	**INFORMAL I**	koboreyoo	koboremai
	II	koboreru daroo	koborenai daroo
	FORMAL I	koboremasyoo	koboremasumai
	II	koboreru desyoo	koborenai desyoo
Provisional	**INFORMAL**	koborereba	koborenakereba
	FORMAL	koboremaseba	koboremaseñ nara
		koboremasureba	
Gerund	**INFORMAL I**	koborete	koborenai de
	II		koborenakute
	FORMAL	koboremasite	koboremaseñ de
Past Ind.	**INFORMAL**	koboreta	koborenakatta
	FORMAL	koboremasita	koboremaseñ desita
Past Presump.	**INFORMAL**	koboretaroo	koborenakattaroo
		koboreta daroo	koborenakatta daroo
	FORMAL	koboremasitaroo	koboremaseñ desitaroo
		koboreta desyoo	koborenakatta desyoo
Conditional	**INFORMAL**	koboretara	koborenakattara
	FORMAL	koboremasitara	koboremaseñ desitara
Alternative	**INFORMAL**	koboretari	koborenakattari
	FORMAL	koboremasitari	koboremaseñ desitari

	INFORMAL AFFIRMATIVE INDICATIVE
Passive	koborerareru
Potential	koborerareru
Causative	koboresaseru
Causative Pass.	
Honorific	
Humble	

			AFFIRMATIVE	NEGATIVE
Indicative	INFORMAL		kobosu	kobosanai
	FORMAL		kobosimasu	kobosimaseñ
Imperative	INFORMAL	I	kobose	kobosu na
		II	kobosinasai	kobosinasaru na
		III		
	FORMAL			
Presumptive	INFORMAL	I	kobosoo	kobosumai
		II	kobosu daroo	kobosanai daroo
	FORMAL	I	kobosimasyoo	kobosimasumai
		II	kobosu desyoo	kobosanai desyoo
Provisional	INFORMAL		koboseba	kobosanakereba
	FORMAL		kobosimaseba	kobosimaseñ nara
			kobosimasureba	
Gerund	INFORMAL	I	kobosite	kobosanai de
		II		kobosanakute
	FORMAL		kobosimasite	kobosimaseñ de
Past Ind.	INFORMAL		kobosita	kobosanakatta
	FORMAL		kobosimasita	kobosimaseñ desita
Past Presump.	INFORMAL		kobositaroo	kobosanakattaroo
			kobosita daroo	kobosanakatta daroo
	FORMAL		kobosimasitaroo	kobosimaseñ desitaroo
			kobosita desyoo	kobosanakatta desyoo
Conditional	INFORMAL		kobositara	kobosanakattara
	FORMAL		kobosimasitara	kobosimaseñ desitara
Alternative	INFORMAL		kobositari	kobosanakattari
	FORMAL		kobosimasitari	kobosimaseñ desitari

	INFORMAL AFFIRMATIVE INDICATIVE
Passive	kobosareru
Potential	koboseru
Causative	kobosaseru
Causative Pass.	kobosaserareru

Honorific	I	okobosi ni naru
	II	okobosi nasaru
Humble	I	okobosi suru
	II	okobosi itasu

		AFFIRMATIVE	NEGATIVE
Indicative	INFORMAL	komaru	komaranai
	FORMAL	komarimasu	komarimaseñ
Imperative	INFORMAL I	komare	komaru na
	II		
	III		
	FORMAL		
Presumptive	INFORMAL I	komaroo	komarumai
	II	komaru daroo	komaranai daroo
	FORMAL I	komarimasyoo	komarimasumai
	II	komaru desyoo	komaranai desyoo
Provisional	INFORMAL	komareba	komaranakereba
	FORMAL	komarimaseba	komarimaseñ nara
		komarimasureba	
Gerund	INFORMAL I	komatte	komaranai de
	II		komaranakute
	FORMAL	komarimasite	komarimaseñ de
Past Ind.	INFORMAL	komatta	komaranakatta
	FORMAL	komarimasita	komarimaseñ desita
Past Presump.	INFORMAL	komattaroo	komaranakattaroo
		komatta daroo	komaranakatta daroo
	FORMAL	komarimasitaroo	komarimaseñ desitaroo
		komatta desyoo	komaranakatta desyoo
Conditional	INFORMAL	komattara	komaranakattara
	FORMAL	komarimasitara	komarimaseñ desitara
Alternative	INFORMAL	komattari	komaranakattari
	FORMAL	komarimasitari	komarimaseñ desitari

	INFORMAL AFFIRMATIVE INDICATIVE
Passive	komarareru
Potential	
Causative	komaraseru
Causative Pass.	komaraserareru

Honorific	I	okomari ni naru
	II	okomari nasaru
Humble		

komi

kom.u

to become crowded

		AFFIRMATIVE	NEGATIVE
Indicative	**INFORMAL**	komu	komanai
	FORMAL	komimasu	komimaseñ
Imperative	**INFORMAL I**		
	II		
	III		
	FORMAL		
Presumptive	**INFORMAL I**	komoo	komumai
	II	komu daroo	komanai daroo
	FORMAL I	komimasyoo	komimasumai
	II	komu desyoo	komanai desyoo
Provisional	**INFORMAL**	komeba	komanakereba
	FORMAL	komimaseba	komimaseñ nara
		komimasureba	
Gerund	**INFORMAL I**	koñde	komanai de
	II		komanakute
	FORMAL	komimasite	komimaseñ de
Past Ind.	**INFORMAL**	koñda	komanakatta
	FORMAL	komimasita	komimaseñ desita
Past Presump.	**INFORMAL**	koñdaroo	komanakattaroo
		koñda daroo	komanakatta daroo
	FORMAL	komimasitaroo	komimaseñ desitaroo
		koñda desyoo	komanakatta desyoo
Conditional	**INFORMAL**	koñdara	komanakattara
	FORMAL	komimasitara	komimaseñ desitara
Alternative	**INFORMAL**	koñdari	komanakattari
	FORMAL	komimasitari	komimaseñ desitari

INFORMAL AFFIRMATIVE INDICATIVE

Passive

Potential

Causative

Causative Pass.

Honorific

Humble

konom.u
to like TRANSITIVE

			AFFIRMATIVE	NEGATIVE
Indicative	INFORMAL		konomu	konomanai
	FORMAL		konomimasu	konomimaseñ
Imperative	INFORMAL	I	konome	konomu na
		II	konominasai	konominasaru na
		III	konoñde kudasai	konomanai de kudasai
	FORMAL		okonomi nasaimase	okonomi nasaimasu na
Presumptive	INFORMAL	I	konomoo	konomumai
		II	konomu daroo	konomanai daroo
	FORMAL	I	konomimasyoo	konomimasumai
		II	konomu desyoo	konomanai desyoo
Provisional	INFORMAL		konomeba	konomanakereba
	FORMAL	.	konomimaseba	konomimaseñ nara
			konomimasureba	
Gerund	INFORMAL	I	konoñde	konomanai de
		II		konomanakute
	FORMAL		konomimasite	konomimaseñ de
Past Ind.	INFORMAL		konoñda	konomanakatta
	FORMAL		konomimasita	konomimaseñ desita
Past Presump.	INFORMAL		konoñdaroo	konomanakattaroo
			konoñda daroo	konomanakatta daroo
	FORMAL		konomimasitaroo	konomimaseñ desitaroo
			konoñda desyoo	konomanakatta desyoo
Conditional	INFORMAL		konoñdara	konomanakattara
	FORMAL		konomimasitara	konomimaseñ desitara
Alternative	INFORMAL		konoñdari	konomanakattari
	FORMAL		konomimasitari	konomimaseñ desitari

	INFORMAL AFFIRMATIVE INDICATIVE
Passive	konomareru
Potential	konomeru
Causative	konomaseru
Causative Pass.	konomaserareru

Honorific	I	okonomi ni naru
	II	okonomi nasaru
Humble		

		AFFIRMATIVE	NEGATIVE
Indicative	**INFORMAL**	kooru	kooranai
	FORMAL	koorimasu	koorimaseñ
Imperative	**INFORMAL I**	koore	kooru na
	II		
	III		
	FORMAL		
Presumptive	**INFORMAL I**	kooroo	koorumai
	II	kooru daroo	kooranai daroo
	FORMAL I	koorimasyoo	koorimasumai
	II	kooru desyoo	kooranai desyoo
Provisional	**INFORMAL**	kooreba	kooranakereba
	FORMAL	koorimaseba	koorimaseñ nara
		koorimasureba	
Gerund	**INFORMAL I**	kootte	kooranai de
	II		kooranakute
	FORMAL	koorimasite	koorimaseñ de
Past Ind.	**INFORMAL**	kootta	kooranakatta
	FORMAL	koorimasita	koorimaseñ desita
Past Presump.	**INFORMAL**	koottaroo	kooranakattaroo
		kootta daroo	kooranakatta daroo
	FORMAL	koorimasitaroo	koorimaseñ desitaroo
		kootta desyoo	kooranakatta desyoo
Conditional	**INFORMAL**	koottara	kooranakattara
	FORMAL	koorimasitara	koorimaseñ desitara
Alternative	**INFORMAL**	koottari	kooranakattari
	FORMAL	koorimasitari	koorimaseñ desitari

	INFORMAL AFFIRMATIVE INDICATIVE
Passive	koorareru
Potential	kooreru
Causative	kooraseru
Causative Pass.	kooraserareru

Honorific

Humble

koros.u
to kill   TRANSITIVE

			AFFIRMATIVE	NEGATIVE
Indicative	**INFORMAL**		korosu	korosanai
	FORMAL		korosimasu	korosimaseñ
Imperative	**INFORMAL**	I	korose	korosu na
		II	korosinasai	korosinasaru na
		III	korosite kudasai	korosanai de kudasai
	FORMAL		okorosi nasaimase	okorosi nasaimasu na
Presumptive	**INFORMAL**	I	korosoo	korosumai
		II	korosu daroo	korosanai daroo
	FORMAL	I	korosimasyoo	korosimasumai
		II	korosu desyoo	korosanai desyoo
Provisional	**INFORMAL**		koroseba	korosanakereba
	FORMAL		korosimaseba	korosimaseñ nara
			korosimasureba	
Gerund	**INFORMAL**	I	korosite	korosanai de
		II		korosanakute
	FORMAL		korosimasite	korosimaseñ de
Past Ind.	**INFORMAL**		korosita	korosanakatta
	FORMAL		korosimasita	korosimaseñ desita
Past Presump.	**INFORMAL**		korositaroo	korosanakattaroo
			korosita daroo	korosanakatta daroo
	FORMAL		korosimasitaroo	korosimaseñ desitaroo
			korosita desyoo	korosanakatta desyoo
Conditional	**INFORMAL**		korositara	korosanakattara
	FORMAL		korosimasitara	korosimaseñ desitara
Alternative	**INFORMAL**		korositari	korosanakattari
	FORMAL		korosimasitari	korosimaseñ desitari

INFORMAL AFFIRMATIVE INDICATIVE

Passive	korosareru
Potential	koroseru
Causative	korosaseru
Causative Pass.	korosaserareru

Honorific	I	okorosi ni naru
	II	okorosi nasaru
Humble	I	okorosi suru
	II	okorosi itasu

		AFFIRMATIVE	NEGATIVE
Indicative	INFORMAL	kotaeru	kotaenai
	FORMAL	kotaemasu	kotaemaseñ
Imperative	INFORMAL I	kotaero	kotaeru na
	II	kotaenasai	kotaenasaru na
	III	kotaete kudasai	kotaenai de kudasai
	FORMAL	okotae nasaimase	okotae nasaimasu na
Presumptive	INFORMAL I	kotaeyoo	kotaemai
	II	kotaeru daroo	kotaenai daroo
	FORMAL I	kotaemasyoo	kotaemasumai
	II	kotaeru desyoo	kotaenai desyoo
Provisional	INFORMAL	kotaereba	kotaenakereba
	FORMAL	kotaemaseba	kotaemaseñ nara
		kotaemasureba	
Gerund	INFORMAL I	kotaete	kotaenai de
	II		kotaenakute
	FORMAL	kotaemasite	kotaemaseñ de
Past Ind.	INFORMAL	kotaeta	kotaenakatta
	FORMAL	kotaemasita	kotaemaseñ desita
Past Presump.	INFORMAL	kotaetaroo	kotaenakattaroo
		kotaeta daroo	kotaenakatta daroo
	FORMAL	kotaemasitaroo	kotaemaseñ desitaroo
		kotaeta desyoo	kotaenakatta desyoo
Conditional	INFORMAL	kotaetara	kotaenakattara
	FORMAL	kotaemasitara	kotaemaseñ desitara
Alternative	INFORMAL	kotaetari	kotaenakattari
	FORMAL	kotaemasitari	kotaemaseñ desitari

INFORMAL AFFIRMATIVE INDICATIVE	
Passive	kotaerareru
Potential	kotaerareru
Causative	kotaesaseru
Causative Pass.	kotaesaserareru

Honorific	I	okotae ni naru
	II	okotae nasaru
Humble	I	okotae suru
	II	okotae itasu

kotowar.u
to refuse TRANSITIVE

		AFFIRMATIVE	NEGATIVE
Indicative	**INFORMAL**	kotowaru	kotowaranai
	FORMAL	kotowarimasu	kotowarimaseñ
Imperative	**INFORMAL I**	kotoware	kotowaru na
	II	kotowarinasai	kotowarinasaru na
	III	kotowatte kudasai	kotowaranai de kudasai
	FORMAL	okotowari nasaimase	okotowari nasaimasu na
Presumptive	**INFORMAL I**	kotowaroo	kotowarumai
	II	kotowaru daroo	kotowaranai daroo
	FORMAL I	kotowarimasyoo	kotowarimasumai
	II	kotowaru desyoo	kotowaranai desyoo
Provisional	**INFORMAL**	kotowareba	kotowaranakereba
	FORMAL	kotowarimaseba	kotowarimaseñ nara
		kotowarimasureba	
Gerund	**INFORMAL I**	kotowatte	kotowaranai de
	II		kotowaranakute
	FORMAL	kotowarimasite	kotowarimaseñ de
Past Ind.	**INFORMAL**	kotowatta	kotowaranakatta
	FORMAL	kotowarimasita	kotowarimaseñ desita
Past Presump.	**INFORMAL**	kotowattaroo	kotowaranakattaroo
		kotowatta daroo	kotowaranakatta daroo
	FORMAL	kotowarimasitaroo	kotowarimaseñ desitaroo
		kotowatta desyoo	kotowaranakatta desyoo
Conditional	**INFORMAL**	kotowattara	kotowaranakattara
	FORMAL	kotowarimasitara	kotowarimaseñ desitara
Alternative	**INFORMAL**	kotowattari	kotowaranakattari
	FORMAL	kotowarimasitari	kotowarimaseñ desitari

INFORMAL AFFIRMATIVE INDICATIVE

Passive	kotowarareru
Potential	kotowareru
Causative	kotowaraseru
Causative Pass.	kotowaraserareru

Honorific	**I**	okotowari ni naru
	II	okotowari nasaru
Humble	**I**	okotowari suru
	II	okotowani itasu

			AFFIRMATIVE	NEGATIVE
Indicative	**INFORMAL**		kowareru	kowarenai
	FORMAL		kowaremasu	kowaremaseñ
Imperative	**INFORMAL**	I	kowarero	kowareru na
		II		
		III		
	FORMAL			
Presumptive	**INFORMAL**	I	kowareyoo	kowaremai
		II	kowareru daroo	kowarenai daroo
	FORMAL	I	kowaremasyoo	kowaremasumai
		II	kowareru desyoo	kowarenai desyoo
Provisional	**INFORMAL**		kowarereba	kowarenakereba
	FORMAL		kowaremaseba	kowaremaseñ nara
Gerund	**INFORMAL**	I	kowarete	kowarenai de
		II		kowarenakute
	FORMAL		kowaremasite	kowaremaseñ de
Past Ind.	**INFORMAL**		kowareta	kowarenakatta
	FORMAL		kowaremasita	kowaremaseñ desita
Past Presump.	**INFORMAL**		kowaretaroo	kowarenakattaroo
			kowareta daroo	kowarenakatta daroo
	FORMAL		kowaremasitaroo	kowaremaseñ desitaroo
			kowareta desyoo	kowarenakatta desyoo
Conditional	**INFORMAL**		kowaretara	kowarenakattara
	FORMAL		kowaremasitara	kowaremaseñ desitara
Alternative	**INFORMAL**		kowaretari	kowarenakattari
	FORMAL		kowaremasitari	kowaremaseñ desitari

INFORMAL AFFIRMATIVE INDICATIVE

Passive	
Potential	kowarerareru
Causative	*
Causative Pass.	*
Honorific	
Humble	

*See *kowas.u*, the transitive verb for 'to break.'

kowas.u
to smash   TRANSITIVE

		AFFIRMATIVE	NEGATIVE
Indicative	**INFORMAL**	kowasu	kowasanai
	FORMAL	kowasimasu	kowasimaseñ
Imperative	**INFORMAL I**	kowase	kowasu na
	II	kowasinasai	kowasinasaru na
	III	kowasite kudasai	kowasanai de kudasai
	FORMAL	okowasi nasaimase	okowasi nasaimasu na
Presumptive	**INFORMAL I**	kowasoo	kowasumai
	II	kowasu daroo	kowasanai daroo
	FORMAL I	kowasimasyoo	kowasimasumai
	II	kowasu desyoo	kowasanai desyoo
Provisional	**INFORMAL**	kowaseba	kowasanakereba
	FORMAL	kowasimaseba	kowasimaseñ nara
		kowasimasureba	
Gerund	**INFORMAL I**	kowasite	kowasanai de
	II		kowasanakute
	FORMAL	kowasimasite	kowasimaseñ de
Past Ind.	**INFORMAL**	kowasita	kowasanakatta
	FORMAL	kowasimasita	kowasimaseñ desita
Past Presump.	**INFORMAL**	kowasitaroo	kowasanakattaroo
		kowasita daroo	kowasanakatta daroo
	FORMAL	kowasimasitaroo	kowasimaseñ desitaroo
		kowasita desyoo	kowasanakatta desyoo
Conditional	**INFORMAL**	kowasitara	kowasanakattara
	FORMAL	kowasimasitara	kowasimaseñ desitara
Alternative	**INFORMAL**	kowasitari	kowasanakattari
	FORMAL	kowasimasitari	kowasimaseñ desitari

INFORMAL AFFIRMATIVE INDICATIVE

Passive	kowasareru
Potential	kowaseru
Causative	kowasaseru
Causative Pass.	kowasaserareru

Honorific	**I**	okowasi ni naru
	II	okowasi nasaru
Humble	**I**	okowasi suru
	II	okowasi itasu

kudasai

kudasar.u
to give (to me)*

		AFFIRMATIVE	NEGATIVE
Indicative	**INFORMAL**	kudasaru	kudasaranai
	FORMAL	kudasaimasu	kudasaimaseñ
Imperative	**INFORMAL** I	kudasai	kudasaru na
	II		
	III		
	FORMAL	kudasaimase	kudasaimasu na
Presumptive	**INFORMAL** I	kudasaroo	kudasarumai
	II	kudasaru daroo	kudasaranai daroo
	FORMAL I	kudasaimasyoo	kudasaimasumai
	II	kudasaru desyoo	kudasaranai desyoo
Provisional	**INFORMAL**	kudasareba	kudasaranakereba
	FORMAL	kudasaimaseba	kudasaimaseñ nara
		kudasaimasureba	
Gerund	**INFORMAL** I	kudasatte	kudasaranai de
	II		kudasaranakute
	FORMAL	kudasaimasite	kudasaimaseñ de
Past Ind.	**INFORMAL**	kudasatta	kudasaranakatta
	FORMAL	kudasaimasita	kudasaimaseñ desita
Past Presump.	**INFORMAL**	kudasattaroo	kudasaranakattaroo
		kudasatta daroo	kudasaranakatta daroo
	FORMAL	kudasaimasitaroo	kudasaimaseñ desitaroo
		kudasatta desyoo	kudasaranakatta desyoo
Conditional	**INFORMAL**	kudasattara	kudasaranakattara
	FORMAL	kudasaimasitara	kudasaimaseñ desitara
Alternative	**INFORMAL**	kudasattari	kudasaranakattari
	FORMAL	kudasaimasitari	kudasaimaseñ desitari

	INFORMAL AFFIRMATIVE INDICATIVE
Passive	kudasareru
Potential	
Causative	
Causative Pass.	
Honorific	
Humble	

*Or to a member of my "in group."

kumor.u
to get cloudy

		AFFIRMATIVE	NEGATIVE
Indicative	**INFORMAL**	kumoru	kumoranai
	FORMAL	kumorimasu	kumorimaseñ
Imperative	**INFORMAL I**	kumore	kumoru na
	II		
	III		
	FORMAL		
Presumptive	**INFORMAL I**	kumoroo	kumorumai
	II	kumoru daroo	kumoranai daroo
	FORMAL I	kumorimasyoo	kumorimasumai
	II	kumoru desyoo	kumoranai desyoo
Provisional	**INFORMAL**	kumoreba	kumoranakereba
	FORMAL	kumorimaseba	kumorimaseñ nara
		kumorimasureba	
Gerund	**INFORMAL I**	kumotte	kumoranai de
	II		kumoranakute
	FORMAL	kumorimasite	kumorimaseñ de
Past Ind.	**INFORMAL**	kumotta	kumoranakatta
	FORMAL	kumorimasita	kumorimaseñ desita
Past Presump.	**INFORMAL**	kumottaroo	kumoranakattaroo
		kumotta daroo	kumoranakatta daroo
	FORMAL	kumorimasitaroo	kumorimaseñ desitaroo
		kumotta desyoo	kumoranakatta desyoo
Conditional	**INFORMAL**	kumottara	kumoranakattara
	FORMAL	kumorimasitara	kumorimaseñ desitara
Alternative	**INFORMAL**	kumottari	kumoranakattari
	FORMAL	kumorimasitari	kumorimaseñ desitari

	INFORMAL AFFIRMATIVE INDICATIVE
Passive	kumorareru
Potential	
Causative	kumoraseru
Causative Pass.	kumoraserareru
Honorific	
Humble	

kurabe.ru

TRANSITIVE *to compare*

			AFFIRMATIVE	NEGATIVE
Indicative	INFORMAL		kuraberu	kurabenai
	FORMAL		kurabemasu	kurabemaseñ
Imperative	INFORMAL	I	kurabero	kuraberu na
		II	kurabenasai	kurabenasaru na
		III	kurabete kudasai	kurabenai de kudasai
	FORMAL		okurabe nasaimase	okurabe nasaimasu na
Presumptive	INFORMAL	I	kurabeyoo	kurabemai
		II	kuraberu daroo	kurabenai daroo
	FORMAL	I	kurabemasyoo	kurabemasumai
		II	kuraberu desyoo	kurabenai desyoo
Provisional	INFORMAL		kurabereba	kurabenakereba
	FORMAL		kurabemaseba	kurabemaseñ nara
			kurabemasureba	
Gerund	INFORMAL	I	kurabete	kurabenai de
		II		kurabenakute
	FORMAL		kurabemasite	kurabemaseñ de
Past Ind.	INFORMAL		kurabeta	kurabenakatta
	FORMAL		kurabemasita	kurabemaseñ desita
Past Presump.	INFORMAL		kurabetaroo	kurabenakattaroo
			kurabeta daroo	kurabenakatta daroo
	FORMAL		kurabemasitaroo	kurabemaseñ desitaroo
			kurabeta desyoo	kurabenakatta desyoo
Conditional	INFORMAL		kurabetara	kurabenakattara
	FORMAL		kurabemasitara	kurabemaseñ desitara
Alternative	INFORMAL		kurabetari	kurabenakattari
	FORMAL		kurabemasitari	kurabemaseñ desitari

INFORMAL AFFIRMATIVE INDICATIVE

Passive kuraberareru

Potential kuraberareru

Causative kurabesaseru

Causative Pass. kurabesaserareru

Honorific I okurabe ni naru
II okurabe nasaru

Humble I okurabe suru
II okurabe itasu

79

kure.ru
to give (the giver is someone other than the speaker)   TRANSITIVE

			AFFIRMATIVE	NEGATIVE
Indicative	**INFORMAL**		kureru	kurenai
	FORMAL		kuremasu	kuremaseñ
Imperative	**INFORMAL**	I	kure	kureru na
		II	kurenasai	kurenasaru na
		III		
	FORMAL			
Presumptive	**INFORMAL**	I	kureyoo	kuremai
		II	kureru daroo	kurenai daroo
	FORMAL	I	kuremasyoo	kuremasumai
		II	kureru desyoo	kurenai desyoo
Provisional	**INFORMAL**		kurereba	kurenakereba
	FORMAL		kuremaseba	kuremaseñ nara
			kuremasureba	
Gerund	**INFORMAL**	I	kurete	kurenai de
		II		kurenakute
	FORMAL		kuremasite	kuremaseñ de
Past Ind.	**INFORMAL**		kureta	kurenakatta
	FORMAL		kuremasita	kuremaseñ desita
Past Presump.	**INFORMAL**		kuretaroo	kurenakattaroo
			kureta daroo	kurenakatta daroo
	FORMAL		kuremasitaroo	kuremaseñ desitaroo
			kureta desyoo	kurenakatta desyoo
Conditional	**INFORMAL**		kuretara	kurenakattara
	FORMAL		kuremasitara	kuremaseñ desitara
Alternative	**INFORMAL**		kuretari	kurenakattari
	FORMAL		kuremasitari	kuremaseñ desitari

INFORMAL AFFIRMATIVE INDICATIVE

Passive	kurerareru
Potential	kurerareru
Causative	kuresaseru
Causative Pass.	kuresaserareru

Honorific

Humble

		AFFIRMATIVE	NEGATIVE
Indicative	INFORMAL	kuru	konai
	FORMAL	kimasu	kimaseñ
Imperative	INFORMAL I	koi	kuru na
	II	kinasai	kinasaru na
	III	kite kudasai	konai de kudasai
	FORMAL	oide nasaimase	oide nasaimasu na
Presumptive	INFORMAL I	koyoo	kurumai
	II	kuru daroo	konai daroo
	FORMAL I	kimasyoo	kimasumai
	II	kuru desyoo	konai desyoo
Provisional	INFORMAL	kureba	konakereba
	FORMAL	kimaseba	kimaseñ nara
		kimasureba	
Gerund	INFORMAL I	kite	konai de
	II		konakute
	FORMAL	kimasite	kimaseñ de
Past Ind.	INFORMAL	kita	konakatta
	FORMAL	kimasita	kimaseñ desita
Past Presump.	INFORMAL	kitaroo	konakattaroo
		kita daroo	konakatta daroo
	FORMAL	kimasitaroo	kimaseñ desitaroo
		kita desyoo	konakatta desyoo
Conditional	INFORMAL	kitara	konakattara
	FORMAL	kimasitara	kimaseñ desitara
Alternative	INFORMAL	kitari	konakattari
	FORMAL	kimasitari	kimaseñ desitari

INFORMAL AFFIRMATIVE INDICATIVE	
Passive	korareru
Potential	korareru
Causative	kosaseru
Causative Pass.	kosaserareru

Honorific	irassyaru	{ oide ni naru (I) { oide nasaru (II)
Humble	mairu	

magar.u
to turn a corner (transitive) *to bend* (intransitive)

			AFFIRMATIVE	NEGATIVE
Indicative	INFORMAL		magaru	magaranai
	FORMAL		magarimasu	magarimaseñ
Imperative	INFORMAL	I	magare	magaru na
		II	magarinasai	magarinasaru na
		III	magatte kudasai	magaranai de kudasai
	FORMAL		omagari nasaimase	omagari nasaimasu na
Presumptive	INFORMAL	I	magaroo	magarumai
		II	magaru daroo	magaranai daroo
	FORMAL	I	magarimasyoo	magarimasumai
		II	magaru desyoo	magaranai desyoo
Provisional	INFORMAL		magareba	magaranakereba
	FORMAL		magarimaseba	magarimaseñ nara
			magarimasureba	
Gerund	INFORMAL	I	magatte	magaranai de
		II		magaranakute
	FORMAL		magarimasite	magarimaseñ de
Past Ind.	INFORMAL		magatta	magaranakatta
	FORMAL		magarimasita	magarimaseñ desita
Past Presump.	INFORMAL		magattaroo	magaranakattaroo
			magatta daroo	magaranakatta daroo
	FORMAL		magarimasitaroo	magarimaseñ desitaroo
			magatta desyoo	magaranakatta desyoo
Conditional	INFORMAL		magattara	magaranakattara
	FORMAL		magarimasitara	magarimaseñ desitara
Alternative	INFORMAL		magattari	magaranakattari
	FORMAL		magarimasitari	magarimaseñ desitari

INFORMAL AFFIRMATIVE INDICATIVE

Passive		
Potential		magareru
Causative		magaraseru
Causative Pass.		magaraserareru

Honorific	I	omagari ni naru
	II	omagari nasaru
Humble		

		AFFIRMATIVE	NEGATIVE
Indicative	INFORMAL	mageru	magenai
	FORMAL	magemasu	magemaseñ
Imperative	INFORMAL I	magero	mageru na
	II	magenasai	magenasaru na
	III	magete kudasai	magenai de kudasai
	FORMAL	omage nasaimase	omage nasaimasu na
Presumptive	INFORMAL I	mageyoo	magemai
	II	mageru daroo	magenai daroo
	FORMAL I	magemasyoo	magemasumai
	II	mageru desyoo	magenai desyoo
Provisional	INFORMAL	magereba	magenakereba
	FORMAL	magemaseba	magemaseñ nara
		magemasureba	
Gerund	INFORMAL I	magete	magenai de
	II		magenakute
	FORMAL	magemasite	magemaseñ de
Past Ind.	INFORMAL	mageta	magenakatta
	FORMAL	magemasita	magemaseñ desita
Past Presump.	INFORMAL	magetaroo	magenakattaroo
		mageta daroo	magenakatta daroo
	FORMAL	magemasitaroo	magemaseñ desitaroo
		mageta desyoo	magenakatta desyoo
Conditional	INFORMAL	magetara	magenakattara
	FORMAL	magemasitara	magemaseñ desitara
Alternative	INFORMAL	magetari	magenakattari
	FORMAL	magemasitari	magemaseñ desitari

INFORMAL AFFIRMATIVE INDICATIVE

Passive	magerareru
Potential	magerareru
Causative	magesaseru
Causative Pass.	magesaserareru

Honorific	I	omage ni naru
	II	omage nasaru
Humble	I	omage suru
	II	omage itasu

mair.u
to come or go (humble)

mairi (top right)

		AFFIRMATIVE	NEGATIVE
Indicative	INFORMAL	mairu	mairanai
	FORMAL	mairimasu	mairimaseñ
Imperative	INFORMAL I	maire	mairu na
	II		
	III		
	FORMAL		
Presumptive	INFORMAL I	mairoo	mairumai
	II	mairu daroo	mairanai daroo
	FORMAL I	mairimasyoo	mairimasumai
	II	mairu desyoo	mairanai desyoo
Provisional	INFORMAL	maireba	mairanakereba
	FORMAL	mairimaseba	mairimaseñ nara
		mairimasureba	
Gerund	INFORMAL I	maitte	mairanai de
	II		mairanakute
	FORMAL	mairimasite	mairimaseñ de
Past Ind.	INFORMAL	maitta	mairanakatta
	FORMAL	mairimasita	mairimaseñ desita
Past Presump.	INFORMAL	maittaroo	mairanakattaroo
		maitta daroo	mairanakatta daroo
	FORMAL	mairimasitaroo	mairimaseñ desitaroo
		maitta desyoo	mairanakatta desyoo
Conditional	INFORMAL	maittara	mairanakattara
	FORMAL	mairimasitara	mairimaseñ desitara
Alternative	INFORMAL	maittari	mairanakattari
	FORMAL	mairimasitari	mairimaseñ desitari

INFORMAL AFFIRMATIVE INDICATIVE

Passive	
Potential	
Causative	mairaseru
Causative Pass.	mairaserareru
Honorific	
Humble	

84

		AFFIRMATIVE	NEGATIVE
Indicative	**INFORMAL**	makasu	makasanai
	FORMAL	makasimasu	makasimaseñ
Imperative	**INFORMAL I**	makase	makasu na
	II	makasinasai	makasinasaru na
	III	makasite kudasai	makasanai de kudasai
	FORMAL	omakasi nasaimase	omakasi nasaimasu na
Presumptive	**INFORMAL I**	makasoo	makasumai
	II	makasu daroo	makasanai daroo
	FORMAL I	makasimasyoo	makasimasumai
	II	makasu desyoo	makasanai desyoo
Provisional	**INFORMAL**	makaseba	makasanakereba
	FORMAL	makasimaseba	makasimaseñ nara
		makasimasureba	
Gerund	**INFORMAL I**	makasite	makasanai de
	II		makasanakute
	FORMAL	makasimasite	makasimaseñ de
Past Ind.	**INFORMAL**	makasita	makasanakatta
	FORMAL	makasimasita	makasimaseñ desita
Past Presump.	**INFORMAL**	makasitaroo	makasanakattaroo
		makasita daroo	makasanakatta daroo
	FORMAL	makasimasitaroo	makasimaseñ desitaroo
		makasita desyoo	makasanakatta desyoo
Conditional	**INFORMAL**	makasitara	makasanakattara
	FORMAL	makasimasitara	makasimaseñ desitara
Alternative	**INFORMAL**	makasitari	makasanakattari
	FORMAL	makasimasitari	makasimaseñ desitari

INFORMAL AFFIRMATIVE INDICATIVE

Passive	makasareru
Potential	makaseru
Causative	
Causative Pass.	

Honorific	**I**	omakasi ni naru
	II	omakasi nasaru
Humble	**I**	omakasi suru
	II	omakasi itasu

make.ru
to be defeated, to be bested

		AFFIRMATIVE	NEGATIVE
Indicative	**INFORMAL**	makeru	makenai
	FORMAL	makemasu	makemaseñ
Imperative	**INFORMAL I**	makero	makeru na
	II	makenasai	makenasaru na
	III	makete kudasai	makenai de kudasai
	FORMAL	omake nasaimase	omake nasaimasu na
Presumptive	**INFORMAL I**	makeyoo	makemai
	II	makeru daroo	makenai daroo
	FORMAL I	makemasyoo	makemasumai
	II	makeru desyoo	makenai desyoo
Provisional	**INFORMAL**	makereba	makenakereba
	FORMAL	makemaseba	makemaseñ nara
		makemasureba	
Gerund	**INFORMAL I**	makete	makenai de
	II		makenakute
	FORMAL	makemasite	makemaseñ de
Past Ind.	**INFORMAL**	maketa	makenakatta
	FORMAL	makemasita	makemasen desita
Past Presump.	**INFORMAL**	maketaroo	makenakattaroo
		maketa daroo	makenakatta daroo
	FORMAL	makemasitaroo	makemaseñ desitaroo
		maketa desyoo	makenakatta desyoo
Conditional	**INFORMAL**	maketara	makenakattara
	FORMAL	makemasitara	makemaseñ desitara
Alternative	**INFORMAL**	maketari	makenakattari
	FORMAL	makemasitari	makemaseñ desitari

	INFORMAL AFFIRMATIVE INDICATIVE
Passive	makerareru
Potential	makerareru
Causative	makesaseru
Causative Pass.	makesaserareru

Honorific	**I**	omake ni naru
	II	omake nasaru
Humble	**I**	omake suru
	II	omake itasu

		AFFIRMATIVE	NEGATIVE
Indicative	**INFORMAL**	matigau	matigawanai
	FORMAL	matigaimasu	matigaimaseñ
Imperative	**INFORMAL I**		
	II		
	III		
	FORMAL		
Presumptive	**INFORMAL I**	matigaoo	matigaumai
	II	matigau daroo	matigawanai daroo
	FORMAL I	matigaimasyoo	matigaimasumai
	II	matigau desyoo	matigawanai desyoo
Provisional	**INFORMAL**	matigaeba	matigawanakereba
	FORMAL	matigaimaseba	matigaimasen nara
		matigaimasureba	
Gerund	**INFORMAL I**	matigatte	matigawanai de
	II		matigawanakute
	FORMAL	matigaimasite	matigaimaseñ de
Past Ind.	**INFORMAL**	matigatta	matigawanakatta
	FORMAL	matigaimasita	matigaimaseñ desita
Past Presump.	**INFORMAL**	matigattaroo	matigawanakattaroo
		matigatta daroo	matigawanakatta daroo
	FORMAL	matigaimasitaroo	matigaimaseñ desitaroo
		matigatta desyoo	matigawanakatta desyoo
Conditional	**INFORMAL**	matigattara	matigawanakattara
	FORMAL	matigaimasitara	matigaimaseñ desitara
Alternative	**INFORMAL**	matigattari	matigawanakattari
	FORMAL	matigaimasitari	matigaimaseñ desitari

	INFORMAL AFFIRMATIVE INDICATIVE
Passive	matigawareru
Potential	matigaeru
Causative	matigawaseru
Causative Pass.	matigawaserareru

Honorific

Humble

mat.u
to wait TRANSITIVE

			AFFIRMATIVE	NEGATIVE
Indicative	INFORMAL		matu	matanai
	FORMAL		matimasu	matimaseñ
Imperative	INFORMAL	I	mate	matu na
		II	matinasai	matinasaru na
		III	matte kudasai	matanai de kudasai
	FORMAL		omati nasaimase	omati nasaimasu na
Presumptive	INFORMAL	I	matoo	matumai
		II	matu daroo	matanai daroo
	FORMAL	I	matimasyoo	matimasumai
		II	matu desyoo	matanai desyoo
Provisional	INFORMAL		mateba	matanakereba
	FORMAL		matimaseba	matimaseñ nara
			matimasureba	
Gerund	INFORMAL	I	matte	matanai de
		II		matanakute
	FORMAL		matimasite	matimaseñ de
Past Ind.	INFORMAL		matta	matanakatta
	FORMAL		matimasita	matimaseñ desita
Past Presump.	INFORMAL		mattaroo	matanakattaroo
			matta daroo	matanakatta daroo
	FORMAL		matimasitaroo	matimaseñ desitaroo
			matta desyoo	matanakatta desyoo
Conditional	INFORMAL		mattara	matanakattara
	FORMAL		matimasitara	matimaseñ desitara
Alternative	INFORMAL		mattari	matanakattari
	FORMAL		matimasitari	matimaseñ desitari

INFORMAL AFFIRMATIVE INDICATIVE

Passive	matareru
Potential	materu
Causative	mataseru
Causative Pass.	mataserareru

Honorific	I	omati ni naru
	II	omati nasaru
Humble	I	omati suru
	II	omati itasu

		AFFIRMATIVE	NEGATIVE
Indicative	**INFORMAL**	mazeru	mazenai
	FORMAL	mazemasu	mazemaseñ
Imperative	**INFORMAL** I	mazero	mazeru na
	II	mazenasai	mazenasaru na
	III	mazete kudasai	mazenai de kudasai
	FORMAL	omaze nasaimase	omaze nasaimasu na
Presumptive	**INFORMAL** I	mazeyoo	mazemai
	II	mazeru daroo	mazenai daroo
	FORMAL I	mazemasyoo	mazemasumai
	II	mazeru desyoo	mazenai desyoo
Provisional	**INFORMAL**	mazereba	mazenakereba
	FORMAL	mazemaseba	mazemaseñ nara
		mazemasureba	
Gerund	**INFORMAL** I	mazete	mazenai de
	II		mazenakute
	FORMAL	mazemasite	mazemaseñ de
Past Ind.	**INFORMAL**	mazeta	mazenakatta
	FORMAL	mazemasita	mazemaseñ desita
Past Presump.	**INFORMAL**	mazetaroo	mazenakattaroo
		mazeta daroo	mazenakatta daroo
	FORMAL	mazemasitaroo	mazemaseñ desitaroo
		mazeta desyoo	mazenakatta desyoo
Conditional	**INFORMAL**	mazetara	mazenakattara
	FORMAL	mazemasitara	mazemaseñ desitara
Alternative	**INFORMAL**	mazetari	mazenakattari
	FORMAL	mazemasitari	mazemaseñ desitari

INFORMAL AFFIRMATIVE INDICATIVE

Passive	mazerareru
Potential	mazerareru
Causative	mazesaseru
Causative Pass.	mazesaserareru

Honorific	I	omaze ni naru
	II	omaze nasaru
Humble	I	omaze suru
	II	omaze itasu

to be visible, to be able to see, honorific for to visit

		AFFIRMATIVE	NEGATIVE
Indicative	INFORMAL	mieru	mienai
	FORMAL	miemasu	miemaseñ
Imperative	INFORMAL I		
	II		
	III		
	FORMAL		
Presumptive	INFORMAL I	mieyoo	miemai
	II	mieru daroo	mienai daroo
	FORMAL I	miemasyoo	miemasumai
	II	mieru desyoo	mienai desyoo
Provisional	INFORMAL	miereba	mienakereba
	FORMAL	miemaseba	miemaseñ nara
		miemasureba	
Gerund	INFORMAL I	miete	mienai de
	II		mienakute
	FORMAL	miemasite	miemaseñ de
Past Ind.	INFORMAL	mieta	mienakatta
	FORMAL	miemasita	miemaseñ desita
Past Presump.	INFORMAL	mietaroo	mienakattaroo
		mieta daroo	mienakatta daroo
	FORMAL	miemasitaroo	miemaseñ desitaroo
		mieta desyoo	mienakatta desyoo
Conditional	INFORMAL	mietara	mienakattara
	FORMAL	miemasitara	miemaseñ desitara
Alternative	INFORMAL	mietari	mienakattari
	FORMAL	miemasitari	miemaseñ desitari

INFORMAL AFFIRMATIVE INDICATIVE

Passive

Potential

Causative

Causative Pass.

Honorific	I	omie ni naru
	II	omie nasaru

Humble

		AFFIRMATIVE	NEGATIVE
Indicative	**INFORMAL**	migaku	migakanai
	FORMAL	migakimasu	migakimaseñ
Imperative	**INFORMAL** I	migake	migaku na
	II	migakinasai	migakinasaru na
	III	migaite kudasai	migakanai de kudasai
	FORMAL	omigaki nasaimase	omigaki nasaimasu na
Presumptive	**INFORMAL** I	migakoo	migakumai
	II	migaku daroo	migakanai daroo
	FORMAL I	migakimasyoo	migakimasumai
	II	migaku desyoo	migakanai desyoo
Provisional	**INFORMAL**	migakeba	migakanakereba
	FORMAL	migakimaseba	migakimaseñ nara
		migakimasureba	
Gerund	**INFORMAL** I	migaite	migakanai de
	II		migakanakute
	FORMAL	migakimasite	migakimaseñ de
Past Ind.	**INFORMAL**	migaita	migakanakatta
	FORMAL	migakimasita	migakimaseñ desita
Past Presump.	**INFORMAL**	migaitaroo	migakanakattaroo
		migaita daroo	migakanakatta daroo
	FORMAL	migakimasitaroo	migakimaseñ desitaroo
		migaita desyoo	migakanakatta desyoo
Conditional	**INFORMAL**	migaitara	migakanakattara
	FORMAL	migakimasitara	migakimaseñ desitara
Alternative	**INFORMAL**	migaitari	migakanakattari
	FORMAL	migakimasitari	migakimaseñ desitari

	INFORMAL AFFIRMATIVE INDICATIVE
Passive	migakareru
Potential	migakeru
Causative	migakaseru
Causative Pass.	migakaserareru

Honorific	I	omigaki ni naru
	II	omigaki nasaru
Humble	I	omigaki suru
	II	omigaki itasu

mi.ru

to look (at) *to see*   TRANSITIVE

			AFFIRMATIVE	NEGATIVE
Indicative	**INFORMAL**		miru	minai
	FORMAL		mimasu	mimaseñ
Imperative	**INFORMAL**	**I**	miro	miru na
		II	minasai	minasaru na
		III	mite kudasai	minai de kudasai
	FORMAL		gorañ nasaimase	goran nasaimasu na
Presumptive	**INFORMAL**	**I**	miyoo	mimai
		II	miru daroo	minai daroo
	FORMAL	**I**	mimasyoo	mimasumai
		II	miru desyoo	minai desyoo
Provisional	**INFORMAL**		mireba	minakereba
	FORMAL		mimaseba	mimaseñ nara
			mimasureba	
Gerund	**INFORMAL**	**I**	mite	minai de
		II		minakute
	FORMAL		mimasite	mimaseñ de
Past Ind.	**INFORMAL**		mita	minakatta
	FORMAL		mimasita	mimaseñ desita
Past Presump.	**INFORMAL**		mitaroo	minakattaroo
			mita daroo	minakatta daroo
	FORMAL		mimasitaroo	mimaseñ desitaroo
			mita desyoo	minakatta desyoo
Conditional	**INFORMAL**		mitara	minakattara
	FORMAL		mimasitara	mimaseñ desitara
Alternative	**INFORMAL**		mitari	minakattari
	FORMAL		mimasitari	mimaseñ desitari

		INFORMAL AFFIRMATIVE INDICATIVE
Passive		mirareru
Potential		mirareru*
Causative		misaseru
Causative Pass.		misaserareru
Honorific	**I**	gorañ ni naru
	II	gorañ nasaru
Humble	**I**	haikeñ suru
	II	haikeñ itasu

*This form means 'can be seen' in the sense that it exists at the time one wants to look at it. 'To visible' is a separate verb *mieru*.

			AFFIRMATIVE	NEGATIVE
Indicative	**INFORMAL**		miseru	misenai
	FORMAL		misemasu	misemaseñ
Imperative	**INFORMAL**	**I**	misero	miseru na
		II	misenasai	misenasaru na
		III	misete kudasai	misenai de kudasai
	FORMAL		omise nasaimase	omise nasaimasu na
Presumptive	**INFORMAL**	**I**	miseyoo	misemai
		II	miseru daroo	misenai daroo
	FORMAL	**I**	misemasyoo	misemasumai
		II	miseru desyoo	misenai desyoo
Provisional	**INFORMAL**		misereba	misenakereba
	FORMAL		misemaseba	misemaseñ nara
			misemasureba	
Gerund	**INFORMAL**	**I**	misete	misenai de
		II		misenakute
	FORMAL		misemasite	misemaseñ de
Past Ind.	**INFORMAL**		miseta	misenakatta
	FORMAL		misemasita	misemaseñ desita
Past Presump.	**INFORMAL**		misetaroo	misenakattaroo
			miseta daroo	misenakatta daroo
	FORMAL		misemasitaroo	misemaseñ desitaroo
			miseta desyoo	misenakatta desyoo
Conditional	**INFORMAL**		misetara	misenakattara
	FORMAL		misemasitara	misemaseñ desitara
Alternative	**INFORMAL**		misetari	misenakattari
	FORMAL		misemasitari	misemaseñ desitari

	INFORMAL AFFIRMATIVE INDICATIVE
Passive	miserareru
Potential	miserareru
Causative	misesaseru
Causative Pass.	misesaserareru

Honorific	**I**	omise ni naru
	II	omise nasaru
Humble		gorañ ni ireru

			AFFIRMATIVE	NEGATIVE
Indicative	INFORMAL		mitomeru	mitomenai
	FORMAL		mitomemasu	mitomemaseñ
Imperative	INFORMAL	I	mitomero	mitomeru na
		II	mitomeru daroo	mitomenai daroo
		III	mitomete kudasai	mitomenai de kudasai
	FORMAL		omitome nasaimase	omitome nasaimasu na
Presumptive	INFORMAL	I	mitomeyoo	mitomemai
		II	mitomeru daroo	mitomenai daroo
	FORMAL	I	mitomemasyoo	mitomemasumai
		II	mitomeru desyoo	mitomenai desyoo
Provisional	INFORMAL		mitomereba	mitomenakereba
	FORMAL		mitomemaseba	mitomemaseñ nara
			mitomemasureba	
Gerund	INFORMAL	I	mitomete	mitomenai de
		II		mitomenakute
	FORMAL		mitomemasite	mitomemaseñ de
Past Ind.	INFORMAL		mitometa	mitomenakatta
	FORMAL		mitomemasita	mitomemaseñ desita
Past Presump.	INFORMAL		mitometaroo	mitomenakattaroo
			mitometa daroo	mitomenakatta daroo
	FORMAL		mitomemasitaroo	mitomemaseñ desitaroo
			mitometa desyoo	mitomenakatta desyoo
Conditional	INFORMAL		mitometara	mitomenakattara
	FORMAL		mitomemasitara	mitomemaseñ desitara
Alternative	INFORMAL		mitometari	mitomenakattari
	FORMAL		mitomemasitari	mitomemaseñ desitari

	INFORMAL AFFIRMATIVE INDICATIVE
Passive	mitomerareru
Potential	mitomerareru
Causative	mitomesaseru
Causative Pass.	mitomesaserareru

Honorific	I	omitome ni naru
	II	omitome nasaru

Humble

		AFFIRMATIVE	NEGATIVE
Indicative	**INFORMAL**	mitukaru	mitukaranai
	FORMAL	mitukarimasu	mitukarimaseñ
Imperative	**INFORMAL I**		
	II		
	III		
	FORMAL		
Presumptive	**INFORMAL I**	mitukaroo	mitukarumai
	II	mitukaru daroo	mitukaranai daroo
	FORMAL I	mitukarimasyoo	mitukarimasumai
	II	mitukaru desyoo	mitukaranai desyoo
Provisional	**INFORMAL**	mitukareba	mitukaranakereba
	FORMAL	mitukarimaseba	mitukarimaseñ nara
		mitukarimasureba	
Gerund	**INFORMAL I**	mitukatte	mitukaranai de
	II		mitukaranakute
	FORMAL	mitukarimasite	mitukarimaseñ de
Past Ind.	**INFORMAL**	mitukatta	mitukaranakatta
	FORMAL	mitukarimasita	mitukarimaseñ desita
Past Presump.	**INFORMAL**	mitukattaroo	mitukaranakattaroo
		mitukatta daroo	mitukaranakatta daroo
	FORMAL	mitukarimasitaroo	mitukarimaseñ desitaroo
		mitukatta desyoo	mitukaranakatta desyoo
Conditional	**INFORMAL**	mitukattara	mitukaranakattara
	FORMAL	mitukarimasitara	mitukarimaseñ desitara
Alternative	**INFORMAL**	mitukattari	mitukaranakattari
	FORMAL	mitukarimasitari	mitukarimaseñ desitari

INFORMAL AFFIRMATIVE INDICATIVE

Passive

Potential

Causative

Causative Pass.

Honorific

Humble

to find   TRANSITIVE

		AFFIRMATIVE	NEGATIVE
Indicative	**INFORMAL**	mitukeru	mitukenai
	FORMAL	mitukemasu	mitukemaseñ
Imperative	**INFORMAL I**	mitukero	mitukeru na
	II	mitukenasai	mitukenasaru na
	III	mitukete kudasai	mitukenai de kudasai
	FORMAL	omituke nasaimase	omituke nasaimasu na
Presumptive	**INFORMAL I**	mitukeyoo	mitukemai
	II	mitukeru daroo	mitukenai daroo
	FORMAL I	mitukemasyoo	mitukemasumai
	II	mitukeru desyoo	mitukenai desyoo
Provisional	**INFORMAL**	mitukereba	mitukenakereba
	FORMAL	mitukemaseba	mitukemaseñ nara
		mitukemasureba	
Gerund	**INFORMAL I**	mitukete	mitukenai de
	II		mitukenakute
	FORMAL	mitukemasite	mitukemaseñ de
Past Ind.	**INFORMAL**	mituketa	mitukenakatta
	FORMAL	mitukemasita	mitukemaseñ desita
Past Presump.	**INFORMAL**	mituketaroo	mitukenakattaroo
		mituketa daroo	mitukenakatta daroo
	FORMAL	mitukemasitaroo	mitukemaseñ desitaroo
		mituketa desyoo	mitukenakatta desyoo
Conditional	**INFORMAL**	mituketara	mitukenakattara
	FORMAL	mitukemasitara	mitukemaseñ desitara
Alternative	**INFORMAL**	mituketari	mitukenakattari
	FORMAL	mitukemasitari	mitukemaseñ desitari

		INFORMAL AFFIRMATIVE INDICATIVE
Passive		mitukerareru
Potential		mitukerareru
Causative		mitukesaseru
Causative Pass.		mitukesaserareru

Honorific	**I**	omituke ni naru
	II	omituke nasaru
Humble		

TRANSITIVE   *to profit, to make money*

		AFFIRMATIVE	NEGATIVE
Indicative	**INFORMAL**	mookeru	mookenai
	FORMAL	mookemasu	mookemaseñ
Imperative	**INFORMAL** I	mookero	mookeru na
	II	mookenasai	mookenasaru na
	III	mookete kudasai	mookenai de kudasai
	FORMAL	omooke nasaimase	omooke nasaimasu na
Presumptive	**INFORMAL** I	mookeyoo	mookemai
	II	mookeru daroo	mookenai daroo
	FORMAL I	mookemasyoo	mookemasumai
	II	mookeru desyoo	mookenai desyoo
Provisional	**INFORMAL**	mookereba	mookenakereba
	FORMAL	mookemaseba	mookemaseñ nara
		mookemasureba	
Gerund	**INFORMAL** I	mookete	mookenai de
	II		mookenakute
	FORMAL	mookemasite	mookemaseñ de
Past Ind.	**INFORMAL**	mooketa	mookenakatta
	FORMAL	mookemasita	mookemaseñ desita
Past Presump.	**INFORMAL**	mooketaroo	mookenakattaroo
		mooketa daroo	mookenakatta daroo
	FORMAL	mookemasitaroo	mookemaseñ desitaroo
		mooketa desyoo	mookenakatta desyoo
Conditional	**INFORMAL**	mooketara	mookenakattara
	FORMAL	mookemasitara	mookemaseñ desitara
Alternative	**INFORMAL**	mooketari	mookenakattari
	FORMAL	mookemasitari	mookemaseñ desitari

	INFORMAL AFFIRMATIVE INDICATIVE
Passive	mookerareru
Potential	mookerareru
Causative	mookesaseru
Causative Pass.	mookesaserareru

Honorific	I	omooke ni naru
	II	omooke nasaru
Humble		

			AFFIRMATIVE	NEGATIVE
Indicative	**INFORMAL**		morau	morawanai
	FORMAL		moraimasu	moraimaseñ
Imperative	**INFORMAL**	**I**	morae	morau na
		II	morainasai	morainasaru na
		III	moratte kudasai	morawanai de kudasai
	FORMAL		omorai nasaimase	omorai nasaimasu na
Presumptive	**INFORMAL**	**I**	moraoo	moraumai
		II	morau daroo	morawanai daroo
	FORMAL	**I**	moraimasyoo	moraimasumai
		II	morau desyoo	morawanai desyoo
Provisional	**INFORMAL**		moraeba	morawanakereba
	FORMAL		moraimaseba	moraimaseñ nara
			moraimasureba	
Gerund	**INFORMAL**	**I**	moratte	morawanai de
		II		morawanakute
	FORMAL		moraimasite	moraimaseñ de
Past Ind.	**INFORMAL**		moratta	morawanakatta
	FORMAL		moraimasita	moraimaseñ desita
Past Presump.	**INFORMAL**		morattaroo	morawanakattaroo
			moratta daroo	morawanakatta daroo
	FORMAL		moraimasitaroo	moraimaseñ desitaroo
			moratta desyoo	morawanakatta desyoo
Conditional	**INFORMAL**		morattara	morawanakattara
	FORMAL		moraimasitara	moraimaseñ desitara
Alternative	**INFORMAL**		morattari	morawanakattari
	FORMAL		moraimasitari	moraimaseñ desitari

	INFORMAL AFFIRMATIVE INDICATIVE
Passive	morawareru
Potential	moraeru
Causative	morawaseru
Causative Pass.	morawaserareru

Honorific	**I**	omorai ni naru
	II	omorai nasaru
Humble		itadaku

			AFFIRMATIVE	NEGATIVE
Indicative	**INFORMAL**		motu	motanai
	FORMAL		motimasu	motimaseñ
Imperative	**INFORMAL**	**I**	mote	motu na
		II	motinasai	motinasaru na
		III	motte kudasai	motanai de kudasai
	FORMAL		omoti nasaimase	omoti nasaimasu na
Presumptive	**INFORMAL**	**I**	motoo	motumai
		II	motu daroo	motanai daroo
	FORMAL	**I**	motimasyoo	motimasumai
		II	motu desyoo	motanai desyoo
Provisional	**INFORMAL**		moteba	motanakereba
	FORMAL		motimaseba	motimaseñ nara
			motimasureba	
Gerund	**INFORMAL**	**I**	motte	motanai de
		II		motanakute
	FORMAL		motimasite	motimaseñ de
Past Ind.	**INFORMAL**		motta	motanakatta
	FORMAL		motimasita	motimaseñ desita
Past Presump.	**INFORMAL**		mottaroo	motanakattaroo
			motta daroo	motanakatta daroo
	FORMAL		motimasitaroo	motimaseñ desitaroo
			motta desyoo	motanakatta desyoo
Conditional	**INFORMAL**		mottara	motanakattara
	FORMAL		motimasitara	motimaseñ desitara
Alternative	**INFORMAL**		mottari	motanakattari
	FORMAL		motimasitari	motimaseñ desitari

	INFORMAL AFFIRMATIVE INDICATIVE
Passive	motareru
Potential	moteru
Causative	motaseru
Causative Pass.	motaserareru

Honorific	**I**	omoti ni naru
	II	omoti nasaru
Humble	**I**	omoti suru
	II	omoti itasu

			AFFIRMATIVE	NEGATIVE
Indicative	INFORMAL		naku	nakanai
	FORMAL		nakimasu	nakimaseñ
Imperative	INFORMAL	I	nake	naku na
		II	nakinasai	nakinasaru na
		III	naite kudasai	nakanai de kudasai
	FORMAL		onaki nasaimase	onaki nasaimasu na
Presumptive	INFORMAL	I	nakoo	nakumai
		II	naku daroo	nakanai daroo
	FORMAL	I	nakimasyoo	nakimasumai
		II	naku desyoo	nakanai desyoo
Provisional	INFORMAL		nakeba	nakanakereba
	FORMAL		nakimaseba	nakimaseñ nara
			nakimasureba	
Gerund	INFORMAL	I	naite	nakanai de
		II		nakanakute
	FORMAL		nakimasite	nakimaseñ de
Past Ind.	INFORMAL		naita	nakanakatta
	FORMAL		nakimasita	nakimaseñ desita
Past Presump.	INFORMAL		naitaroo	nakanakattaroo
			naita daroo	nakanakatta daroo
	FORMAL		nakimasitaroo	nakimaseñ desitaroo
			naita desyoo	nakanakatta desyoo
Conditional	INFORMAL		naitara	nakanakattara
	FORMAL		nakimasitara	nakimaseñ desitara
Alternative	INFORMAL		naitari	nakanakattari
	FORMAL		nakimasitari	nakimaseñ desitari

		INFORMAL AFFIRMATIVE INDICATIVE
Passive		nakareru
Potential		nakeru
Causative		nakaseru
Causative Pass.		nakaserareru

Honorific	I	onaki ni naru
	II	onaki nasaru
Humble		

naor.u

to recover from illness, to be fixed

			AFFIRMATIVE	NEGATIVE
Indicative	**INFORMAL**		naoru	naoranai
	FORMAL		naorimasu	naorimaseñ
Imperative	**INFORMAL**	**I**	naore	naoru na
		II	naorinasai	naorinasaru na
		III	naotte kudasai	naoranai de kudasai
	FORMAL		onaori nasaimase	onaori nasaimasu na
Presumptive	**INFORMAL**	**I**	naoroo	naorumai
		II	naoru daroo	naoranai daroo
	FORMAL	**I**	naorimasyoo	naorimasumai
		II	naoru desyoo	naoranai desyoo
Provisional	**INFORMAL**		naoreba	naoranakereba
	FORMAL		naorimaseba	naorimaseñ nara
			naorimasureba	
Gerund	**INFORMAL**	**I**	naotte	naoranai de
		II		naoranakute
	FORMAL		naorimasite	naorimaseñ de
Past Ind.	**INFORMAL**		naotta	naoranakatta
	FORMAL		naorimasita	naorimaseñ desita
Past Presump.	**INFORMAL**		naottaroo	naoranakattaroo
			naotta daroo	naoranakatta daroo
	FORMAL		naorimasitaroo	naorimaseñ desitaroo
			naotta desyoo	naoranakatta desyoo
Conditional	**INFORMAL**		naottara	naoranakattara
	FORMAL		naorimasitara	naorimaseñ desitara
Alternative	**INFORMAL**		naottari	naoranakattari
	FORMAL		naorimasitari	naorimaseñ desitari

	INFORMAL AFFIRMATIVE INDICATIVE
Passive	naorareru
Potential	naoreru
Causative	naoraseru
Causative Pass.	

Honorific	**I**	onaori ni naru
	II	onaori nasaru
Humble		

naos.u
to repair, cure TRANSITIVE

			AFFIRMATIVE	NEGATIVE
Indicative	INFORMAL		naosu	naosanai
	FORMAL		naosimasu	naosimaseñ
Imperative	INFORMAL	I	naose	naosu na
		II	naosinasai	naosinasaru na
		III	naosite kudasai	naosanai de kudasai
	FORMAL		onasosi nasaimase	onaosi nasaimasu na
Presumptive	INFORMAL	I	naosoo	naosumai
		II	naosu daroo	naosanai daroo
	FORMAL	I	naosimasyoo	naosimasumai
		II	naosu desyoo	naosanai desyoo
Provisional	INFORMAL		naoseba	naosanakereba
	FORMAL		naosimaseba	naosimaseñ nara
			naosimasureba	
Gerund	INFORMAL	I	naosite	naosanai de
		II		naosanakute
	FORMAL		naosimasite	naosimaseñ de
Past Ind.	INFORMAL		naosita	naosanakatta
	FORMAL		naosimasita	naosimaseñ desita
Past Presump.	INFORMAL		naositaroo	naosanakattaroo
			naosita daroo	naosanakatta daroo
	FORMAL		naosimasitaroo	naosimaseñ desitaroo
			naosita desyoo	naosanakatta desyoo
Conditional	INFORMAL		naositara	naosanakattara
	FORMAL		naosimasitara	naosimaseñ desitara
Alternative	INFORMAL		naositari	naosanakattari
	FORMAL		naosimasitari	naosimaseñ desitari

	INFORMAL AFFIRMATIVE INDICATIVE
Passive	naosareru
Potential	naoseru
Causative	naosaseru
Causative Pass.	naosaserareru

Honorific	I	onaosi ni naru
	II	onaosi nasaru
Humble	I	onaosi suru
	II	onaosi itasu

narabe

narabe.ru

TRANSITIVE *to arrange in order*

		AFFIRMATIVE	NEGATIVE
Indicative	**INFORMAL**	naraberu	narabenai
	FORMAL	narabemasu	narabemaseñ
Imperative	**INFORMAL I**	narabero	naraberu na
	II	narabenasai	narabenasaru na
	III	narabete kudasai	narabenai de kudasai
	FORMAL	onarabe nasaimase	onarabe nasaimasu na
Presumptive	**INFORMAL I**	narabeyoo	narabemai
	II	naraberu daroo	narabenai daroo
	FORMAL I	narabemasyoo	narabemasumai
	II	naraberu desyoo	narabenai desyoo
Provisional	**INFORMAL**	narabereba	narabenakereba
	FORMAL	narabemaseba	narabemaseñ nara
		narabemasureba	
Gerund	**INFORMAL I**	narabete	narabenai de
	II		narabenakute
	FORMAL	narabemasite	narabemaseñ de
Past Ind.	**INFORMAL**	narabeta	narabenakatta
	FORMAL	narabemasita	narabemaseñ desita
Past Presump.	**INFORMAL**	narabetaroo	narabenakattaroo
		narabeta daroo	narabenakatta daroo
	FORMAL	narabemasitaroo	narabemaseñ desitaroo
		narabeta desyoo	narabenakatta desyoo
Conditional	**INFORMAL**	narabetara	narabenakattara
	FORMAL	narabemasitara	narabemaseñ desitara
Alternative	**INFORMAL**	narabetari	narabenakattari
	FORMAL	narabemasitari	narabemaseñ desitari

	INFORMAL AFFIRMATIVE INDICATIVE
Passive	naraberareru
Potential	naraberareru
Causative	narabesaseru
Causative Pass.	narabesaserareru

Honorific	**I**	onarabe ni naru
	II	onarabe nasaru
Humble	**I**	onarabe suru
	II	onarabe itasu

103

			AFFIRMATIVE	NEGATIVE
Indicative	INFORMAL		narau	narawanai
	FORMAL		naraimasu	naraimaseñ
Imperative	INFORMAL	I	narae	narau na
		II	narainasai	narainasaru na
		III	naratte kudasai	narwanai de kudasai
	FORMAL		onarai nasaimase	onarai nasaimasu na
Presumptive	INFORMAL	I	naraoo	naraumai
		II	narau daroo	narawanai daroo
	FORMAL	I	naraimasyoo	naraimasumai
		II	narau desyoo	narawanai desyoo
Provisional	INFORMAL		naraeba	narawanakereba
	FORMAL		naraimaseba	naraimaseñ nara
			naraimasureba	
Gerund	INFORMAL	I	naratte	narawanai de
		II		narawanakute
	FORMAL		naraimasite	naraimaseñ de
Past Ind.	INFORMAL		naratta	narawanakatta
	FORMAL		naraimasita	naraimaseñ desita
Past Presump.	INFORMAL		narattaroo	narawanakattaroo
			naratta daroo	narawanakatta daroo
	FORMAL		naraimasitaroo	naraimaseñ desitaroo
			naratta desyoo	narawanakatta desyoo
Conditional	INFORMAL		narattara	narawanakattara
	FORMAL		naraimasitara	naraimaseñ desitara
Alternative	INFORMAL		narattari	narawanakattari
	FORMAL		naraimasitari	naraimaseñ desitari

	INFORMAL AFFIRMATIVE INDICATIVE
Passive	narawareru
Potential	naraeru
Causative	narawaseru
Causative Pass.	narawaserareru

Honorific	I	onarai ni naru
	II	onarai nasaru
Humble		

			AFFIRMATIVE	NEGATIVE
Indicative	**INFORMAL**		naru	naranai
	FORMAL		narimasu	narimaseñ
Imperative	**INFORMAL**	**I**	nare	naru na
		II	narinasai	narinasaru na
		III	natte kudasai	narainai de kudasai
	FORMAL		onari nasaimase	onari nasaimasu na
Presumptive	**INFORMAL**	**I**	naroo	narumai
		II	naru daroo	naranai daroo
	FORMAL	**I**	narimasyoo	narimasumai
		II	naru desyoo	naranai desyoo
Provisional	**INFORMAL**		nareba	naranakereba
	FORMAL		narimaseba	narimaseñ nara
			narimasureba	
Gerund	**INFORMAL**	**I**	natte	naranai de
		II		naranakute
	FORMAL		narimasite	narimaseñ de
Past Ind.	**INFORMAL**		natta	naranakatta
	FORMAL		narimasita	narimaseñ desita
Past Presump.	**INFORMAL**		nattaroo	naranakattaroo
			natta daroo	naranakatta daroo
	FORMAL		narimasitaroo	narimaseñ desitaroo
			natta desyoo	naranakatta desyoo
Conditional	**INFORMAL**		nattara	naranakattara
	FORMAL		narimasitara	narimaseñ desitara
Alternative	**INFORMAL**		nattari	naranakattari
	FORMAL		narimasitari	narimaseñ desitari

INFORMAL AFFIRMATIVE INDICATIVE

Passive	narareru
Potential	nareru
Causative	naraseru
Causative Pass.	naraserareru

Honorific	**I**	onari ni naru
	II	onari nasaru
Humble		

nasar.u   **nasai**
to do (honorific)   TRANSITIVE

		AFFIRMATIVE	NEGATIVE
Indicative	**INFORMAL**	nasaru	nasaranai
	FORMAL	nasaimasu	nasaimaseñ
Imperative	**INFORMAL I**	nasai	nasaru na
	II		
	III	nasatte kudasai	nasaranai de kudasai
	FORMAL	nasaimase	nasaimasu na
Presumptive	**INFORMAL I**	nasaroo	nasarumai
	II	nasaru daroo	nasaranai daroo
	FORMAL I	nasaimasyoo	nasaimasumai
	II	nasaru desyoo	nasaranai desyoo
Provisional	**INFORMAL**	nasareba	nasaranakereba
	FORMAL	nasaimaseba	nasaimaseñ nara
		nasaimasureba	
Gerund	**INFORMAL I**	nasatte	nasaranai de
	II		nasaranakute
	FORMAL	nasaimasite	nasaimaseñ de
Past Ind.	**INFORMAL**	nasatta	nasaranakatta
	FORMAL	nasaimasita	nasaimaseñ desita
Past Presump.	**INFORMAL**	nasattaroo	nasaranakattaroo
		nasatta daroo	nasaranakatta daroo
	FORMAL	nasaimasitaroo	nasaimaseñ desitaroo
		nasatta desyoo	nasaranakatta desyoo
Conditional	**INFORMAL**	nasattara	nasaranakattara
	FORMAL	nasaimasitara	nasaimaseñ desitara
Alternative	**INFORMAL**	nasattari	nasaranakattari
	FORMAL	nasaimasitari	nasaimaseñ desitari

	INFORMAL AFFIRMATIVE INDICATIVE
Passive	nasarareru
Potential	nasareru
Causative	
Causative Pass.	
Honorific	
Humble	

		AFFIRMATIVE	NEGATIVE
Indicative	**INFORMAL**	neru	nenai
	FORMAL	nemasu	nemaseñ
Imperative	**INFORMAL I**	nero	neru na
	II	nenasai	nenasaru na
	III	nete kudasai	nenai de kudasai
	FORMAL*	oyasumi nasaimase	oyasumi nasaimasu na
Presumptive	**INFORMAL I**	neyoo	nemai
	II	neru daroo	nenai daroo
	FORMAL I	nemasyoo	nemasumai
	II	neru desyoo	nenai desyoo
Provisional	**INFORMAL**	nereba	nenakereba
	FORMAL	nemaseba	nemaseñ nara
		nemasureba	
Gerund	**INFORMAL I**	nete	nenai de
	II		nenakute
	FORMAL	nemasite	nemaseñ de
Past Ind.	**INFORMAL**	neta	nenakatta
	FORMAL	nemasita	nemaseñ desita
Past Presump.	**INFORMAL**	netaroo	nenakattaroo
		neta daroo	nenakatta daroo
	FORMAL	nemasitaroo	nemaseñ desitaroo
		neta desyoo	nenakatta desyoo
Conditional	**INFORMAL**	netara	nenakattara
	FORMAL	nemasitara	nemaseñ desitara
Alternative	**INFORMAL**	netari	nenakattari
	FORMAL	nemasitari	nemaseñ desitari

	INFORMAL AFFIRMATIVE INDICATIVE
Passive	nerareru
Potential	nerareru
Causative	nesaseru
Causative Pass.	nesaserareru

Honorific*	**I**	oyasumi ni naru
	II	oyasumi nasaru
Humble		

*The formal imperative forms and honorific equivalents for *neru* are the same as those of its synonym *yasumu*.

		AFFIRMATIVE	NEGATIVE
Indicative	INFORMAL	nigeru	nigenai
	FORMAL	nigemasu	nigemaseñ
Imperative	INFORMAL I	nigero	nigeru na
	II	nigenasai	nigenasaru na
	III	nigete kudasai	nigenai de kudasai
	FORMAL	onige nasaimase	onige nasaimasu na
Presumptive	INFORMAL I	nigeyoo	nigemai
	II	nigeru daroo	nigenai daroo
	FORMAL I	nigemasyoo	nigemasumai
	II	nigeru desyoo	nigenai desyoo
Provisional	INFORMAL	nigereba	nigenakereba
	FORMAL	nigemaseba	nigemaseñ nara
		nigemasureba	
Gerund	INFORMAL I	nigete	nigenai de
	II		nigenakute
	FORMAL	nigemasite	nigemaseñ de
Past Ind.	INFORMAL	nigeta	nigenakatta
	FORMAL	nigemasita	nigemaseñ desita
Past Presump.	INFORMAL	nigetaroo	nigenakattaroo
		nigeta daroo	nigenakatta daroo
	FORMAL	nigemasitaroo	nigemaseñ desitaroo
		nigeta desyoo	nigenakatta desyoo
Conditional	INFORMAL	nigetara	nigenakattara
	FORMAL	nigemasitara	nigemaseñ desitara
Alternative	INFORMAL	nigetari	nigenakattari
	FORMAL	nigemasitari	nigemaseñ desitari

	INFORMAL AFFIRMATIVE INDICATIVE
Passive	nigerareru
Potential	nigerareru
Causative	nigesaseru
Causative Pass.	nigesaserareru

Honorific	I	onige ni naru
	II	onige nasaru
Humble		

nigiri

TRANSITIVE
to grasp

		AFFIRMATIVE	NEGATIVE
Indicative	**INFORMAL**	nigiru	nigiranai
	FORMAL	nigirimasu	nigirimáseñ
Imperative	**INFORMAL I**	nigire	nigiru na
	II	nigirinasai	nigirinasaru na
	III	nigitte kudasai	nigiranai de kudasai
	FORMAL	onigiri nasaimase	onigiri nasaimasu na
Presumptive	**INFORMAL I**	nigiroo	nigirumai
	II	nigiru daroo	nigiranai daroo
	FORMAL I	nigirimasyoo	nigirimasumai
	II	nigiru desyoo	nigiranai desyoo
Provisional	**INFORMAL**	nigireba	nigiranakereba
	FORMAL	nigirimaseba	nigirimaseñ nara
		nigirimasureba	
Gerund	**INFORMAL I**	nigitte	nigiranai de
	II		nigiranakute
	FORMAL	nigirimasite	nigirimaseñ de
Past Ind.	**INFORMAL**	nigitta	nigiranakatta
	FORMAL	nigirimasita	nigirimaseñ desita
Past Presump.	**INFORMAL**	nigittaroo	nigiranakattaroo
		nigitta daroo	nigiranakatta daroo
	FORMAL	nigirimasitaroo	nigirimaseñ desitaroo
		nigitta desyoo	nigiranakatta desyoo
Conditional	**INFORMAL**	nigittara	nigiranakattara
	FORMAL	nigirimasitara	nigirimaseñ desitara
Alternative	**INFORMAL**	nigittari	nigiranakattari
	FORMAL	nigirimasitari	nigirimaseñ desitari

	INFORMAL AFFIRMATIVE INDICATIVE
Passive	nigirareru
Potential	nigireru
Causative	nigiraseru
Causative Pass.	nigiraserareru

Honorific	**I**	onigiri ni naru
	II	onigiri nasaru
Humble	**I**	onigiri suru
	II	onigiri itasu

		AFFIRMATIVE	NEGATIVE
Indicative	INFORMAL	noboru	noboranai
	FORMAL	noborimasu	noborimaseñ
Imperative	INFORMAL I	nobore	noboru na
	II	noborinasai	noborinasaru na
	III	nobotte kudasai	noboranai de kudasai
	FORMAL	onobori nasaimase	onobori nasaimasu na
Presumptive	INFORMAL I	noboroo	noborumai
	II	noboru daroo	noboranai daroo
	FORMAL I	noborimasyoo	noborimasumai
	II	noboru desyoo	noboranai desyoo
Provisional	INFORMAL	noboreba	noboranakereba
	FORMAL	noborimaseba	noborimaseñ nara
		noborimasureba	
Gerund	INFORMAL I	nobotte	noboranai de
	II		noboranakute
	FORMAL	noborimasite	noborimaseñ de
Past Ind.	INFORMAL	nobotta	noboranakatta
	FORMAL	noborimasita	noborimaseñ desita
Past Presump.	INFORMAL	nobottaroo	noboranakattaroo
		nobotta daroo	noboranakatta daroo
	FORMAL	noborimasitaroo	noborimaseñ desitaroo
		nobotta desyoo	noboranakatta desyoo
Conditional	INFORMAL	nobottara	noboranakattara
	FORMAL	noborimasitara	noborimaseñ desitara
Alternative	INFORMAL	nobottari	noboranakattari
	FORMAL	noborimasitari	noborimaseñ desitari

	INFORMAL AFFIRMATIVE INDICATIVE
Passive	nobareru
Potential	noboreru
Causative	noboraseru
Causative Pass.	noboraserareru

Honorific	I	onobori ni naru
	II	onobori nasaru
Humble		

			AFFIRMATIVE	NEGATIVE
Indicative	**INFORMAL**		nokoru	nokoranai
	FORMAL		nokorimasu	nokorimaseñ
Imperative	**INFORMAL**	I	nokore	nokoruna
		II	nokorinasai	nokorinasaru na
		III	nokotte kudasai	nokoranaide kudasai
	FORMAL			
Presumptive	**INFORMAL**	I	nokoroo	nokorumai
		II	nokoru daroo	nokoranai daroo
	FORMAL	I	nokorimasyoo	nokorimasumai
		II	nokoru desyoo	nokoranai desyoo
Provisional	**INFORMAL**		nokoreba	nokoranakereba
	FORMAL		nokorimaseba	nokorimaseñ nara
			nokorimasureba	
Gerund	**INFORMAL**	I	nokotte	nokoranai de
		II		nokoranakute
	FORMAL		nokorimasite	nokorimaseñ de
Past Ind.	**INFORMAL**		nokotta	nokoranakatta
	FORMAL		nokorimasita	nokorimaseñ desita
Past Presump.	**INFORMAL**		nokottaroo	nokoranakattaroo
			nokotta daroo	nokoranakatta daroo
	FORMAL		nokorimasitaroo	nokorimaseñ desitaroo
			nokotta desyoo	nokoranakatta desyoo
Conditional	**INFORMAL**		nokottara	nokoranakattara
	FORMAL		nokorimasitara	nokorimaseñ desitara
Alternative	**INFORMAL**		nokottari	nokoranakattari
	FORMAL		nokorimasitari	nokorimaseñ desitari

	INFORMAL AFFIRMATIVE INDICATIVE
Passive	nokorareru
Potential	nokoreru
Causative	nokoraseru
Causative Pass.	nokoraserareru

Honorific	I	onokori ni naru
	II	onokori nasaru
Humble		

to drink, to smoke (cigarettes etc.)   TRANSITIVE

			AFFIRMATIVE	NEGATIVE
Indicative	**INFORMAL**		nomu	nomanai
	FORMAL		nomimasu	nomimaseñ
Imperative	**INFORMAL**	**I**	nome	nomu na
		II	nominasai	nominasaru na
		III	noñde kudasai	nomanai de kudasai
	FORMAL		mesiagarimase	mesiagarimasu na
			onomi nasaimase	onomi nasaimasu na
Presumptive	**INFORMAL**	**I**	nomoo	nomumai
		II	nomu daroo	nomanai daroo
	FORMAL	**I**	nomimasyoo	nomimasumai
		II	nomu desyoo	nomanai desyoo
Provisional	**INFORMAL**		nomeba	nomanakereba
	FORMAL		nomimaseba	nomimaseñ nara
			nomimasureba	
Gerund	**INFORMAL**	**I**	noñde	nomanai de
		II		nomanakute
	FORMAL		nomimasite	nomimaseñ de
Past Ind.	**INFORMAL**		noñda	nomanakatta
	FORMAL		nomimasita	nomimaseñ desita
Past Presump.	**INFORMAL**		noñdaroo	nomanakattaroo
			noñda daroo	nomanakatta daroo
	FORMAL		nomimasitaroo	nomimaseñ desitaroo
			noñda desyoo	nomanakatta desyoo
Conditional	**INFORMAL**		noñdara	nomanakattara
	FORMAL		nomimasitara	nomimaseñ desitara
Alternative	**INFORMAL**		noñdari	nomanakattari
	FORMAL		nomimasitari	nomimaseñ desitari

INFORMAL AFFIRMATIVE INDICATIVE

Passive	nomareru
Potential	nomeru
Causative	nomaseru
Causative Pass.	nomaserareru

Honorific	mesiagaru	**I**	onomi ni naru
		II	onomi nasaru
Humble	itadaku		

112

		AFFIRMATIVE	NEGATIVE
Indicative	**INFORMAL**	noru	noranai
	FORMAL	norimasu	norimaseñ
Imperative	**INFORMAL I**	nore	noru na
	II	norinasai	norinasaru na
	III	notte kudasai	noranai de kudasai
	FORMAL	onori nasaimase	onori nasaimasu na
Presumptive	**INFORMAL I**	noroo	norumai
	II	noru daroo	noranai daroo
	FORMAL I	norimasyoo	norimasumai
	II	noru desyoo	noranai desyoo
Provisional	**INFORMAL**	noreba	noranakereba
	FORMAL	norimaseba	norimaseñ nara
		norimasureba	
Gerund	**INFORMAL I**	notte	noranai de
	II		noranakute
	FORMAL	norimasite	norimaseñ de
Past Ind.	**INFORMAL**	notta	noranakatta
	FORMAL	norimasita	norimaseñ desita
Past Presump.	**INFORMAL**	nottaroo	noranakattaroo
		notta daroo	noranakatta daroo
	FORMAL	norimasitaroo	norimaseñ desitaroo
		notta desyoo	noranakatta desyoo
Conditional	**INFORMAL**	nottara	noranakattara
	FORMAL	norimasitara	norimaseñ desitara
Alternative	**INFORMAL**	nottari	noranakattari
	FORMAL	norimasitari	norimaseñ desitari

	INFORMAL AFFIRMATIVE INDICATIVE
Passive	norareru
Potential	noreru
Causative	noraseru
Causative Pass.	noraserareru

Honorific	**I**	onori ni naru
	II	onori nasaru
Humble		

to put (on top of), *to put on board*   TRANSITIVE

		AFFIRMATIVE	NEGATIVE
Indicative	**INFORMAL**	noseru	nosenai
	FORMAL	nosemasu	nosemaseñ
Imperative	**INFORMAL I**	nosero	noseru na
	II	nosenasai	nosenasaru na
	III	nosete kudasai	nosenai de kudasai
	FORMAL	onose nasaimase	onose nasaimasu na
Presumptive	**INFORMAL I**	noseyoo	nosemai
	II	noseru daroo	nosenai daroo
	FORMAL I	nosemasyoo	nosemasumai
	II	noseru desyoo	nosenai desyoo
Provisional	**INFORMAL**	nosereba	nosenakereba
	FORMAL	nosemaseba	nosemaseñ nara
		nosemasureba	
Gerund	**INFORMAL I**	nosete	nosenai de
	II		nosenakute
	FORMAL	nosemasite	nosemaseñ de
Past Ind.	**INFORMAL**	noseta	nosenakatta
	FORMAL	nosemasita	nosemaseñ desita
Past Presump.	**INFORMAL**	nosetaroo	nosenakattaroo
		noseta daroo	nosenakatta daroo
	FORMAL	nosemasitaroo	nosemaseñ desitaroo
		noseta desyoo	nosenakatta desyoo
Conditional	**INFORMAL**	nosetara	nosenakattara
	FORMAL	nosemasitara	nosemaseñ desitara
Alternative	**INFORMAL**	nosetari	nosenakattari
	FORMAL	nosemasitari	nosemaseñ desitari

	INFORMAL AFFIRMATIVE INDICATIVE
Passive	noserareru
Potential	noserareru
Causative	nosesaseru
Causative Pass.	nosesaserareru

Honorific	**I**	onose ni naru
	II	onose nasaru
Humble	**I**	onose suru
	II	onose itasu

		AFFIRMATIVE	NEGATIVE
Indicative	**INFORMAL**	nureru	nurenai
	FORMAL	nuremasu	nuremaseñ
Imperative	**INFORMAL I**	nurero	nureruna
	II		
	III		
	FORMAL		
Presumptive	**INFORMAL I**	nureyoo	nuremai
	II	nureru daroo	nurenai daroo
	FORMAL I	nuremasyoo	nuremasumai
	II	nureru desyoo	nurenai desyoo
Provisional	**INFORMAL**	nurereba	nurenakereba
	FORMAL	nuremaseba	nuremaseñ nara
		nuremasureba	
Gerund	**INFORMAL I**	nurete	nurenai de
	II		nurenakute
	FORMAL	nuremasite	nuremaseñ de
Past Ind.	**INFORMAL**	nureta	nurenakatta
	FORMAL	nuremasita	nuremaseñ desita
Past Presump.	**INFORMAL**	nuretaroo	nurenakattaroo
		nureta daroo	nurenakatta daroo
	FORMAL	nuremasitaroo	nuremaseñ desitaroo
		nureta desyoo	nurenakatta desyoo
Conditional	**INFORMAL**	nuretara	nurenakattara
	FORMAL	nuremasitara	nuremaseñ desitara
Alternative	**INFORMAL**	nuretari	nurenakattari
	FORMAL	nuremasitari	nuremaseñ desitari

INFORMAL AFFIRMATIVE INDICATIVE

Passive	nurerareru
Potential	nurerareru
Causative	nuresaseru
Causative Pass.	nuresaserareru

Honorific	**I**	onure ni naru
	II	onure nasaru
Humble		

to smear on   TRANSITIVE

			AFFIRMATIVE	NEGATIVE
Indicative	**INFORMAL**		nuru	nuranai
	FORMAL		nurimasu	nurimaseñ
Imperative	**INFORMAL**	**I**	nure	nuru na
		II	nurinasai	nurinasaru na
		III	nutte kudasai	nuranai de kudasai
	FORMAL		onuri nasaimase	onuri nasaimasu na
Presumptive	**INFORMAL**	**I**	nuroo	nurumai
		II	nuru daroo	nuranai daroo
	FORMAL	**I**	nurimasyoo	nurimasumai
		II	nuru desyoo	nuranai desyoo
Provisional	**INFORMAL**		nureba	nuranakereba
	FORMAL		nurimaseba	nurimaseñ nara
			nurimasureba	
Gerund	**INFORMAL**	**I**	nutte	nuranai de
		II		nuranakute
	FORMAL		nurimasite	nurimaseñ de
Past Ind.	**INFORMAL**		nutta	nuranakatta
	FORMAL		nurimasita	nurimaseñ desita
Past Presump.	**INFORMAL**		nuttaroo	nuranakattaroo
			nutta daroo	nuranakatta daroo
	FORMAL		nurimasitaroo	nurimaseñ desitaroo
			nutta desyoo	nuranakatta desyoo
Conditional	**INFORMAL**		nuttara	nuranakattara
	FORMAL		nurimasitara	nurimaseñ desitara
Alternative	**INFORMAL**		nuttari	nuranakattari
	FORMAL		nurimasitari	nurimaseñ desitari

		INFORMAL AFFIRMATIVE INDICATIVE
Passive		nurareru
Potential		nureru
Causative		nuraseru
Causative Pass.		nuraserareru

Honorific	**I**	onuri ni naru
	II	onuri nasaru
Humble	**I**	onuri suru
	II	onuri itasu

			AFFIRMATIVE	NEGATIVE
Indicative	INFORMAL		nusumu	nusumanai
	FORMAL		nusumimasu	nusumimaseñ
Imperative	INFORMAL	I	nusume	nusumu na
		II	nusumimasai	nusuminasaru na
		III	nusuñde kudasai	nusumanai de kudasai
	FORMAL		onusumi nasaimase	onusumi nasaimasu na
Presumptive	INFORMAL	I	nusumoo	nusumumai
		II	nusumu daroo	nusumanai daroo
	FORMAL	I	nusumimasyoo	nusumimasumai
		II	nusumu desyoo	nusumanai desyoo
Provisional	INFORMAL		nusumeba	nusumanakereba
	FORMAL		nusumimaseba	nusumimaseñ nara
			nusumimasureba	
Gerund	INFORMAL	I	nusuñde	nusumanai de
		II		nusumanakute
	FORMAL		nusumimasite	nusumimaseñ de
Past Ind.	INFORMAL		nusuñda	nusumanakatta
	FORMAL		nusumimasita	nusumimaseñ desita
Past Presump.	INFORMAL		nusuñdaroo	nusumanakattaroo
	FORMAL		nusuñda daroo	nusumanakatta daroo
			nusumimasitaroo	nusumimaseñ desitaroo
			nusuñda desyoo	nusumanakatta desyoo
Conditional	INFORMAL		nusuñdara	nusumanakattara
	FORMAL		nusumimasitara	nusimimaseñ desitara
Alternative	INFORMAL		nusuñdari	nusumanakattari
	FORMAL		nusumimasitari	nusumimaseñ desitari

	INFORMAL AFFIRMATIVE INDICATIVE
Passive	nusumareru
Potential	nusumeru
Causative	nusumaseru
Causative Pass.	nusumaserareru

Honorific	I	onusumi ni naru
	II	onusumi nasaru
Humble		

117

			AFFIRMATIVE	NEGATIVE
Indicative	INFORMAL		oboeru	oboenai
	FORMAL		oboemasu	oboemaseñ
Imperative	INFORMAL	I	oboero	oboeru na
		II	oboenasai	oboenasaru na
		III	oboete kudasai	oboenai de kudasai
	FORMAL		oboe nasaimase	oboe nasaimasu na
Presumptive	INFORMAL	I	oboeyoo	oboe‐nai
		II	oboeru daroo	oboenai daroo
	FORMAL	I	oboemasyoo	oboemasumai
		II	oboeru desyoo	oboenai desyoo
Provisional	INFORMAL		oboereba	oboenakereba
	FORMAL		oboemaseba	oboemaseñ nara
			oboemasureba	
Gerund	INFORMAL	I	oboete	oboenai de
		II		oboenakute
	FORMAL		oboemasite	oboemaseñ de
Past Ind.	INFORMAL		oboeta	oboenakatta
	FORMAL		oboemasita	oboemaseñ desita
Past Presump.	INFORMAL		oboetaroo	oboenakattaroo
			oboeta daroo	oboenakatta daroo
	FORMAL		oboemasitaroo	oboemaseñ desitaroo
			oboeta desyoo	oboenakatta desyoo
Conditional	INFORMAL		oboetara	oboenakattara
	FORMAL		oboemasitara	oboemaseñ desitara
Alternative	INFORMAL		oboetari	oboenakattari
	FORMAL		oboemasitari	oboemaseñ desitari

		INFORMAL AFFIRMATIVE INDICATIVE
Passive		oboerareru
Potential		oboerareru
Causative		oboesaseru
Causative Pass.		oboesaserareru

Honorific	I	ooboe ni naru
	II	ooboe nasaru
Humble		

		AFFIRMATIVE	**NEGATIVE**
Indicative	INFORMAL	odoroku	odorokanai
	FORMAL	odorokimasu	odorokimaseñ
Imperative	INFORMAL I	odoroke	odorokuna
	II	odorokinasai	
	III		
	FORMAL		
Presumptive	INFORMAL I	odorokoo	odorokumai
	II	odoroku daroo	odorokanai daroo
	FORMAL I	odorokimasyoo	odorokimasumai
	II	odoroku desyoo	odorokanai desyoo
Provisional	INFORMAL	odorokeba	odorokanakereba
	FORMAL	odorokimaseba	odorokimaseñ nara
		odorokimasureba	
Gerund	INFORMAL I	odoroite	odorokanai de
	II		odorokanakute
	FORMAL	odorokimasite	odorokimaseñ de
Past Ind.	INFORMAL	odoroita	odorokanakatta
	FORMAL	odorokimasita	odorokimaseñ desita
Past Presump.	INFORMAL	odoroitaroo	odorokanakattaroo
		odoroita daroo	odorokanakatta daroo
	FORMAL	odorokimasitaroo	odorokimaseñ desitaroo
		odoroita desyoo	odorokanakatta desyoo
Conditional	INFORMAL	odoroitara	odorokanakattara
	FORMAL	odorokimasitara	odorokimaseñ desitara
Alternative	INFORMAL	odoroitari	odorokanakattari
	FORMAL	odorokimasitari	odorokimaseñ desitari

INFORMAL AFFIRMATIVE INDICATIVE	
Passive	odorokareru
Potential	odorokeru
Causative	odorokaseru
Causative Pass.	odorokaserareru

Honorific	I	oodoroki ni naru
	II	oodoroki nasaru
Humble		

			AFFIRMATIVE	NEGATIVE
Indicative	INFORMAL		odoru	odoranai
	FORMAL		odorimasu	odorimaseñ
Imperative	INFORMAL	I	odore	odoru na
		II	odorinasai	odorinasaru na
		III	odotte kudasai	odoranai de kudasai
	FORMAL		oodori nasaimase	oodori nasaimasu na
Presumptive	INFORMAL	I	odoroo	odorumai
		II	odoru daroo	odoranai daroo
	FORMAL	I	odorimasyoo	odorimasumai
		II	odoru desyoo	odoranai desyoo
Provisional	INFORMAL		odoreba	odoranakereba
	FORMAL		odorimaseba	odorimaseñ nara
			odorimasureba	
Gerund	INFORMAL	I	odotte	odoranai de
		II		odoranakute
	FORMAL		odorimasite	odorimaseñ de
Past Ind.	INFORMAL		odotta	odoranakatta
	FORMAL		odorimasita	odorimaseñ desita
Past Presump.	INFORMAL		odottaroo	odoranakattaroo
			odotta daroo	odoranakatta daroo
	FORMAL		odorimasitaroo	odorimaseñ desitaroo
			odotta desyoo	odoranakatta desyoo
Conditional	INFORMAL		odottara	odoranakattara
	FORMAL		odorimasitara	odorimaseñ desitara
Alternative	INFORMAL		odottari	odoranakattari
	FORMAL		odorimasitari	odorimaseñ desitari

INFORMAL AFFIRMATIVE INDICATIVE

Passive	odorareru
Potential	odoreru
Causative	odoraseru
Causative Pass.	odoraserareru

Honorific	I	oodori ni naru
	II	oodori nasaru
Humble		

		AFFIRMATIVE	NEGATIVE
Indicative	INFORMAL	okiru	okinai
	FORMAL	okimasu	okimaseñ
Imperative	INFORMAL I	okiro	okiru na
	II	okinasai	okinasaru na
	III	okite kudasai	okinai de kudasai
	FORMAL	ooki nasaimase	ooki nasaimasu na
Presumptive	INFORMAL I	okiyoo	okimai
	II	okiru daroo	okinai daroo
	FORMAL I	okimasyoo	okimasumai
	II	okiru desyoo	okinai desyoo
Provisional	INFORMAL	okireba	okinakereba
	FORMAL	okimaseba	okimaseñ nara
		okimasureba	
Gerund	INFORMAL I	okite	okinai de
	II		okinakute
	FORMAL	okimasite	okimaseñ de
Past Ind.	INFORMAL	okita	okinakatta
	FORMAL	okimasita	okimaseñ desita
Past Presump.	INFORMAL	okitaroo	okinakattaroo
		okita daroo	okinakatta daroo
	FORMAL	okimasitaroo	okimaseñ desitaroo
		okita desyoo	okinakatta desyoo
Conditional	INFORMAL	okitara	okinakattara
	FORMAL	okimasitara	okimaseñ desitara
Alternative	INFORMAL	okitari	okinakattari
	FORMAL	okimasitari	okimaseñ desitari

	INFORMAL AFFIRMATIVE INDICATIVE
Passive	okirareru
Potential	okirareru
Causative	okisaseru
Causative Pass.	okisaserareru

Honorific	I	ooki ni naru
	II	ooki nasaru
Humble	I	ooki suru
	II	ooki itasu

to raise up, to cause to get up   TRANSITIVE

			AFFIRMATIVE	NEGATIVE
Indicative	**INFORMAL**		okosu	okosanai
	FORMAL		okosimasu	okosimaseñ
Imperative	**INFORMAL**	**I**	okose	okosu na
		II	okosinasai	okosinasaru na
		III	okosite kudasai	okosanai de kudasai
	FORMAL		ookosi nasaimase	ookosi nasaimasu na
Presumptive	**INFORMAL**	**I**	okosoo	okosumai
		II	okosu daroo	okosanai daroo
	FORMAL	**I**	okosimasyoo	okosimasumai
		II	okosu daroo	okosanai daroo
Provisional	**INFORMAL**		okoseba	okosanakereba
	FORMAL		okosimaseba	okosimaseñ nara
			okosimasureba	
Gerund	**INFORMAL**	**I**	okosite	okosanai de
		II		okosanakute
	FORMAL		okosimasite	okosimaseñ de
Past Ind.	**INFORMAL**		okosita	okosanakatta
	FORMAL		okosimasita	okosimaseñ desita
Past Presump.	**INFORMAL**		okositaroo	okosanakattaroo
			okosita daroo	okosanakatta daroo
	FORMAL		okosimasitaroo	okosimaseñ desitaroo
			okosita desyoo	okosanakatta desyoo
Conditional	**INFORMAL**		okositara	okosanakattara
	FORMAL		okosimasitara	okosimaseñ desitara
Alternative	**INFORMAL**		okositari	okosanakattari
	FORMAL		okosimasitari	okosimaseñ desitari

		INFORMAL AFFIRMATIVE INDICATIVE
Passive		okosareru
Potential		okoseru
Causative		okosaseru
Causative Pass.		okosaserareru

Honorific	**I**	ookosi ni naru
	II	ookosi nasaru
Humble	**I**	ookosi suru
	II	ookosi itasu

TRANSITIVE   *to put, place*

		AFFIRMATIVE	**NEGATIVE**
Indicative	**INFORMAL**	oku	okanai
	FORMAL	okimasu	okimaseñ
Imperative	**INFORMAL I**	oke	oku na
	II	okinasai	okinasaru na
	III	oite kudasai	okanai de kudasai
	FORMAL	ooki nasaimase	ooki nasaimasu na
Presumptive	**INFORMAL I**	okoo	okumai
	II	oku daroo	okanai daroo
	FORMAL I	okimasyoo	okimasumai
	II	oku desyoo	okanai desyoo
Provisional	**INFORMAL**	okeba	okanakereba
	FORMAL	okimaseba	okimaseñ nara
		okimasureba	
Gerund	**INFORMAL I**	oite	okanai de
	II		okanakute
	FORMAL	okimasite	okimaseñ de
Past Ind.	**INFORMAL**	oita	okanakatta
	FORMAL	okimasita	okimaseñ desita
Past Presump.	**INFORMAL**	oitaroo	okanakattaroo
		oita daroo	okanakatta daroo
	FORMAL	okimasitaroo	okimaseñ desitaroo
		oita desyoo	okanakatta desyoo
Conditional	**INFORMAL**	oitara	okanakattara
	FORMAL	okimasitara	okimaseñ desitara
Alternative	**INFORMAL**	oitari	okanakattari
	FORMAL	okimasitari	okimaseñ desitari

		INFORMAL AFFIRMATIVE INDICATIVE
Passive		okareru
Potential		okeru
Causative		okaseru
tive Pass.		okaserareru
Honorific	**I**	ooki ni naru
	II	ooki nasaru
Humble	**I**	ooki suru
	II	ooki itasu

okur.u

to send (a package), *to escort* (a person)   TRANSITIVE

okuri

			AFFIRMATIVE	NEGATIVE
Indicative	**INFORMAL**		okuru	okuranai
	FORMAL		okurimasu	okurimaseñ
Imperative	**INFORMAL**	I	okure	okuru na
		II	okurinasai	okurinasaru na
		III	okutte kudasai	okuranai de kudasai
	FORMAL		ookuri nasaimase	ookuri nasaimasu na
Presumptive	**INFORMAL**	I	okuroo	okurumai
		II	okuru daroo	okuranai daroo
	FORMAL	I	okurimasyoo	okurimasumai
		II	okuru desyoo	okuranai desyoo
Provisional	**INFORMAL**		okureba	okuranakereba
	FORMAL		okurimaseba	okurimaseñ nara
			okurimasureba	
Gerund	**INFORMAL**	I	okutte	okuranai de
		II		okuranakute
	FORMAL		okurimasite	okurimaseñ de
Past Ind.	**INFORMAL**		okutta	okuranakatta
	FORMAL		okurimasita	okurimaseñ desita
Past Presump.	**INFORMAL**		okuttaroo	okuranakattaroo
			okutta daroo	okuranakatta daroo
	FORMAL		okurimasitaroo	okurimaseñ desitaroo
			okutta desyoo	okuranakatta desyoo
Conditional	**INFORMAL**		okuttara	okuranakattara
	FORMAL		okurimasitara	okurimaseñ desitara
Alternative	**INFORMAL**		okuttari	okuranakattari
	FORMAL		okurimasitari	okurimaseñ desitari

INFORMAL AFFIRMATIVE INDICATIVE

Passive	okurareru
Potential	okureru
Causative	okuraseru
Causative Pass.	okuraserareru

Honorific	I	ookuri ni naru
	II	ookuri nasaru
Humble	I	ookuri suru
	II	ookuri itasu

			AFFIRMATIVE	**NEGATIVE**
Indicative	**INFORMAL**		omou	omowanai
	FORMAL		omoimasu	omoimaseñ
Imperative	**INFORMAL**	I	omoe	omou na
		II	omoinasai	omoi nasaru na
		III	omotte kudasai	omowanai de kudasai
	FORMAL		oomoi nasaimase	oomoi nasaimasu na
Presumptive	**INFORMAL**	I	omooo	omoumai
		II	omou daroo	omowanai daroo
	FORMAL	I	omoimasyoo	omoimasumai
		II	omou desyoo	omowanai desyoo
Provisional	**INFORMAL**		omoeba	omowanakereba
	FORMAL		omoimaseba	omoimaseñ nara
			omoimasureba	
Gerund	**INFORMAL**	I	omotte	omowanai de
		II		omowanakute
	FORMAL		omoimasite	omoimaseñ de
Past Ind.	**INFORMAL**		omotta	omowanakatta
	FORMAL		omoimasita	omoimaseñ desita
Past Presump.	**INFORMAL**		omottaroo	omowanakattaroo
			omotta daroo	omowanakatta daroo
	FORMAL		omoimasitaroo	omoimasen desitaroo
			omotta desyoo	omowanakatta desyoo
Conditional	**INFORMAL**		omottara	omowanakattara
	FORMAL		omoimasitara	omoimaseñ desitara
Alternative	**INFORMAL**		omottari	omowanakattari
	FORMAL		omoimasitari	omoimaseñ desitari

	INFORMAL AFFIRMATIVE INDICATIVE	
Passive	omowareru	
Potential	omoeru	
Causative	omowaseru	
Causative Pass.	omowaserareru	

Honorific		obosimesu	I oomoi ni naru
			II oomoi nasaru
Humble	I	oomoi suru	
	II	oomoi itasu	

ori.ru
to debark from, to descend from

			AFFIRMATIVE	NEGATIVE
Indicative	INFORMAL		oriru	orinai
	FORMAL		orimasu	orimaseñ
Imperative	INFORMAL	I	oriro	oriru na
		II	orinasai	orinasaru na
		III	orite kudasai	orinai de kudasai
	FORMAL		oori nasaimase	oori nasaimasu na
Presumptive	INFORMAL	I	oriyoo	orimai
		II	oriru daroo	orinai daroo
	FORMAL	I	orimasyoo	orimasumai
		II	oriru desyoo	orinai desyoo
Provisional	INFORMAL		orireba	orinakereba
	FORMAL		orimaseba	orimaseñ nara
			orimasureba	
Gerund	INFORMAL	I	orite	orinai de
		II		orinakute
	FORMAL		orimasite	orimaseñ de
Past Ind.	INFORMAL		orita	orinakatta
	FORMAL		orimasita	orimaseñ desita
Past Presump.	INFORMAL		oritaroo	orinakattaroo
			orita daroo	orinakatta daroo
	FORMAL		orimasitaroo	orimaseñ desitaroo
			orita desyoo	orinakatta desyoo
Conditional	INFORMAL		oritara	orinakattara
	FORMAL		orimasitara	orimaseñ desitara
Alternative	INFORMAL		oritari	orinakattari
	FORMAL		orimasitari	orimaseñ desitari

		INFORMAL AFFIRMATIVE INDICATIVE
Passive		orirareru
Potential		orirareru
Causative		orisaseru
Causative Pass.		orisaserareru

Honorific	I	oori ni naru
	II	oori nasaru
Humble		

osie.ru

to teach, to inform   TRANSITIVE

		AFFIRMATIVE	NEGATIVE
Indicative	**INFORMAL**	osieru	osienai
	FORMAL	osiemasu	osiemaseñ
Imperative	**INFORMAL I**	osiero	osiemai
	II	osienasai	osienasaru na
	III	osiete kudasai	osienai de kudasai
	FORMAL	oosie nasaimase	oosie nasaimasu na
Presumptive	**INFORMAL I**	osieyoo	osiemai
	II	osieru daroo	osienai daroo
	FORMAL I	osiemasyoo	osiemasumai
	II	osieru desyoo	osienai desyoo
Provisional	**INFORMAL**	osiereba	osienakereba
	FORMAL	osiemaseba	osiemaseñ nara
		osiemasureba	
Gerund	**INFORMAL I**	osiete	osienai de
	II		osienakute
	FORMAL	osiemasite	osiemaseñ de
Past Ind.	**INFORMAL**	osieta	osienakatta
	FORMAL	osiemasita	osiemaseñ desita
Past Presump.	**INFORMAL**	osietaroo	osienakattaroo
		osieta daroo	osienakatta daroo
	FORMAL	osiemasitaroo	osiemaseñ desitaroo
		osieta desyoo	osienakatta desyoo
Conditional	**INFORMAL**	osietara	osienakattara
	FORMAL	osiemasitara	osiemaseñ desitara
Alternative	**INFORMAL**	osietari	osienakattari
	FORMAL	osiemasitari	osiemaseñ desitari

	INFORMAL AFFIRMATIVE INDICATIVE
Passive	osierareru
Potential	osierareru
Causative	osiesaseru
Causative Pass.	osiesaserareru

Honorific	**I**	oosie ni naru
	II	oosie nasaru
Humble	**I**	oosie suru
	II	oosie itasu

			AFFIRMATIVE	NEGATIVE
Indicative	**INFORMAL**		ossyaru	ossyaranai
	FORMAL		ossyaimasu	ossyaimaseñ
Imperative	**INFORMAL**	I	ossyai	ossyaru na
		II		
		III	ossyatte kudasai	ossyaranai de kudasai
	FORMAL		ossyaimase	ossyaimasu na
Presumptive	**INFORMAL**	I	ossyaroo	ossyarumai
		II	ossyaru daroo	ossyaranai daroo
	FORMAL	I	ossyaimasyoo	ossyaimasumai
		II	ossyaru desyoo	ossyaranai desyoo
Provisional	**INFORMAL**		ossyareba	ossyaranakereba
	FORMAL		ossyaimaseba	ossyaimaseñ nara
			ossyaimasureba	
Gerund	**INFORMAL**	I	ossyatte	ossyaranai de
		II		ossyaranakute
	FORMAL		ossyaimasite	ossyaimaseñ de
Past Ind.	**INFORMAL**		ossyatta	ossyaranakatta
	FORMAL		ossyaimasita	ossyaimaseñ desita
Past Presump.	**INFORMAL**		ossyattaroo	ossyaranakattaroo
			ossyatta daroo	ossyaranakatta daroo
	FORMAL		ossyaimasitaroo	ossyaimaseñ desitaroo
			ossyatta desyoo	ossyaranakatta desyoo
Conditional	**INFORMAL**		ossyattara	ossyaranakattara
	FORMAL		ossyaimasitara	ossyaimaseñ desitara
Alternative	**INFORMAL**		ossyattari	ossyaranakattari
	FORMAL		ossyaimasitari	ossyaimaseñ desitari

	INFORMAL AFFIRMATIVE INDICATIVE
Passive	ossyarareru
Potential	
Causative	
Causative Pass.	
Honorific	
Humble	

		AFFIRMATIVE	NEGATIVE
Indicative	**INFORMAL**	otiru	otinai
	FORMAL	otimasu	otimaseñ
Imperative	**INFORMAL I**	otiro	otiru na
	II		otinasaru na
	III		otinai de kudasai
	FORMAL		ooti nasaimasu na
Presumptive	**INFORMAL I**	otiyoo	otimai
	II	otiru daroo	otinai daroo
	FORMAL I	otimasyoo	otimasumai
	II	otiru desyoo	otinai desyoo
Provisional	**INFORMAL**	otireba	otinakereba
	FORMAL	otimaseba	otimaseñ nara
		otimasureba	
Gerund	**INFORMAL I**	otite	otinai de
	II		otinakute
	FORMAL	otimasite	otimaseñ de
Past Ind.	**INFORMAL**	otita	otinakatta
	FORMAL	otimasita	otimaseñ desita
Past Presump.	**INFORMAL**	otitaroo	otinakattaroo
		otita daroo	otinakatta daroo
	FORMAL	otimasitaroo	otimaseñ desitaroo
		otita desyoo	otinakatta desyoo
Conditional	**INFORMAL**	otitara	otinakattara
	FORMAL	otimasitara	otimaseñ desitara
Alternative	**INFORMAL**	otitari	otinakattari
	FORMAL	otimasitari	otimaseñ desitari

INFORMAL AFFIRMATIVE INDICATIVE	
Passive	otirareru
Potential	
Causative	otisaseru
Causative Pass.	otisaserareru

Honorific	**I**	ooti ni naru
	II	ooti nasaru
Humble		

to drop, to lose   TRANSITIVE

			AFFIRMATIVE	NEGATIVE
Indicative	INFORMAL		otosu	otosanai
	FORMAL		otosimasu	otosimaseñ
Imperative	INFORMAL	I	otose	otosu na
		II	otosinasai	otosinasaru na
		III	otosite kudasai	otosanai de kudasai
	FORMAL		ootosi nasaimase	ootosi nasaimasu na
Presumptive	INFORMAL	I	otosoo	otosumai
		II	otosu daroo	otosanai daroo
	FORMAL	I	otosimasyoo	otosimasumai
		II	otosu desyoo	otosanai desyoo
Provisional	INFORMAL		otoseba	otosanakereba
	FORMAL		otosimaseba	otosimaseñ nara
			otosimasureba	
Gerund	INFORMAL	I	otosite	otosanai de
		II		otosanakute
	FORMAL		otosimasite	otosimaseñ de
Past Ind.	INFORMAL		otosita	otosanakatta
	FORMAL		otosimasita	otosimaseñ desita
Past Presump.	INFORMAL		otositaroo	otosanakattaroo
			otosita daroo	otosanakatta daroo
	FORMAL		otosimasitaroo	otosimaseñ desitaroo
			otosita desyoo	otosanakatta desyoo
Conditional	INFORMAL		otositara	otosanakattara
	FORMAL		otosimasitara	otosimaseñ desitara
Alternative	INFORMAL		otositari	otosanakattari
	FORMAL		otosimasitari	otosimaseñ desitari

		INFORMAL AFFIRMATIVE INDICATIVE
Passive		otosareru
Potential		otoseru
Causative		otosaseru
Causative Pass.		otosaserareru

Honorific	I	ootosi ni naru
	II	ootosi nasaru
Humble	I	ootosi suru
	II	ootosi itasu

		AFFIRMATIVE	NEGATIVE
Indicative	**INFORMAL**	owaru	owaranai
	FORMAL	owarimasu	owarimaseñ
Imperative	**INFORMAL I**	oware	owaru na
	II		
	III		
	FORMAL		
Presumptive	**INFORMAL I**	owaroo	owarumai
	II	owaru daroo	owaranai daroo
	FORMAL I	owarimasyoo	owarimasumai
	II	owaru desyoo	owaranai desyoo
Provisional	**INFORMAL**	owareba	owaranakereba
	FORMAL	owarimaseba	owarimaseñ nara
		owarimasureba	
Gerund	**INFORMAL I**	owatte	owaranai de
	II		owaranakute
	FORMAL	owarimasite	owarimaseñ de
Past Ind.	**INFORMAL**	owatta	owaranakatta
	FORMAL	owarimasita	owarimaseñ desita
Past Presump.	**INFORMAL**	owattaroo	owaranakattaroo
		owatta daroo	owaranakatta daroo
	FORMAL	owarimasitaroo	owarimaseñ desitaroo
		owatta desyoo	owaranakatta desyoo
Conditional	**INFORMAL**	owattara	owaranakattara
	FORMAL	owarimasitara	owarimaseñ desitara
Alternative	**INFORMAL**	owattari	owaranakattari
	FORMAL	owarimasitari	owarimaseñ desitari

	INFORMAL AFFIRMATIVE INDICATIVE
Passive	
Potential	
Causative	owaraseru
Causative Pass.	owaraserareru
Honorific	
Humble	

		AFFIRMATIVE	NEGATIVE
Indicative	INFORMAL	oyogu	oyoganai
	FORMAL	oyogimasu	oyogimaseñ
Imperative	INFORMAL I	oyoge	oyogu na
	II	oyoginasai	oyoginasaru na
	III	oyoide kudasai	oyoganai de kudasai
	FORMAL	ooyogi nasaimase	ooyogi nasaimasu na
Presumptive	INFORMAL I	oyogoo	oyogumai
	II	oyogu daroo	oyoganai daroo
	FORMAL I	oyogimasyoo	oyogimasumai
	II	oyogu desyoo	oyoganai desyoo
Provisional	INFORMAL	oyogeba	oyoganakereba
	FORMAL	oyogimaseba	oyogimaseñ nara
		oyogimasureba	
Gerund	INFORMAL I	oyoide	oyoganai de
	II		oyoganakute
	FORMAL	oyogimasite	oyogimaseñ de
Past Ind.	INFORMAL	oyoida	oyoganakatta
	FORMAL	oyogimasita	oyogimaseñ desita
Past Presump.	INFORMAL	oyoidaroo	oyoganakattaroo
		oyoida daroo	oyoganakatta daroo
	FORMAL	oyogimasitaroo	oyogimaseñ desitaroo
		oyoida desyoo	oyoganakatta desyoo
Conditional	INFORMAL	oyoidara	oyoganakattara
	FORMAL	oyogimasitara	oyogimaseñ desitara
Alternative	INFORMAL	oyoidari	oyoganakattari
	FORMAL	oyogimasitari	oyogimaseñ desitari

	INFORMAL AFFIRMATIVE INDICATIVE
Passive	oyogareru
Potential	oyogeru
Causative	oyogaseru
Causative Pass.	oyogaserareru

Honorific	I	ooyogi ni naru
	II	ooyogi nasaru

Humble

		AFFIRMATIVE	NEGATIVE
Indicative	**INFORMAL**	sagasu	sagasanai
	FORMAL	sagasimasu	sagasimaseñ
Imperative	**INFORMAL** I	sagase	sagasu na
	II	sagasinasai	sagasinasaru na
	III	sagasite kudasai	sagasanai de kudasai
	FORMAL	osagasi nasaimase	osagasi nasaimasu na
Presumptive	**INFORMAL** I	sagasoo	sagasumai
	II	sagasu daroo	sagasanai daroo
	FORMAL I	sagasimasyoo	sagasimasumai
	II	sagasu desyoo	sagasanai desyoo
Provisional	**INFORMAL**	sagaseba	sagasanakereba
	FORMAL	sagasimaseba	sagasimaseñ nara
		sagasimasureba	
Gerund	**INFORMAL** I	sagasite	sagasanai de
	II		sagasanakute
	FORMAL	sagasimasite	sagasimaseñ de
Past Ind.	**INFORMAL**	sagasita	sagasanakatta
	FORMAL	sagasimasita	sagasimaseñ desita
Past Presump.	**INFORMAL**	sagasitaroo	sagasanakattaroo
		sagasita daroo	sagasanakatta daroo
	FORMAL	sagasimasitaroo	sagasimaseñ desitaroo
		sagasita desyoo	sagasanakatta desyoo
Conditional	**INFORMAL**	sagasitara	sagasanakattara
	FORMAL	sagasimasitara	sagasimaseñ desitara
Alternative	**INFORMAL**	sagasitari	sagasanakattari
	FORMAL	sagasimasitari	sagasimaseñ desitari

	INFORMAL AFFIRMATIVE INDICATIVE
Passive	sagasareru
Potential	sagaseru
Causative	sagasaseru
Causative Pass.	sagasaserareru

Honorific	I	osagasi ni naru
	II	osagasi nasaru
Humble	I	osagasi suru
	II	osagasi itasu

sak.u
to bloom

			AFFIRMATIVE	NEGATIVE
Indicative	INFORMAL		saku	sakanai
	FORMAL		sakimasu	sakimaseñ
Imperative	INFORMAL	I	sake	sakuna
		II		
		III		
	FORMAL			
Presumptive	INFORMAL	I	sakoo	sakumai
		II	saku daroo	sakanai daroo
	FORMAL	I	sakimasyoo	sakimasumai
		II	saku desyoo	sakanai desyoo
Provisional	INFORMAL		sakeba	sakanakereba
	FORMAL		sakimaseba sakimasureba	sakimaseñ nara
Gerund	INFORMAL	I	saite	sakanai de
		II		sakanakute
	FORMAL		sakimasite	sakimaseñ de
Past Ind.	INFORMAL		saita	sakanakatta
	FORMAL		sakimasita	sakimaseñ desita
Past Presump.	INFORMAL		saitaroo saita daroo	sakanakattaroo sakanakatta daroo
	FORMAL		sakimasitaroo saita desyoo	sakimaseñ desitaroo sakanakatta desyoo
Conditional	INFORMAL		saitara	sakanakattara
	FORMAL		sakimasitara	sakimaseñ desitara
Alternative	INFORMAL		saitari	sakanakattari
	FORMAL		sakimasitari	sakimaseñ desitari

INFORMAL AFFIRMATIVE INDICATIVE

Passive	
Potential	sakeru
Causative	sakaseru
Causative Pass.	sakaserareru

Honorific

Humble

			AFFIRMATIVE	NEGATIVE
Indicative	INFORMAL		sawagu	sawaganai
	FORMAL		sawagimasu	sawagimaseñ
Imperative	INFORMAL	I	sawage	sawagu na
		II	sawaginasai	sawaginasaru na
		III	sawaide kudasai	sawaganai de kudasai
	FORMAL		osawagi nasaimase	osawagi nasaimasu na
Presumptive	INFORMAL	I	sawagoo	sawagumai
		II	sawagu daroo	sawaganai daroo
	FORMAL	I	sawagimasyoo	sawagimasumai
		II	sawagu desyoo	sawaganai desyoo
Provisional	INFORMAL		sawageba	sawaganakereba
	FORMAL		sawagimaseba	sawagimaseñ nara
			sawagimasureba	
Gerund	INFORMAL	I	sawaide	sawaganai de
		II		sawaganakute
	FORMAL		sawagimasite	sawagimaseñ de
Past Ind.	INFORMAL		sawaida	sawaganakatta
	FORMAL		sawagimasita	sawagimaseñ desita
Past Presump.	INFORMAL		sawaidaroo	sawaganakattaroo
			sawaida daroo	sawaganakatta daroo
	FORMAL		sawagimasitaroo	sawagimaseñ desitaroo
			sawaida desyoo	sawaganakatta desyoo
Conditional	INFORMAL		sawaidara	sawaganakattara
	FORMAL		sawagimasitara	sawagimaseñ desitara
Alternative	INFORMAL		sawaidari	sawaganakattari
	FORMAL		sawagimasitari	sawagimaseñ desitari

		INFORMAL AFFIRMATIVE INDICATIVE
Passive		sawagareru
Potential		sawageru
Causative		sawagaseru
Causative Pass.		sawagaserareru

Honorific	I	osawagi ni naru
	II	osawagi nasaru
Humble		

135

		AFFIRMATIVE	NEGATIVE
Indicative	INFORMAL	sibaru	sibaranai
	FORMAL	sibarimasu	sibarimaseñ
Imperative	INFORMAL I	sibare	sibaru na
	II	sibarinasai	sibarinasaru na
	III	sibatte kudasai	sibaranai de kudasai
	FORMAL	osibari nasaimase	osibari nasaimasu na
Presumptive	INFORMAL I	sibaroo	sibarumai
	II	sibaru daroo	sibaranai daroo
	FORMAL I	sibarimasyoo	sibarimasumai
	II	sibaru desyoo	sibaranai desyoo
Provisional	INFORMAL	sibareba	sibaranakereba
	FORMAL	sibarimaseba	sibarimaseñ nara
		sibarimasureba	
Gerund	INFORMAL I	sibatte	sibaranai de
	II		sibaranakute
	FORMAL	sibarimasite	sibarimaseñ de
Past Ind.	INFORMAL	sibatta	sibaranakatta
	FORMAL	sibarimasita	sibarimaseñ desita
Past Presump.	INFORMAL	sibattaroo	sibaranakattaroo
		sibatta daroo	sibaranakatta daroo
	FORMAL	sibarimasitaroo	sibarimaseñ desitaroo
		sibatta desyoo	sibaranakatta desyoo
Conditional	INFORMAL	sibattara	sibaranakattara
	FORMAL	sibarimasitara	sibarimaseñ desitara
Alternative	INFORMAL	sibattari	sibaranakattari
	FORMAL	sibarimasitari	sibarimaseñ desitari

INFORMAL AFFIRMATIVE INDICATIVE

Passive	sibarareru
Potential	sibareru
Causative	sibaraseru
Causative Pass.	sibaraserareru

Honorific	I	osibari ni naru
	II	osibari nasaru
Humble	I	osibari suru
	II	osibari itasu

			AFFIRMATIVE	**NEGATIVE**
Indicative	**INFORMAL**		sikaru	sikaranai
	FORMAL		sikarimasu	sikarimaseñ
Imperative	**INFORMAL**	I	sikare	sikaru na
		II	sikarinasai	sikarinasaru na
		III	sikatte kudasai	sikaranai de kudasai
	FORMAL		osikari nasaimase	osikari nasaimasu na
Presumptive	**INFORMAL**	I	sikaroo	sikarumai
		II	sikaru daroo	sikaranai daroo
	FORMAL	I	sikarimasyoo	sikarimasumai
		II	sikaru desyoo	sikaranai desyoo
Provisional	**INFORMAL**		sikareba	sikaranakereba
	FORMAL		sikarimaseba	sikarimaseñ nara
			sikarimasureba	
Gerund	**INFORMAL**	I	sikatte	sikaranai de
		II		sikaranakute
	FORMAL		sikarimasite	sikarimaseñ de
Past Ind.	**INFORMAL**		sikatta	sikaranakatta
	FORMAL		sikarimasita	sikarimaseñ desita
Past Presump.	**INFORMAL**		sikattaroo	sikaranakattaroo
			sikatta daroo	sikaranakatta daroo
	FORMAL		sikarimasitaroo	sikarimaseñ desitaroo
			sikatta desyoo	sikaranakatta desyoo
Conditional	**INFORMAL**		sikattara	sikaranakattara
	FORMAL		sikarimasitara	sikarimaseñ desitara
Alternative	**INFORMAL**		sikattari	sikaranakattari
	FORMAL		sikarimasitari	sikarimaseñ desitari

	INFORMAL AFFIRMATIVE INDICATIVE
Passive	sikarareru
Potential	sikareru
Causative	sikaraseru
Causative Pass.	sikaraserareru

Honorific	I	osikari ni naru
	II	osikari nasaru
Humble	I	osikari suru
	II	osikari itasu

to spread out flat (as a quilt)   TRANSITIVE

		AFFIRMATIVE	NEGATIVE
Indicative	INFORMAL	siku	sikanai
	FORMAL	sikimasu	sikimaseñ
Imperative	INFORMAL I	sike	siku na
	II	sikinasai	sikinasaru na
	III	siite kudasai	sikanai de kudasai
	FORMAL	osiki nasaimase	osiki nasaimasu na
Presumptive	INFORMAL I	sikoo	sikumai
	II	siku daroo	sikanai daroo
	FORMAL I	sikimasyoo	sikimasumai
	II	siku desyoo	sikanai desyoo
Provisional	INFORMAL	sikeba	sikanakereba
	FORMAL	sikimaseba	sikimaseñ nara
		simimasureba	
Gerund	INFORMAL I	siite	sikanai de
	II		sikanakute
	FORMAL	sikimasite	sikimaseñ de
Past Ind.	INFORMAL	siita	sikanakatta
	FORMAL	sikimasita	sikimaseñ desita
Past Presump.	INFORMAL	siitaroo	sikanakattaroo
		siita daroo	sikanakatta daroo
	FORMAL	sikimasitaroo	sikimaseñ desitaroo
		siita desyoo	sikanakatta desyoo
Conditional	INFORMAL	siitara	sikanakattara
	FORMAL	sikimasitara	sikimaseñ desitara
Alternative	INFORMAL	siitari	sikanakattari
	FORMAL	sikimasitari	sikimaseñ desitari

	INFORMAL AFFIRMATIVE INDICATIVE
Passive	sikareru
Potential	sikeru
Causative	sikaseru
Causative Pass.	sikaserareru

Honorific	I	osiki ni naru
	II	osiki nasaru
Humble	I	osiki suru
	II	osiki itasu

simari

simar.u
to close (by itself)

		AFFIRMATIVE	NEGATIVE
Indicative	INFORMAL	simaru	simaranai
	FORMAL	simarimasu	simarimaseñ
Imperative	INFORMAL I	simare	simaru na
	II		
	III		
	FORMAL		
Presumptive	INFORMAL I	simaroo	simarumai
	II	simaru daroo	simaranai daroo
	FORMAL I	simarimasyoo	simarimasumai
	II	simaru desyoo	simaranai desyoo
Provisional	INFORMAL	simareba	simaranakereba
	FORMAL	simarimaseba	simarimaseñ nara
		simarimasureba	
Gerund	INFORMAL I	simatte	simaranai de
	II		simaranakute
	FORMAL	simarimasite	simarimaseñ de
Past Ind.	INFORMAL	simatta	simaranakatta
	FORMAL	simarimasita	simarimaseñ desita
Past Presump.	INFORMAL	simattaroo	simaranakattaroo
		simatta daroo	simaranakatta daroo
	FORMAL	simarimasitaroo	simarimaseñ desitaroo
		simatta desyoo	simaranakatta desyoo
Conditional	INFORMAL	simattara	simaranakattara
	FORMAL	simarimasitara	simarimaseñ desitara
Alternative	INFORMAL	simattari	simaranakattari
	FORMAL	simarimasitari	simarimaseñ desitari

INFORMAL AFFIRMATIVE INDICATIVE

Passive	
Potential	
Causative	
Causative Pass.	

Honorific	
Humble	

to put away, to pack away   TRANSITIVE

		AFFIRMATIVE	NEGATIVE
Indicative	INFORMAL	simau	simawanai
	FORMAL	simaimasu	simaimaseñ
Imperative	INFORMAL I	simae	simau na
	II	simainasai	simainasaru na
	III	simatte kudasai	simawanai de kudasai
	FORMAL	osimai nasaimase	osimai nasaimasu na
Presumptive	INFORMAL I	simaoo	simaumai
	II	simau daroo	simawanai daroo
	FORMAL I	simaimasyoo	simaimasumai
	II	simau desyoo	simawanai desyoo
Provisional	INFORMAL	simaeba	simawanakereba
	FORMAL	simaimaseba	simaimaseñ nara
		simaimasureba	
Gerund	INFORMAL I	simatte	simawanai de
	II		simawanakute
	FORMAL	simaimasite	simaimaseñ de
Past Ind.	INFORMAL	simatta	simawanakatta
	FORMAL	simaimasita	simaimaseñ desita
Past Presump.	INFORMAL	simattaroo	simawanakattaroo
		simatta daroo	simawanakatta daroo
	FORMAL	simaimasitaroo	simaimaseñ desitaroo
		simatta desyoo	simawanakatta desyoo
Conditional	INFORMAL	simattara	simawanakattara
	FORMAL	simaimasitara	simaimaseñ desitara
Alternative	INFORMAL	simattari	simawanakattari
	FORMAL	simaimasitari	simaimaseñ desitari

		INFORMAL AFFIRMATIVE INDICATIVE
Passive		simawareru
Potential		simaeru
Causative		simawaseru
Causative Pass.		simawaserareru

Honorific	I	osimai ni naru
	II	osimai nasaru
Humble	I	osimai suru
	II	osimai itasu

sime

sime.ru

TRANSITIVE *to shut*

		AFFIRMATIVE	NEGATIVE
Indicative	**INFORMAL**	simeru	simenai
	FORMAL	simemasu	simemaseñ
Imperative	**INFORMAL** I	simero	simeru na
	II	simenasai	simenasaru na
	III	simete kudasai	simenai de kudasai
	FORMAL	osime nasaimase	osime nasaimasu na
Presumptive	**INFORMAL** I	simeyoo	simemai
	II	simeru daroo	simenai daroo
	FORMAL I	simemasyoo	simemasumai
	II	simeru desyoo	simenai desyoo
Provisional	**INFORMAL**	simereba	simenakereba
	FORMAL	simemaseba	simemaseñ nara
		simemasureba	
Gerund	**INFORMAL** I	simete	simenai de
	II		simenakute
	FORMAL	simemasite	simemaseñ de
Past Ind.	**INFORMAL**	simeta	simenakatta
	FORMAL	simemasita	simemaseñ desita
Past Presump.	**INFORMAL**	simetaroo	simenakattaroo
		simeta daroo	simenakatta daroo
	FORMAL	simemasitaroo	simemaseñ desitaroo
		simeta desyoo	simenakatta desyoo
Conditional	**INFORMAL**	simetara	simenakattara
	FORMAL	simemasitara	simemaseñ desitara
Alternative	**INFORMAL**	simetari	simenakattari
	FORMAL	simemasitari	simemaseñ desitari

INFORMAL AFFIRMATIVE INDICATIVE

Passive		simerareru
Potential		simerareru
Causative		simesaseru
Causative Pass.		simesaserareru

Honorific	I	osime ni naru
	II	osime nasaru
Humble	I	osime suru
	II	osime itasu

141

			AFFIRMATIVE	**NEGATIVE**
Indicative	**INFORMAL**		sinu	sinanai
	FORMAL		sinimasu	sinimaseñ
Imperative	**INFORMAL**	**I**	sine	sinu na
		II	sininasai	sininasaru na
		III	siñde kudasai	sinanai de kudasai
	FORMAL			osini nasaimasu na
Presumptive	**INFORMAL**	**I**	sinoo	sinumai
		II	sinu daroo	sinanai daroo
	FORMAL	**I**	sinimasyoo	sinimasumai
		II	sinu desyoo	sinanai desyoo
Provisional	**INFORMAL**		sineba	sinanakereba
	FORMAL		sinimaseba	sinimaseñ nara
			sinimasureba	
Gerund	**INFORMAL**	**I**	siñde	sinanai de
		II		sinanakute
	FORMAL		sinimasite	sinimaseñ de
Past Ind.	**INFORMAL**		siñda	sinanakatta
	FORMAL		sinimasita	sinimaseñ desita
Past Presump.	**INFORMAL**		siñdaroo	sinanakattaroo
			siñda daroo	sinanakatta daroo
	FORMAL		sinimasitaroo	sinimaseñ desitaroo
			siñda desyoo	sinanakatta desyoo
Conditional	**INFORMAL**		siñdara	sinanakattara
	FORMAL		sinimasitara	sinimaseñ desitara
Alternative	**INFORMAL**		siñdari	sinanakattari
	FORMAL		sinimasitari	sinimaseñ desitari

INFORMAL AFFIRMATIVE INDICATIVE

Passive	sinareru
Potential	sineru
Causative	sinaseru
Causative Pass.	sinaserareru

Honorific	**I**	onakunari ni naru
	II	onakunari nasaru
Humble		

		AFFIRMATIVE	NEGATIVE
Indicative	**INFORMAL**	siraberu	sirabenai
	FORMAL	sirabemasu	sirabemaseñ
Imperative	**INFORMAL I**	sirabero	siraberu na
	II	sirabenasai	sirabenasaru na
	III	sirabete kudasai	sirabenai de kudasai
	FORMAL	osirabe nasaimase	osirabe nasaimasu na
Presumptive	**INFORMAL I**	sirabeyoo	sirabemai
	II	siraberu daroo	sirabenai daroo
	FORMAL I	sirabemasyoo	sirabemasumai
	II	siraberu desyoo	sirabenai desyoo
Provisional	**INFORMAL**	sirabereba	sirabenakereba
	FORMAL	sirabemaseba	sirabemaseñ nara
		sirabemasureba	
Gerund	**INFORMAL I**	sirabete	sirabenai de
	II		sirabenakute
	FORMAL	sirabemasite	sirabemaseñ de
Past Ind.	**INFORMAL**	sirabeta	sirabenakatta
	FORMAL	sirabemasita	sirabemaseñ desita
Past Presump.	**INFORMAL**	sirabetaroo	sirabenakattaroo
		sirabeta daroo	sirabenakatta daroo
	FORMAL	sirabemasitaroo	sirabemaseñ desitaroo
		sirabeta desyoo	sirabenakatta desyoo
Conditional	**INFORMAL**	sirabetara	sirabenakattara
	FORMAL	sirabemasitara	sirabemaseñ desitara
Alternative	**INFORMAL**	sirabetari	sirabenakattari
	FORMAL	sirabemasitari	sirabemaseñ desitari

	INFORMAL AFFIRMATIVE INDICATIVE
Passive	siraberareru
Potential	siraberareru
Causative	sirabesaseru
Causative Pass.	sirabesaserareru

Honorific	**I**	osirabe ni naru
	II	osirabe nasaru
Humble	**I**	osirabe suru
	II	osirabe itasu

		AFFIRMATIVE	NEGATIVE
Indicative	INFORMAL	siru	siranai
	FORMAL	sirimasu	sirimaseñ
Imperative	INFORMAL I	sire	
	II		
	III		
	FORMAL		
Presumptive	INFORMAL I	siroo	sirumai
	II	siru daroo	siranai daroo
	FORMAL I	sirimasyoo	sirimasumai
	II	siru desyoo	siranai desyoo
Provisional	INFORMAL	sireba	siranakereba
	FORMAL	sirimaseba	sirimaseñ nara
		sirimasureba	
Gerund	INFORMAL I	sitte	siranai de
	II		siranakute
	FORMAL	sirimasite	sirimaseñ de
Past Ind.	INFORMAL	sitta	siranakatta
	FORMAL	sirimasita	sirimaseñ desita
Past Presump.	INFORMAL	sittaroo	siranakattaroo
		sitta daroo	siranakatta daroo
	FORMAL	sirimasitaroo	sirimaseñ desitaroo
		sitta desyoo	siranakatta desyoo
Conditional	INFORMAL	sittara	siranakattara
	FORMAL	sirimasitara	sirimaseñ desitara
Alternative	INFORMAL	sittari	siranakattari
	FORMAL	sirimasitari	sirimaseñ desitari

	INFORMAL AFFIRMATIVE INDICATIVE
Passive	sirareru
Potential	sireru
Causative	siraseru
Causative Pass.	siraserareru

Honorific	gozoñzi de irassyaru
Humble	zoñziru

144

		AFFIRMATIVE	NEGATIVE
Indicative	INFORMAL	sizumu	sizumanai
	FORMAL	sizumimasu	sizumimaseñ
Imperative	INFORMAL I	sizume	sizumu na
	II	sizuminasai	sizuminasaru na
	III	sizuñde kudasai	sizumanai de kudasai
	FORMAL	osizumi nasaimase	osizumi nasaimasu na
Presumptive	INFORMAL I	sizumoo	sizumumai
	II	sizumu daroo	sizumanai daroo
	FORMAL I	sizumimasyoo	sizumimasumai
	II	sizumu daroo	sizumanai daroo
Provisional	INFORMAL	sizumeba	sizumanakereba
	FORMAL	sizumimaseba	sizumimaseñ nara
		sizumimasureba	
Gerund	INFORMAL I	sizuñde	sizumanai de
	II		sizumanakute
	FORMAL	sizumimasite	sizumimaseñ de
Past Ind.	INFORMAL	sizuñda	sizumanakatta
	FORMAL	sizumimasita	sizumimaseñ desita
Past Presump.	INFORMAL	sizuñdaroo	sizumanakattaroo
		sizuñda daroo	sizumanakatta daroo
	FORMAL	sizumimasitaroo	sizumimaseñ desitaroo
		sizuñda desyoo	sizumanakatta desyoo
Conditional	INFORMAL	sizuñdara	sizumanakattara
	FORMAL	sizumimasitara	sizumimaseñ desitara
Alternative	INFORMAL	sizuñdari	sizumanakattari
	FORMAL	sizumimasitari	sizumimaseñ desitari

INFORMAL AFFIRMATIVE INDICATIVE

Passive	sizumareru
Potential	sizumeru
Causative	sizumaseru
Causative Pass.	sizumaserareru

Honorific	I	osizumi ni naru
	II	osizumi nasaru
Humble		

to raise a child   TRANSITIVE

		AFFIRMATIVE	NEGATIVE
Indicative **INFORMAL**		sodateru	sodatenai
FORMAL		sodatemasu	sodatemaseñ
Imperative **INFORMAL** I		sodatero	sodatemai
II		sodatenasai	sodatenasaru na
III		sodatete kudasai	sodatenai de kudasai
FORMAL		osodate nasaimase	osodate nasaimasu na
Presumptive **INFORMAL** I		sodateyoo	sodatemai
II		sodateru daroo	sodatenai daroo
FORMAL I		sodatemasyoo	sodatemasumai
II		sodateru desyoo	sodatenai desyoo
Provisional **INFORMAL**		sodatereba	sodatenakereba
FORMAL		sodatemaseba	sodatemaseñ nara
		sodatemasureba	
Gerund **INFORMAL** I		sodatete	sodatenai de
II			sodatenakute
FORMAL		sodatemasite	sodatemaseñ de
Past Ind. **INFORMAL**		sodateta	sodatenakatta
FORMAL		sodatemasita	sodatemaseñ desita
Past Presump. **INFORMAL**		sodatetaroo	sodatenakattaroo
		sodateta daroo	sodatenakatta daroo
FORMAL		sodatemasitaroo	sodatemaseñ desitaroo
		sodateta desyoo	sodatenakatta desyoo
Conditional **INFORMAL**		sodatetara	sodatenakattara
FORMAL		sodatemasitara	sodatemaseñ desitara
Alternative **INFORMAL**		sodatetari	sodatenakattari
FORMAL		sodatemasitari	sodatemaseñ desitari

		INFORMAL AFFIRMATIVE INDICATIVE
Passive		sodaterareru
Potential		sodaterareru
Causative		sodatesaseru
Causative Pass.		sodatesaserareru

Honorific	I	osodate ni naru
	II	osodate nasaru
Humble	I	osodate suru
	II	osodate itasu

			AFFIRMATIVE	NEGATIVE
Indicative	**INFORMAL**		sugiru	suginai
	FORMAL		sugimasu	sugimaseñ
Imperative	**INFORMAL**	I	sugiro	sugiru na
		II	suginasai	suginasaru na
		III	sugite kudasai	suginai de kudasai
	FORMAL		osugi nasaimase	osugi nasaimasu na
Presumptive	**INFORMAL**	I	sugiyoo	sugimai
		II	sugiru daroo	suginai daroo
	FORMAL	I	sugimasyoo	sugimasumai
		II	sugiru desyoo	suginai desyoo
Provisional	**INFORMAL**		sugireba	suginakereba
	FORMAL		sugimaseba	sugimaseñ nara
			sugimasureba	
Gerund	**INFORMAL**	I	sugite	suginai de
		II		suginakute
	FORMAL		sugimasite	sugimaseñ de
Past Ind.	**INFORMAL**		sugita	suginakatta
	FORMAL		sugimasita	sugimaseñ desita
Past Presump.	**INFORMAL**		sugitaroo	suginakattaroo
			sugita daroo	suginakatta daroo
	FORMAL		sugimasitaroo	sugimaseñ desitaroo
			sugita desyoo	suginakatta desyoo
Conditional	**INFORMAL**		sugitara	suginakattara
	FORMAL		sugimasitara	sugimaseñ desitara
Alternative	**INFORMAL**		sugitari	suginakattari
	FORMAL		sugimasitari	sugimaseñ desitari

INFORMAL AFFIRMATIVE INDICATIVE

Passive		
Potential		
Causative		
Causative Pass.		

Honorific	I	osugi ni naru
	II	osugi nasaru
Humble		

		AFFIRMATIVE	NEGATIVE
Indicative	**INFORMAL**	suku	sukanai
	FORMAL	sukimasu	sukimaseñ
Imperative	**INFORMAL I**		
	II		
	III		
	FORMAL		
Presumptive	**INFORMAL I**	sukoo	sukumai
	II	suku daroo	sukanai daroo
	FORMAL I	sukimasyoo	sukimasumai
	II	suku desyoo	sukanai desyoo
Provisional	**INFORMAL**	sukeba	sukanakereba
	FORMAL	sukimaseba	sukimaseñ nara
		sukimasureba	
Gerund	**INFORMAL I**	suite	sukanai de
	II		sukanakute
	FORMAL	sukimasite	sukimaseñ de
Past Ind.	**INFORMAL**	suita	sukanakatta
	FORMAL	sukimasita	sukimaseñ desita
Past Presump.	**INFORMAL**	suitaroo	sukanakattaroo
		suita daroo	sukanakatta daroo
	FORMAL	sukimasitaroo	sukimaseñ desitaroo
		suita desyoo	sukanakatta desyoo
Conditional	**INFORMAL**	suitara	sukanakattara
	FORMAL	sukimasitara	sukimaseñ desitara
Alternative	**INFORMAL**	suitari	sukanakattari
	FORMAL	sukimasitari	sukimaseñ desitari

INFORMAL AFFIRMATIVE INDICATIVE

Passive	
Potential	
Causative	sukaseru
Causative Pass.	sukaserareru
Honorific	
Humble	

		AFFIRMATIVE	NEGATIVE
Indicative	**INFORMAL**	sumaseru	sumasenai
	FORMAL	sumasemasu	sumasemaseñ
Imperative	**INFORMAL** I	sumasero	sumaseru na
	II	sumasenasai	sumasenasaru na
	III	sumasete kudasai	sumasenai de kudasai
	FORMAL	osumase nasaimase	osumase nasaimasu na
Presumptive	**INFORMAL** I	sumaseyoo	sumasemai
	II	sumaseru daroo	sumasenai daroo
	FORMAL I	sumasemasyoo	sumasemasumai
	II	sumaseru desyoo	sumasenai desyoo
Provisional	**INFORMAL**	sumasereba	sumasenakereba
	FORMAL	sumasemaseba	sumasemaseñ nara
		sumasemasureba	
Gerund	**INFORMAL** I	sumasete	sumasenai de
	II		sumasenakute
	FORMAL	sumasemasite	sumasemaseñ de
Past Ind.	**INFORMAL**	sumaseta	sumasenakatta
	FORMAL	sumasemasita	sumasemaseñ desita
Past Presump.	**INFORMAL**	sumasetaroo	sumasenakattaroo
		sumaseta daroo	sumasenakatta daroo
	FORMAL	sumasemasitaroo	sumasemaseñ desitaroo
		sumaseta desyoo	sumasenakatta desyoo
Conditional	**INFORMAL**	sumasetara	sumasenakattara
	FORMAL	sumasemasitara	sumasemaseñ desitara
Alternative	**INFORMAL**	sumasetari	sumasenakattari
	FORMAL	sumasemasitari	sumasemaseñ desitari

INFORMAL AFFIRMATIVE INDICATIVE

Passive	sumaserareru
Potential	sumaserareru
Causative	
Causative Pass.	

Honorific	I	osumase ni naru
	II	osumase nasaru
Humble		

This is the causative form of *sum.u* 'to end' and is given to illustrate the full range of inflection found in this type of derived verb.

		AFFIRMATIVE	NEGATIVE
Indicative	**INFORMAL**	sumu	sumanai
	FORMAL	sumimasu	sumimaseñ
Imperative	**INFORMAL I**	sume	sumu na
	II	suminasai	suminasaru na
	III	suñde kudasai	sumanai de kudasai
	FORMAL	osumi nasaimase	osumi nasaimasu na
Presumptive	**INFORMAL I**	sumoo	sumumai
	II	sumu daroo	sumanai daroo
	FORMAL I	sumimasyoo	sumimasumai
	II	sumu desyoo	sumanai desyoo
Provisional	**INFORMAL**	sumeba	sumanakereba
	FORMAL	sumimaseba	sumimaseñ nara
		sumimasureba	
Gerund	**INFORMAL I**	suñde	sumanai de
	II		sumanakute
	FORMAL	sumimasite	sumimaseñ de
Past Ind.	**INFORMAL**	suñda	sumanakatta
	FORMAL	sumimasita	sumimaseñ desita
Past Presump.	**INFORMAL**	suñdaroo	sumanakattaroo
		suñda daroo	sumanakatta daroo
	FORMAL	sumimasitaroo	sumimaseñ desitaroo
		suñda desyoo	sumanakatta desyoo
Conditional	**INFORMAL**	suñdara	sumanakattara
	FORMAL	sumimasitara	sumimaseñ desitara
Alternative	**INFORMAL**	suñdari	sumanakattari
	FORMAL	sumimasitari	sumimaseñ desitari

INFORMAL AFFIRMATIVE INDICATIVE

Passive	sumareru
Potential	sumeru
Causative	sumaseru
Causative Pass.	sumaserareru

Honorific	**I**	osumi ni naru
	II	osumi nasaru
Humble		

			AFFIRMATIVE	NEGATIVE
Indicative	**INFORMAL**		suru	sinai
	FORMAL		simasu	simaseñ
Imperative	**INFORMAL**	**I**	siro	suru na
		II	sinasai	sinasaru na
		III	site kudasai	sinai de kudasai
	FORMAL		nasaimase	nasaimasu na
Presumptive	**INFORMAL**	**I**	siyoo	surumai
		II	suru daroo	sinai daroo
	FORMAL	**I**	simasyoo	simasumai
		II	suru desyoo	sinai desyoo
Provisional	**INFORMAL**		sureba	sinakereba
	FORMAL		simaseba	simaseñ nara
			simasureba	
Gerund	**INFORMAL**	**I**	site	sinai de
		II		sinakute
	FORMAL		simasite	simaseñ de
Past Ind.	**INFORMAL**		sita	sinakatta
	FORMAL		simasita	simaseñ desita
Past Presump.	**INFORMAL**		sitaroo	sinakattaroo
			sita daroo	sinakatta daroo
	FORMAL		simasitaroo	simaseñ desitaroo
			sita desyoo	sinakatta desyoo
Conditional	**INFORMAL**		sitara	sinakattara
	FORMAL		simasitara	simaseñ desitara
Alternative	**INFORMAL**		sitari	sinakattari
	FORMAL		simasitari	simaseñ desitari

	INFORMAL AFFIRMATIVE INDICATIVE
Passive	sareru
Potential	dekiru
Causative	saseru
Causative Pass.	saserareru
Honorific	nasaru
Humble	itasu

*This is used to derive verbs from many Sino-Japanese nouns. For example, *kekkoñ* ('marriage') plus *su.ru* becomes *kekkoñ-suxu* 'to get married.'

to abandon, to throw away   TRANSITIVE

			AFFIRMATIVE	NEGATIVE
Indicative	**INFORMAL**		suteru	sutenai
	FORMAL		sutemasu	sutemaseñ
Imperative	**INFORMAL**	I	sutero	suteru na
		II	sutenasai	sutenasaru na
		III	sutete kudasai	sutenai de kudasai
	FORMAL		osute nasaimase	osute nasaimasu na
Presumptive	**INFORMAL**	I	suteyoo	sutemai
		II	suteru daroo	sutenai daroo
	FORMAL	I	sutemasyoo	sutemasumai
		II	suteru desyoo	sutenai desyoo
Provisional	**INFORMAL**		sutereba	sutenakereba
	FORMAL		sutemaseba	sutemaseñ nara
			sutemasureba	
Gerund	**INFORMAL**	I	sutete	sutenai de
		II		sutenakute
	FORMAL		sutemasite	sutemaseñ de
Past Ind.	**INFORMAL**		suteta	sutenakatta
	FORMAL		sutemasita	sutemaseñ desita
Past Presump.	**INFORMAL**		sutetaroo	sutenakattaroo
			suteta daroo	sutenakatta daroo
	FORMAL		sutemasitaroo	sutemaseñ desitaroo
			suteta desyoo	sutenakatta desyoo
Conditional	**INFORMAL**		sutetara	sutenakattara
	FORMAL		sutemasitara	sutemaseñ desitara
Alternative	**INFORMAL**		sutetari	sutenakattari
	FORMAL		sutemasitari	sutemaseñ desitari

INFORMAL AFFIRMATIVE INDICATIVE

Passive	suterareru
Potential	suterareru
Causative	sutesaseru
Causative Pass.	sutesaserareru

Honorific	I	osute ni naru
	II	osute nasaru
Humble	I	osute suru
	II	osute itasu

			AFFIRMATIVE	NEGATIVE
Indicative	**INFORMAL**		suwaru	suwaranai
	FORMAL		suwarimasu	suwarimaseñ
Imperative	**INFORMAL**	I	suware	suwaru na
		II	suwarinasai	suwarinasaru na
		III	suwatte kudasai	suwaranai de kudasai
	FORMAL		osuwari nasaimase	osuwari nasaimasu na
Presumptive	**INFORMAL**	I	suwaroo	suwarumai
		II	suwaru daroo	suwaranai daroo
	FORMAL	I	suwarimasyoo	suwarimasumai
		II	suwaru desyoo	suwaranai desyoo
Provisional	**INFORMAL**		suwareba	suwaranakereba
	FORMAL		suwarimaseba	suwarimaseñ nara
			suwarimasureba	
Gerund	**INFORMAL**	I	suwatte	suwaranai de
		II		suwaranakute
	FORMAL		suwarimasite	suwarimaseñ de
Past Ind.	**INFORMAL**		suwatta	suwaranakatta
	FORMAL		suwarimasita	suwarimaseñ desita
Past Presump.	**INFORMAL**		suwattaroo	suwaranakattaroo
			suwatta daroo	suwaranakatta daroo
	FORMAL		suwarimasitaroo	suwarimaseñ desitaroo
			suwatta desyoo	suwaranakatta desyoo
Conditional	**INFORMAL**		suwattara	suwaranakattara
	FORMAL		suwarimasitara	suwarimaseñ desitara
Alternative	**INFORMAL**		suwattari	suwaranakattari
	FORMAL		suwarimasitari	suwarimaseñ desitari

	INFORMAL AFFIRMATIVE INDICATIVE
Passive	suwarareru
Potential	suwareru
Causative	suwaraseru
Causative Pass.	suwaraserareru

Honorific	I	osuwari ni naru
	II	osuwari nasaru
Humble		

to eat   TRANSITIVE

		AFFIRMATIVE	NEGATIVE
Indicative	**INFORMAL**	taberu	tabenai
	FORMAL	tabemasu	tabemaseñ
Imperative	**INFORMAL I**	tabero	taberu na
	II	tabenasai	tabenasaru na
	III	tabete kudasai	tabenai de kudasai
	FORMAL	mesiagarimase	mesiagarimasu na
Presumptive	**INFORMAL I**	tabeyoo	tabemai
	II	taberu daroo	tabenai daroo
	FORMAL I	tabemasyoo	tabemasumai
	II	taberu desyoo	tabenai desyoo
Provisional	**INFORMAL**	tabereba	tabenakereba
	FORMAL	tabemaseba	tabemaseñ nara
		tabemasureba	
Gerund	**INFORMAL I**	tabete	tabenai de
	II		tabenakute
	FORMAL	tabemasite	tabemaseñ de
Past Ind.	**INFORMAL**	tabeta	tabenakatta
	FORMAL	tabemasita	tabemaseñ desita
Past Presump.	**INFORMAL**	tabetaroo	tabenakattaroo
		tabeta daroo	tabenakatta daroo
	FORMAL	tabemasitaroo	tabemaseñ desitaroo
		tabeta desyoo	tabenakatta desyoo
Conditional	**INFORMAL**	tabetara	tabenakattara
	FORMAL	tabemasitara	tabemaseñ desitara
Alternative	**INFORMAL**	tabetari	tabenakattari
	FORMAL	tabemasitari	tabemaseñ desitari

	INFORMAL AFFIRMATIVE INDICATIVE
Passive	taberareru
Potential	taberareru
Causative	tabesaseru
Causative Pass.	tabesaserareru

Honorific	mesiagaru
Humble	itadaku

		AFFIRMATIVE	NEGATIVE
Indicative	**INFORMAL**	-tagaru	-tagaranai
	FORMAL	-tagarimasu	-tagarimaseñ
Imperative	**INFORMAL I**		
	II		
	III		
	FORMAL		
Presumptive	**INFORMAL I**	-tagaroo	-tagarumai
	II	-tagaru daroo	-tagaranai daroo
	FORMAL I	-tagarimasyoo	-tagarimasumai
	II	-tagaru desyoo	-tagaranai desyoo
Provisional	**INFORMAL**	-tagareba	-tagaranakereba
	FORMAL	-tagarimaseba	-tagarimaseñ nara
		-tagarimasureba	
Gerund	**INFORMAL I**	-tagatte	-tagaranai de
	II		-tagaranakute
	FORMAL	-tagarimasite	-tagarimaseñ de
Past Ind.	**INFORMAL**	-tagatta	-tagaranakatta
	FORMAL	-tagarimasita	-tagarimaseñ desita
Past Presump.	**INFORMAL**	-tagattaroo	-tagaranakattaroo
		-tagatta daroo	-tagaranakatta daroo
	FORMAL	-tagarimasitaroo	-tagarimaseñ desitaroo
		-tagatta desyoo	-tagaranakatta desyoo
Conditional	**INFORMAL**	-tagattara	-tagaranakattara
	FORMAL	-tagarimasitara	-tagarimaseñ desitara
Alternative	**INFORMAL**	-tagattari	-tagaranakattari
	FORMAL	-tagarimasitari	-tagarimaseñ desitari

INFORMAL AFFIRMATIVE INDICATIVE

Passive	
Potential	
Causative	-tagaraseru
Causative Pass.	-tagaraserareru

Honorific	
Humble	

**-tagaru* is added to the infinitive of verbs, and like *-masu* does not have any transitive/intransitive bias of its own.

		AFFIRMATIVE	NEGATIVE
Indicative	INFORMAL	tanomu	tanomanai
	FORMAL	tanomimasu	tanomimaseñ
Imperative	INFORMAL I	tanome	tanomu na
	II	tanominasai	tanominasaru na
	III	tanoñde kudasai	tanomanai de kudasai
	FORMAL	otanomi nasaimase	otanomi nasaimasu na
Presumptive	INFORMAL I	tanomoo	tanomumai
	II	tanomu daroo	tanomanai daroo
	FORMAL I	tanomimasyoo	tanomimasumai
	II	tanomu desyoo	tanomanai desyoo
Provisional	INFORMAL	tanomeba	tanomanakereba
	FORMAL	tanomimaseba tanomimasureba	tanomimaseñ nara
Gerund	INFORMAL I	tanoñde	tanomanai de
	II		tanomanakute
	FORMAL	tanomimasite	tanomimaseñ de
Past Ind.	INFORMAL	tanoñda	tanomanakatta
	FORMAL	tanomimasita	tanomimaseñ desita
Past Presump.	INFORMAL	tanoñdaroo	tanomanakattaroo
		tanoñda daroo	tanomanakatta daroo
	FORMAL	tanomimasitaroo	tanomimaseñ desitaroo
		tanoñda desyoo	tanomanakatta desyoo
Conditional	INFORMAL	tanoñdara	tanomanakattara
	FORMAL	tanomimasitara	tanomimaseñ desitara
Alternative	INFORMAL	tanoñdari	tanomanakattari
	FORMAL	tanomimasitari	tanomimaseñ desitari

INFORMAL AFFIRMATIVE INDICATIVE

Passive	tanomareru
Potential	tanomeru
Causative	tanomaseru
Causative Pass.	tanomaserareru

Honorific	I	otanomi ni naru
	II	otanomi nasaru
Humble	I	otanomi suru
	II	otanomi itasu

156

			AFFIRMATIVE	NEGATIVE
Indicative	**INFORMAL**		taoreru	taorenai
	FORMAL		taoremasu	taoremaseñ
Imperative	**INFORMAL**	I	taorero	taoreru na
		II	taorenasai	taorenasaru na
		III	taorete kudasai	taorenai de kudasai
	FORMAL		otaore nasaimase	otaore nasaimasu na
Presumptive	**INFORMAL**	I	taoreyoo	taoremai
		II	taoreru daroo	taorenai daroo
	FORMAL	I	taoremasyoo	taoremasumai
		II	taoreru desyoo	taorenai desyoo
Provisional	**INFORMAL**		taoreba	taorenakereba
	FORMAL		taoremaseba	taoremaseñ nara
			taoremasureba	
Gerund	**INFORMAL**	I	taorete	taorenai de
		II		taorenakute
	FORMAL		taoremasite	taoremaseñ de
Past Ind.	**INFORMAL**		taoreta	taorenakatta
	FORMAL		taoremasita	taoremaseñ desita
Past Presump.	**INFORMAL**		taoretaroo	taorenakattaroo
			taoreta daroo	taorenakatta daroo
	FORMAL		taoremasitaroo	taoremaseñ desitaroo
			taoreta desyoo	taorenakatta desyoo
Conditional	**INFORMAL**		taoretara	taorenakattara
	FORMAL		taoremasitara	taoremaseñ desitara
Alternative	**INFORMAL**		taoretari	taorenakattari
	FORMAL		taoremasitari	taoremaseñ desitari

		INFORMAL AFFIRMATIVE INDICATIVE
Passive		
Potential		
Causative		taoresaseru
Causative Pass.		taoresaserareru
Honorific	I	otaore ni naru
	II	otaore nasaru
Humble		

			AFFIRMATIVE	NEGATIVE
Indicative	INFORMAL		taosu	taosanai
	FORMAL		taosimasu	taosimaseñ
Imperative	INFORMAL	I	taose	taosu na
		II	taosinasai	taosinasaru na
		III	taosite kudasai	taosanai de kudasai
	FORMAL		otaosi nasaimase	otaosi nasaimasu na
Presumptive	INFORMAL	I	taosoo	taosumai
		II	taosu daroo	taosanai daroo
	FORMAL	I	taosimasyoo	taosimasumai
		II	taosu desyoo	taosanai desyoo
Provisional	INFORMAL		taoseba	taosanakereba
	FORMAL		taosimaseba	taosimaseñ nara
			taosimasureba	
Gerund	INFORMAL	I	taosite	taosanai de
		II		taosanakute
	FORMAL		taosimasite	taosimaseñ de
Past Ind.	INFORMAL		taosita	taosanakatta
	FORMAL		taosimasita	taosimaseñ desita
Past Presump.	INFORMAL		taositaroo	taosanakattaroo
			taosita daroo	taosanakatta daroo
	FORMAL		taosimasitaroo	taosimaseñ desitaroo
			taosita desyoo	taosanakatta desyoo
Conditional	INFORMAL		taositara	taosanakattara
	FORMAL		taosimasitara	taosimaseñ desitara
Alternative	INFORMAL		taositari	taosanakattari
	FORMAL		taosimasitari	taosimaseñ desitari

	INFORMAL AFFIRMATIVE INDICATIVE
Passive	taosareru
Potential	taoseru
Causative	taosaseru
Causative Pass.	taosaserareru

Honorific	I	otaosi ni naru
	II	otaosi nasaru
Humble		

		AFFIRMATIVE	**NEGATIVE**
Indicative	**INFORMAL**	tariru	tarinai
	FORMAL	tarimasu	tarimaseñ
Imperative	**INFORMAL I**		
	II		
	III		
	FORMAL		
Presumptive	**INFORMAL I**	tariyoo	tarimai
	II	tariru daroo	tarinai daroo
	FORMAL I	tarimasyoo	tarimasumai
	II	tariru desyoo	tarinai desyoo
Provisional	**INFORMAL**	tarireba	tarinakereba
	FORMAL	tarimaseba	tarimaseñ nara
		tarimasureba	
Gerund	**INFORMAL I**	tarite	tarinai de
	II		tarinakute
	FORMAL	tarimasite	tarimaseñ de
Past Ind.	**INFORMAL**	tarita	tarinakatta
	FORMAL	tarimasita	tarimaseñ desita
Past Presump.	**INFORMAL**	taritaroo	tarinakattaroo
		tarita daroo	tarinakatta daroo
	FORMAL	tarimasitaroo	tarimaseñ desitaroo
		tarita desyoo	tarinakatta desyoo
Conditional	**INFORMAL**	taritara	tarinakattara
	FORMAL	tarimasitara	tarimaseñ desitara
Alternative	**INFORMAL**	taritari	tarinakattari
	FORMAL	tarimasitari	tarimaseñ desitari

INFORMAL AFFIRMATIVE INDICATIVE

Passive

Potential

Causative

Causative Pass.

Honorific

Humble

			AFFIRMATIVE	NEGATIVE
Indicative	INFORMAL		tasukeru	tasukenai
	FORMAL		tasukemasu	tasukemaseñ
Imperative	INFORMAL	I	tasukero	tasukeru na
		II	tasukenasai	tasukenasaru na
		III	tasukete kudasai	tasukenai de kudasai
	FORMAL		otasuke nasaimase	otasuke nasaimasu na
Presumptive	INFORMAL	I	tasukeyoo	tasukemai
		II	tasukeru daroo	tasukenai daroo
	FORMAL	I	tasukemasyoo	tasukemasumai
		II	tasukeru desyoo	tasukenai desyoo
Provisional	INFORMAL		tasukereba	tasukenakereba
	FORMAL		tasukemaseba	tasukemaseñ nara
			tasukemasureba	
Gerund	INFORMAL	I	tasukete	tasukenai de
		II		tasukenakute
	FORMAL		tasukemasite	tasukemaseñ de
Past Ind.	INFORMAL		tasuketa	tasukenakatta
	FORMAL		tasukemasita	tasukemaseñ desita
Past Presump.	INFORMAL		tasuketaroo	tasukenakattaroo
			tasuketa daroo	tasukenakatta daroo
	FORMAL		tasukemasitaroo	tasukemaseñ desitaroo
			tasuketa desyoo	tasukenakatta desyoo
Conditional	INFORMAL		tasuketara	tasukenakattara
	FORMAL		tasukemasitara	tasukemaseñ desitara
Alternative	INFORMAL		tasuketari	tasukenakattari
	FORMAL		tasukemasitari	tasukemaseñ desitari

		INFORMAL AFFIRMATIVE INDICATIVE
Passive		tasukerareru
Potential		tasukerareru
Causative		tasukesaseru
Causative Pass.		tasukesaserareru

Honorific	I	otasuke ni naru
	II	otasuke nasaru
Humble	I	otasuke suru
	II	otasuke itasu

			AFFIRMATIVE	NEGATIVE
Indicative	**INFORMAL**		tateru	tatenai
	FORMAL		tatemasu	tatemaseñ
Imperative	**INFORMAL**	**I**	tatero	tateru na
		II	tatenasai	tatenasaru na
		III	tatete kudasai	tatenai de kudasai
	FORMAL		otate nasaimase	otate nasaimasu na
Presumptive	**INFORMAL**	**I**	tateyoo	tatemai
		II	tateru daroo	tatenai daroo
	FORMAL	**I**	tatemasyoo	tatemasumai
		II	tateru desyoo	tatenai desyoo
Provisional	**INFORMAL**		tatereba	tatenakereba
	FORMAL		tatemaseba	tatemaseñ nara
			tatemasureba	
Gerund	**INFORMAL**	**I**	tatete	tatenai de
		II		tatenakute
	FORMAL		tatemasite	tatemaseñ de
Past Ind.	**INFORMAL**		tateta	tatenakatta
	FORMAL		tatemasita	tatemasen desita
Past Presump.	**INFORMAL**		tatetaroo	tatenakattaroo
			tateta daroo	tatenakatta daroo
	FORMAL		tatemasitaroo	tatemaseñ desitaroo
			tateta desyoo	tatenakatta desyoo
Conditional	**INFORMAL**		tatetara	tatenakattara
	FORMAL		tatemasitara	tatemaseñ desitara
Alternative	**INFORMAL**		tatetari	tatenakattari
	FORMAL		tatemasitari	tatemaseñ desitari

		INFORMAL AFFIRMATIVE INDICATIVE
Passive		taterareru
Potential		taterareru
Causative		tatesaseru
Causative Pass.		tatesaserareru

Honorific	**I**	otate ni naru
	II	otate nasaru
Humble	**I**	otate suru
	II	otate itasu

tat.u
to stand

tati

			AFFIRMATIVE	NEGATIVE
Indicative	INFORMAL		tatu	tatanai
	FORMAL		tatimasu	tatimaseñ
Imperative	INFORMAL	I	tate	tatu na
		II	tatinasai	tatinasaru na
		III	tatte kudasai	tatanai de kudasai
	FORMAL		otati nasaimase	otati nasaimasu na
Presumptive	INFORMAL	I	tatoo	tatumai
		II	tatu daroo	tatanai daroo
	FORMAL	I	tatimasyoo	tatimasumai
		II	tatu desyoo	tatanai desyoo
Provisional	INFORMAL		tateba	tatanakereba
	FORMAL		tatimaseba	tatimaseñ nara
			tatimasureba	
Gerund	INFORMAL	I	tatte	tatanai de
		II		tatanakute
	FORMAL		tatimasite	tatimaseñ de
Past Ind.	INFORMAL		tatta	tatanakatta
	FORMAL		tatimasita	tatimaseñ desita
Past Presump.	INFORMAL		tattaroo	tatanakattaroo
			tatta daroo	tatanakatta daroo
	FORMAL		tatimasitaroo	tatimaseñ desitaroo
			tatta desyoo	tatanakatta desyoo
Conditional	INFORMAL		tattara	tatanakattara
	FORMAL		tatimasitara	tatimaseñ desitara
Alternative	INFORMAL		tattari	tatanakattari
	FORMAL		tatimasitari	tatimaseñ desitari

INFORMAL AFFIRMATIVE INDICATIVE

Passive	tatareru
Potential	tateru
Causative	tataseru
Causative Pass.	tataserareru

Honorific	I	otati ni naru
	II	otati nasaru
Humble	I	otati suru
	II	otati itasu

162

			AFFIRMATIVE	NEGATIVE
Indicative	**INFORMAL**		tetudau	tetudawanai
	FORMAL		tetudaimasu	tetudaimaseñ
Imperative	**INFORMAL**	I	tetudae	tetudau na
		II	tetudainasai	tetudainasaru na
		III	tetudatte kudasai	tetudawanai de kudasai
	FORMAL		otetudai nasaimase	otedudai nasaimasu na
Presumptive	**INFORMAL**	I	tetudaoo	tetudaumai
		II	tetudau daroo	tetudawanai daroo
	FORMAL	I	tetudaimasyoo	tetudaimasumai
		II	tetudau desyoo	tetudawanai desyoo
Provisional	**INFORMAL**		tetudaeba	tetudawanakereba
	FORMAL		tetudaimaseba	tetudaimaseñ nara
			tetudaimasureba	
Gerund	**INFORMAL**	I	tetudatte	tetudawanai de
		II		tetudawanakute
	FORMAL		tetudaimasite	tetudaimaseñ de
Past Ind.	**INFORMAL**		tetudatta	tetudawanakatta
	FORMAL		tetudaimasita	tetudaimaseñ desita
Past Presump.	**INFORMAL**		tetudattaroo	tetudawanakattaroo
			tetudatta daroo	tetudawanakatta daroo
	FORMAL		tetudaimasitaroo	tetudaimaseñ desitaroo
			tetudatta desyoo	tetudawanakatta desyoo
Conditional	**INFORMAL**		tetudattara	tetudawanakattara
	FORMAL		tetudaimasitara	tetudaimaseñ desitara
Alternative	**INFORMAL**		tetudattari	tetudawanakattari
	FORMAL		tetudaimasitari	tetudaimaseñ desitari

	INFORMAL AFFIRMATIVE INDICATIVE
Passive	tetudawareru
Potential	tetudaeru
Causative	tetudawaseru
Causative Pass.	tetudawaserareru

Honorific	I	otetudai ni naru
	II	otetudai nasaru
Humble	I	otetudai suru
	II	otetudai itasu

		AFFIRMATIVE	NEGATIVE
Indicative	**INFORMAL**	tigau	tigawanai
	FORMAL	tigaimasu	tigaimaseñ
Imperative	**INFORMAL I**		
	II		
	III		
	FORMAL		
Presumptive	**INFORMAL I**	tigaoo	tigaumai
	II	tigau daroo	tigawanai daroo
	FORMAL I	tigaimasyoo	tigaimasumai
	II	tigau desyoo	tigawanai desyoo
Provisional	**INFORMAL**	tigaeba	tigawanakereba
	FORMAL	tigaimaseba	tigaimaseñ nara
		tigaimasureba	
Gerund	**INFORMAL I**	tigatte	tigawanai de
	II		tigawanakute
	FORMAL	tigaimasite	tigaimaseñ de
Past Ind.	**INFORMAL**	tigatta	tigawanakatta
	FORMAL	tigaimasita	tigaimaseñ desita
Past Presump.	**INFORMAL**	tigattaroo	tigawanakattaroo
		tigatta daroo	tigawanakatta daroo
	FORMAL	tigaimasitaroo	tigaimaseñ desitaroo
		tigatta desyoo	tigawanakatta desyoo
Conditional	**INFORMAL**	tigattara	tigawanakattara
	FORMAL	tigaimasitara	tigaimaseñ desitara
Alternative	**INFORMAL**	tigattari	tigawanakattari
	FORMAL	tigaimasitari	tigaimaseñ desitari

INFORMAL AFFIRMATIVE INDICATIVE

Passive	
Potential	tigaeru
Causative	tigawaseru
Causative Pass.	tigawaserareru

Honorific

Humble

		AFFIRMATIVE	NEGATIVE
Indicative	**INFORMAL**	tobu	tobanai
	FORMAL	tobimasu	tobimaseñ
Imperative	**INFORMAL** I	tobe	tobu na
	II	tobinasai	tobinasaru na
	III	toñde kudasai	tobanai de kudasai
	FORMAL	otobi nasaimase	otobi nasaimasu na
Presumptive	**INFORMAL** I	toboo	tobumai
	II	tobu daroo	tobanai daroo
	FORMAL I	tobimasyoo	tobimasumai
	II	tobu desyoo	tobanai desyoo
Provisional	**INFORMAL**	tobeba	tobanakereba
	FORMAL	tobimaseba	tobimaseñ nara
		tobimasureba	
Gerund	**INFORMAL** I	toñde	tobanai de
	II		tobanakute
	FORMAL	tobimasite	tobimaseñ de
Past Ind.	**INFORMAL**	toñda	tobanakatta
	FORMAL	tobimasita	tobimaseñ desita
Past Presump.	**INFORMAL**	toñdaroo	tobanakattaroo
		toñda daroo	tobanakatta daroo
	FORMAL	tobimasitaroo	tobimaseñ desitaroo
		toñda desyoo	tobanakatta desyoo
Conditional	**INFORMAL**	toñdara	tobanakattara
	FORMAL	tobimasitara	tobimaseñ desitara
Alternative	**INFORMAL**	toñdari	tobanakattari
	FORMAL	tobimasitari	tobimaseñ desitari

	INFORMAL AFFIRMATIVE INDICATIVE
Passive	tobareru
Potential	toberu
Causative	tobaseru
Causative Pass.	tobaserareru

Honorific	I	otobi ni naru
	II	otobi nasaru

Humble

		AFFIRMATIVE	NEGATIVE
Indicative	**INFORMAL**	todokeru	todokenai
	FORMAL	todokemasu	todokemaseñ
Imperative	**INFORMAL I**	todokero	todokeru na
	II	todokenasai	todokenasaru na
	III	todokete kudasai	todokenai de kudasai
	FORMAL	otodoke nasaimase	otodoke nasaimasu na
Presumptive	**INFORMAL I**	todokeyoo	todokemai
	II	todokeru daroo	todokenai daroo
	FORMAL I	todokemasyoo	todokemasumai
	II	todokeru desyoo	todokenai desyoo
Provisional	**INFORMAL**	todokereba	todokenakereba
	FORMAL	todokemaseba	todokemaseñ nara
		todokemasureba	
Gerund	**INFORMAL I**	todokete	todokenai de
	II		todokenakute
	FORMAL	todokemasite	todokemaseñ de
Past Ind.	**INFORMAL**	todoketa	todokenakatta
	FORMAL	todokemasita	todokemaseñ desita
Past Presump.	**INFORMAL**	todoketaroo	todokenakattaroo
		todoketa daroo	todokenakatta daroo
	FORMAL	todokemasitaroo	todokemaseñ desitaroo
		todoketa desyoo	todokenakatta desyoo
Conditional	**INFORMAL**	todoketara	todokenakattara
	FORMAL	todokemasitara	todokemaseñ desitara
Alternative	**INFORMAL**	todoketari	todokenakattari
	FORMAL	todokemasitari	todokemaseñ desitari

	INFORMAL AFFIRMATIVE INDICATIVE
Passive	todokerareru
Potential	todokerareru
Causative	todokesaseru
Causative Pass.	todokesaserareru

Honorific	**I**	otodoke ni naru
	II	otodoke nasaru
Humble	**I**	otodoke suru
	II	otodoke itasu

todoki

			AFFIRMATIVE	NEGATIVE
Indicative	**INFORMAL**		todoku	todokanai
	FORMAL		todokimasu	todokimaseñ
Imperative	**INFORMAL**	I	todoke	todoku na
		II	todokinasai	todokinasaru na
		III	todoite kudasai	todokanai de kudasai
	FORMAL		otodoki nasaimase	otodoki nasaimasu na
Presumptive	**INFORMAL**	I	todokoo	todokumai
		II	todoku daroo	todokanai daroo
	FORMAL	I	todokimasyoo	todokimasumai
		II	todoku desyoo	todokanai desyoo
Provisional	**INFORMAL**		todokeba	todokanakereba
	FORMAL		todokimaseba	todokimaseñ nara
			todokimasureba	
Gerund	**INFORMAL**	I	todoite	todokanai de
		II		todokanakute
	FORMAL		todokimasite	todokimaseñ de
Past Ind.	**INFORMAL**		todoita	todokanakatta
	FORMAL		todokimasita	todokimaseñ desita
Past Presump.	**INFORMAL**		todoitaroo	todokanakattaroo
			todoita daroo	todokanakatta daroo
	FORMAL		todokimasitaroo	todokimaseñ desitaroo
			todoita desyoo	todokanakatta desyoo
Conditional	**INFORMAL**		todoitara	todokanakattara
	FORMAL		todokimasitara	todokimaseñ desitara
Alternative	**INFORMAL**		todoitari	todokanakattari
	FORMAL		todokimasitari	todokimaseñ desitari

INFORMAL AFFIRMATIVE INDICATIVE

Passive	
Potential	todokeru
Causative	todokaseru
Causative Pass.	todokaserareru
Honorific	
Humble	

toke.ru
to melt

			AFFIRMATIVE	NEGATIVE
Indicative	INFORMAL		tokeru	tokenai
	FORMAL		tokemasu	tokemaseñ
Imperative	INFORMAL	I	tokero	tokeru na
		II		
		III		
	FORMAL			
Presumptive	INFORMAL	I	tokeyoo	tokemai
		II	tokeru daroo	tokenai daroo
	FORMAL	I	tokemasyoo	tokemasumai
		II	tokeru desyoo	tokenai desyoo
Provisional	INFORMAL		tokereba	tokenakereba
	FORMAL		tokemaseba	tokemaseñ nara
			tokemasureba	
Gerund	INFORMAL	I	tokete	tokenai de
		II		tokenakute
	FORMAL		tokemasite	tokemaseñ de
Past Ind.	INFORMAL		toketa	tokenakatta
	FORMAL		tokemasita	tokemaseñ desita
Past Presump.	INFORMAL		toketaroo	tokenakattaroo
			toketa daroo	tokenakatta daroo
	FORMAL		tokemasitaroo	tokemaseñ desitaroo
			toketa desyoo	tokenakatta desyoo
Conditional	INFORMAL		toketara	tokenakattara
	FORMAL		tokemasitara	tokemaseñ desitara
Alternative	INFORMAL		toketari	tokenakattari
	FORMAL		tokemasitari	tokemaseñ desitari

INFORMAL AFFIRMATIVE INDICATIVE

Passive

Potential

Causative

Causative Pass.

Honorific

Humble

		AFFIRMATIVE	NEGATIVE
Indicative	**INFORMAL**	tomaru	tomaranai
	FORMAL	tomarimasu	tomarimaseñ
Imperative	**INFORMAL I**	tomare	tomaru na
	II	tomarinasai	tomarinasaru na
	III	tomatte kudasai	tomaranai de kudasai
	FORMAL	otomari nasaimase	otomari nasaimasu na
Presumptive	**INFORMAL I**	tomaroo	tomarumai
	II	tomaru daroo	tomaranai daroo
	FORMAL I	tomarimasyoo	tomarimasumai
	II	tomaru desyoo	tomaranai desyoo
Provisional	**INFORMAL**	tomareba	tomaranakereba
	FORMAL	tomarimaseba	tomarimaseñ nara
		tomarimasureba	
Gerund	**INFORMAL I**	tomatte	tomaranai de
	II		tomaranakute
	FORMAL	tomarimasite	tomarimaseñ de
Past Ind.	**INFORMAL**	tomatta	tomaranakatta
	FORMAL	tomarimasita	tomarimaseñ desita
Past Presump.	**INFORMAL**	tomattaroo	tomaranakattaroo
		tomatta daroo	tomaranakatta daroo
	FORMAL	tomarimasitaroo	tomarimaseñ desitaroo
		tomatta desyoo	tomaranakatta desyoo
Conditional	**INFORMAL**	tomattara	tomaranakattara
	FORMAL	tomarimasitara	tomarimaseñ desitara
Alternative	**INFORMAL**	tomattari	tomaranakattari
	FORMAL	tomarimasitari	tomarimaseñ desitari

INFORMAL AFFIRMATIVE INDICATIVE

Passive	tomarareru
Potential	tomareru
Causative	tomaraseru
Causative Pass.	tomaraserareru

Honorific	**I**	otomari ni naru
	II	otomari nasaru
Humble	**I**	otomari suru
	II	otomari itasu

169

		AFFIRMATIVE	NEGATIVE
Indicative	**INFORMAL**	tomeru	tomenai
	FORMAL	tomemasu	tomemaseñ
Imperative	**INFORMAL** I	tomero	tomeru na
	II	tomenasai	tomenasaru na
	III	tomete kudasai	tomenai de kudasai
	FORMAL	otome nasaimase	otome nasaimasu na
Presumptive	**INFORMAL** I	tomeyoo	tomemai
	II	tomeru daroo	tomenai daroo
	FORMAL I	tomemasyoo	tomemasumai
	II	tomeru desyoo	tomenai desyoo
Provisional	**INFORMAL**	tomereba	tomenakereba
	FORMAL	tomemaseba	tomemaseñ nara
		tomemasureba	
Gerund	**INFORMAL** I	tomete	tomenai de
	II		tomenakute
	FORMAL	tomemasite	tomemaseñ de
Past Ind.	**INFORMAL**	tometa	tomenakatta
	FORMAL	tomemasita	tomemaseñ desita
Past Presump.	**INFORMAL**	tometaroo	tomenakattaroo
		tometa daroo	tomenakatta daroo
	FORMAL	tomemasitaroo	tomemaseñ desitaroo
		tometa desyoo	tomenakatta desyoo
Conditional	**INFORMAL**	tometara	tomenakattara
	FORMAL	tomemasitara	tomemaseñ desitara
Alternative	**INFORMAL**	tometari	tomenakattari
	FORMAL	tomemasitari	tomemaseñ desitari

INFORMAL AFFIRMATIVE INDICATIVE

Passive	tomerareru
Potential	tomerareru
Causative	tomesaseru
Causative Pass.	tomesaserareru

Honorific	I	otome ni naru
	II	otome nasaru
Humble	I	otome suru
	II	otome itasu

			AFFIRMATIVE	NEGATIVE
Indicative	**INFORMAL**		tooru	tooranai
	FORMAL		toorimasu	toorimaseñ
Imperative	**INFORMAL**	**I**	toore	tooru na
		II	toorinasai	toorinasaru na
		III	tootte kudasai	tooranai de kudasai
	FORMAL		otoori nasaimase	otoori nasaimasu na
Presumptive	**INFORMAL**	**I**	tooroo	toorumai
		II	tooru daroo	tooranai daroo
	FORMAL	**I**	toorimasyoo	toorimasumai
		II	tooru desyoo	tooranai desyoo
Provisional	**INFORMAL**		tooreba	tooranakereba
	FORMAL		toorimaseba	toorimaseñ nara
			toorimasureba	
Gerund	**INFORMAL**	**I**	tootte	tooranai de
		II		tooranakute
	FORMAL		toorimasite	toorimaseñ de
Past Ind.	**INFORMAL**		tootta	tooranakatta
	FORMAL		toorimasita	toorimaseñ desita
Past Presump.	**INFORMAL**		toottaroo	tooranakattaroo
			tootta daroo	tooranakatta daroo
	FORMAL		toorimasitaroo	toorimaseñ desitaroo
			tootta desyoo	tooranakatta desyoo
Conditional	**INFORMAL**		toottara	tooranakattara
	FORMAL		toorimasitara	toorimaseñ desitara
Alternative	**INFORMAL**		toottari	tooranakattari
	FORMAL		toorimasitari	toorimaseñ desitari

	INFORMAL AFFIRMATIVE INDICATIVE
Passive	toorareru
Potential	tooreru
Causative	tooraseru
Causative Pass.	tooraserareru

Honorific	**I**	otoori ni naru
	II	otoori nasaru
Humble		

to take   TRANSITIVE

			AFFIRMATIVE	NEGATIVE
Indicative	**INFORMAL**		toru	toranai
	FORMAL		torimasu	torimaseñ
Imperative	**INFORMAL**	**I**	tore	toru na
		II	torinasai	torinasaru na
		III	totte kudasai	toranai de kudasai
	FORMAL		otori nasaimase	otori nasaimasu na
Presumptive	**INFORMAL**	**I**	toroo	torumai
		II	toru daroo	toranai daroo
	FORMAL	**I**	torimasyoo	torimasumai
		II	toru desyoo	toranai desyoo
Provisional	**INFORMAL**		toreba	toranakereba
	FORMAL		torimaseba	torimaseñ nara
			torimasureba	
Gerund	**INFORMAL**	**I**	totte	toranai de
		II		toranakute
	FORMAL		torimasite	torimaseñ de
Past Ind.	**INFORMAL**		totta	toranakatta
	FORMAL		torimasita	torimaseñ desita
Past Presump.	**INFORMAL**		tottaroo	toranakattaroo
			totta daroo	toranakatta daroo
	FORMAL		torimasitaroo	torimaseñ desitaroo
			totta desyoo	toranakatta desyoo
Conditional	**INFORMAL**		tottara	toranakattara
	FORMAL		torimasitara	torimaseñ desitara
Alternative	**INFORMAL**		tottari	toranakattari
	FORMAL		torimasitari	torimaseñ desitari

INFORMAL AFFIRMATIVE INDICATIVE

Passive	torareru
Potential	toreru
Causative	toraseru
Causative Pass.	toraserareru

Honorific	**I**	otori ni naru
	II	otori nasaru
Humble	**I**	otori suru
	II	otori itasu

tukamae

tukamae.ru
to catch, to seize

		AFFIRMATIVE	NEGATIVE
Indicative	**INFORMAL**	tukamaeru	tukamaenai
	FORMAL	tukamaemasu	tukamaemaseñ
Imperative	**INFORMAL I**	tukamaero	tukamaeru na
	II	tukamaenasai	tukamaenasaru na
	III	tukamaete kudasai	tukamaenai de kudasai
	FORMAL	otukamae nasaimase	otukamae nasaimasu na
Presumptive	**INFORMAL I**	tukamaeyoo	tukamaemai
	II	tukamaeru daroo	tukamaenai daroo
	FORMAL I	tukamaemasyoo	tukamaemasumai
	II	tukamaeru desyoo	tukamaenai desyoo
Provisional	**INFORMAL**	tukamaereba	tukamaenakereba
	FORMAL	tukamaemaseba	tukamaemaseñ nara
		tukamaemasureba	
Gerund	**INFORMAL I**	tukamaete	tukamaenai de
	II		tukamaenakute
	FORMAL	tukamaemasite	tukamaemaseñ de
Past Ind.	**INFORMAL**	tukamaeta	tukamenakatta
	FORMAL	tukamaemasita	tukamaemaseñ desita
Past Presump.	**INFORMAL**	tukamaetaroo	tukamaenakattaroo
		tukamaeta daroo	tukamaenakatta daroo
	FORMAL	tukamaemasitaroo	tukamaemaseñ desitaroo
		tukamaeta desyoo	tukamaenakatta desyoo
Conditional	**INFORMAL**	tukamaetara	tukamaenakattara
	FORMAL	tukamaemasitara	tukamaemaseñ desitara
Alternative	**INFORMAL**	tukamaetari	tukamaenakattari
	FORMAL	tukamaemasitari	tukamaemaseñ desitari

	INFORMAL AFFIRMATIVE INDICATIVE
Passive	tukamaerareru
Potential	tukamaerareru
Causative	tukamaesaseru
Causative Pass.	tukamaesaserareru

Honorific	**I**	otukamae ni naru
	II	otukamae nasaru
Humble		

		AFFIRMATIVE	NEGATIVE
Indicative	INFORMAL	tukareru	tukarenai
	FORMAL	tukaremasu	tukaremaseñ
Imperative	INFORMAL I		
	II		
	III		
	FORMAL		
Presumptive	INFORMAL I	tukareyoo	tukaremai
	II	tukareru daroo	tukarenai daroo
	FORMAL I	tukaremasyoo	tukaremasumai
	II	tukareru desyoo	tukarenai desyoo
Provisional	INFORMAL	tukarereba	tukarenakereba
	FORMAL	tukaremaseba	tukaremaseñ nara
		tukaremasureba	
Gerund	INFORMAL I	tukarete	tukarenai de
	II		tukarenakute
	FORMAL	tukaremasite	tukaremaseñ de
Past Ind.	INFORMAL	tukareta	tukarenakatta
	FORMAL	tukaremasita	tukaremaseñ desita
Past Presump.	INFORMAL	tukaretaroo	tukarenakattaroo
		tukareta daroo	tukarenakatta daroo
	FORMAL	tukaremasitaroo	tukaremaseñ desitaroo
		tukareta desyoo	tukarenakatta desyoo
Conditional	INFORMAL	tukaretara	tukarenakattara
	FORMAL	tukaremasitara	tukaremaseñ desitara
Alternative	INFORMAL	tukaretari	tukarenakattari
	FORMAL	tukaremasitari	tukaremaseñ desitari

INFORMAL AFFIRMATIVE INDICATIVE

Passive		
Potential		
Causative		tukaresaseru
Causative Pass.		tukaresaserareru

Honorific	I	otukare ni naru
	II	otukare nasaru
Humble	I	otukai suru
	II	otukai itasu

		AFFIRMATIVE	NEGATIVE
Indicative	**INFORMAL**	tukau	tukawanai
	FORMAL	tukaimasu	tukaimaseñ
Imperative	**INFORMAL I**	tukae	tukau na
	II	tukainasai	tukainasaru na
	III	tukatte kudasai	tukawanai de kudasai
	FORMAL	otukai nasaimase	otukai nasaimasu na
Presumptive	**INFORMAL I**	tukaoo	tukaumai
	II	tukau daroo	tukawanai daroo
	FORMAL I	tukaimasyoo	tukaimasumai
	II	tukau desyoo	tukawanai desyoo
Provisional	**INFORMAL**	tukaeba	tukawanakereba
	FORMAL	tukaimaseba	tukaimaseñ nara
		tukaimasureba	
Gerund	**INFORMAL I**	tukatte	tukawanai de
	II		tukawanakute
	FORMAL	tukaimasite	tukaimaseñ de
Past Ind.	**INFORMAL**	tukatta	tukawanakatta
	FORMAL	tukaimasita	tukaimaseñ desita
Past Presump.	**INFORMAL**	tukattaroo	tukawanakattaroo
		tukatta daroo	tukawanakatta daroo
	FORMAL	tukaimasitaroo	tukaimaseñ desitaroo
		tukatta desyoo	tukawanakatta desyoo
Conditional	**INFORMAL**	tukattara	tukawanakattara
	FORMAL	tukaimasitara	tukaimaseñ desitara
Alternative	**INFORMAL**	tukattari	tukawanakattari
	FORMAL	tukaimasitari	tukaimaseñ desitari

INFORMAL AFFIRMATIVE INDICATIVE

Passive	tukawareru
Potential	tukaeru
Causative	tukawaseru
Causative Pass.	tukawaserareru

Honorific	**I**	otukai ni naru
	II	otukai nasaru
Humble	**I**	otukai suru
	II	otukai itasu

			AFFIRMATIVE	NEGATIVE
Indicative	INFORMAL		tukiau	tukiawanai
	FORMAL		tukiaimasu	tukiaimaseñ
Imperative	INFORMAL	I	tukiae	tukiau na
		II	tukiainasai	tukiainasaru na
		III	tukiatte kudasai	tukiawanai de kudasai
	FORMAL		otukiai nasaimase	otukiai nasaimasu na
Presumptive	INFORMAL	I	tukiaoo	tukiaumai
		II	tukiau daroo	tukiawanai daroo
	FORMAL	I	tukiaimasyoo	tukiaimasumai
		II	tukiau desyoo	tukiawanai desyoo
Provisional	INFORMAL		tukiaeba	tukiawanakereba
	FORMAL		tukiaimaseba	tukiaimaseñ nara
			tukiaimasureba	
Gerund	INFORMAL	I	tukiatte	tukiawanai de
		II		tukiawanakute
	FORMAL		tukiaimasite	tukiaimaseñ de
Past Ind.	INFORMAL		tukiatta	tukiawanakatta
	FORMAL		tukiaimasita	tukiaimaseñ desita
Past Presump.	INFORMAL		tukiattaroo	tukiawanakattaroo
			tukiatta daroo	tukiawanakatta daroo
	FORMAL		tukiaimasitaroo	tukiaimaseñ desitaroo
			tukiatta desyoo	tukiawanakatta desyoo
Conditional	INFORMAL		tukiattara	tukiawanakattara
	FORMAL		tukiaimasitara	tukiaimaseñ desitara
Alternative	INFORMAL		tukiattari	tukiawanakattari
	FORMAL		tukiaimasitari	tukiaimaseñ desitari

INFORMAL AFFIRMATIVE INDICATIVE

Passive		
Potential		tukiaeru
Causative		tukiawaseru
Causative Pass.		tukiawaserareru

Honorific	I	otukiai ni naru
	II	otukiai nasaru
Humble	I	otukiai suru
	II	otukiai itasu

			AFFIRMATIVE	NEGATIVE
Indicative	**INFORMAL**		tuku	tukanai
	FORMAL		tukimasu	tukimaseñ
Imperative	**INFORMAL**	**I**	tsuke	tsuku na
		II		
		III		
	FORMAL			
Presumptive	**INFORMAL**	**I**	tukoo	tukumai
		II	tuku daroo	tukanai daroo
	FORMAL	**I**	tukimasyoo	tukimasumai
		II	tuku desyoo	tukanai desyoo
Provisional	**INFORMAL**		tukeba	tukanakereba
	FORMAL		tukimaseba	tukimaseñ nara
			tukimasureba	
Gerund	**INFORMAL**	**I**	tuite	tukanai de
		II		tukanakute
	FORMAL		tukimasite	tukimaseñ de
Past Ind.	**INFORMAL**		tuita	tukanakatta
	FORMAL		tukimasita	tukimaseñ desita
Past Presump.	**INFORMAL**		tuitaroo	tukanakattaroo
			tuita daroo	tukanakatta daroo
	FORMAL		tukimasitaroo	tukimaseñ desitaroo
			tuita desyoo	tukanakatta desyoo
Conditional	**INFORMAL**		tuitara	tukanakattara
	FORMAL		tukimasitara	tukimaseñ desitara
Alternative	**INFORMAL**		tuitari	tukanakattari
	FORMAL		tukimasitari	tukimaseñ desitari

		INFORMAL AFFIRMATIVE INDICATIVE
Passive		
Potential		tukeru
Causative		tsukaseru
Causative Pass.		tsukaserareru

Honorific	**I**	otuki ni naru
	II	otuki nasaru
Humble		

			AFFIRMATIVE	NEGATIVE
Indicative	INFORMAL		tukuru	tukuranai
	FORMAL		tukurimasu	tukurimaseñ
Imperative	INFORMAL	I	tukure	tukuru na
		II	tukurinasai	tukurinasaru na
		III	tukutte kudasai	tukuranai de kudasai
	FORMAL		otukuri nasaimase	otukuri nasaimasu na
Presumptive	INFORMAL	I	tukuroo	tukurumai
		II	tukuru daroo	tukuranai daroo
	FORMAL	I	tukurimasyoo	tukurimasumai
		II	tukuru desyoo	tukuranai desyoo
Provisional	INFORMAL		tukureba	tukuranakereba
	FORMAL		tukurimaseba	tukurimaseñ nara
			tukurimasureba	
Gerund	INFORMAL	I	tukutte	tukuranai de
		II		tukuranakute
	FORMAL		tukurimasite	tukurimaseñ de
Past Ind.	INFORMAL		tukutta	tukuranakatta
	FORMAL		tukurimasita	tukurimaseñ desita
Past Presump.	INFORMAL		tukuttaroo	tukuranakattaroo
			tukutta daroo	tukuranakatta daroo
	FORMAL		tukurimasitaroo	tukurimaseh desitaroo
			tukutta desyoo	tukuranakatta desyoo
Conditional	INFORMAL		tukuttara	tukuranakattara
	FORMAL		tukurimasitara	tukurimaseñ desitara
Alternative	INFORMAL		tukuttari	tukuranakattari
	FORMAL		tukurimasitari	tukurimaseñ desitari

	INFORMAL AFFIRMATIVE INDICATIVE
Passive	tukurareru
Potential	tukureru
Causative	tukuraseru
Causative Pass.	tukuraserareru

Honorific	I	otukuri ni naru
	II	otukuri nasaru
Humble	I	otukuri suru
	II	otukuri itasu

		AFFIRMATIVE	NEGATIVE
Indicative	**INFORMAL**	tumoru	tumoranai
	FORMAL	tumorimasu	tumorimaseñ
Imperative	**INFORMAL I**	tumore	tumoru na
	II		
	III		
	FORMAL		
Presumptive	**INFORMAL I**	tumoroo	tumorumai
	II	tumoru daroo	tumoranai daroo
	FORMAL I	tumorimasyoo	tumorimasumai
	II	tumoru desyoo	tumoranai desyoo
Provisional	**INFORMAL**	tumoreba	tumoranakereba
	FORMAL	tumorimaseba	tumorimaseñ nara
		tumorimasureba	
Gerund	**INFORMAL I**	tumotte	tumoranai de
	II		tumoranakute
	FORMAL	tumorimasite	tumorimaseñ de
Past Ind.	**INFORMAL**	tumotta	tumoranakatta
	FORMAL	tumorimasita	tumorimaseñ desita
Past Presump.	**INFORMAL**	tumottaroo	tumoranakattaroo
		tumotta daroo	tumoranakatta daroo
	FORMAL	tumorimasitaroo	tumorimaseñ desitaroo
		tumotta desyoo	tumoranakatta desyoo
Conditional	**INFORMAL**	tumottara	tumoranakattara
	FORMAL	tumorimasitara	tumorimaseñ desitara
Alternative	**INFORMAL**	tumottari	tumoranakattari
	FORMAL	tumorimasitari	tumorimaseñ desitari

INFORMAL AFFIRMATIVE INDICATIVE

Passive

Potential

Causative

Causative Pass.

Honorific

Humble

tutae.ru
to transmit   TRANSITIVE   **tutae**

			AFFIRMATIVE	NEGATIVE
Indicative	**INFORMAL**		tutaeru	tutaenai
	FORMAL		tutaemasu	tutaemaseñ
Imperative	**INFORMAL**	**I**	tutaero	tutaeru na
		II	tutaenasai	tutaenasaru na
		III	tutaete kudasai	tutaenai de kudasai
	FORMAL		otutae nasaimase	otutae nasaimasu na
Presumptive	**INFORMAL**	**I**	tutaeyoo	tutaemai
		II	tutaeru daroo	tutaenai daroo
	FORMAL	**I**	tutaemasyoo	tutaemasumai
		II	tutaeru desyoo	tutaenai desyoo
Provisional	**INFORMAL**		tutaereba	tutaenakereba
	FORMAL		tutaemaseba	tutaemaseñ nara
			tutaemasureba	
Gerund	**INFORMAL**	**I**	tutaete	tutaenai de
		II		tutaenakute
	FORMAL		tutaemasite	tutaemaseñ de
Past Ind.	**INFORMAL**		tutaeta	tutaenakatta
	FORMAL		tutaemasita	tutaemaseñ desita
Past Presump.	**INFORMAL**		tutaetaroo	tutaenakattaroo
			tutaeta daroo	tutaenakatta daroo
	FORMAL		tutaemasitaroo	tutaemaseñ desitaroo
			tutaeta desyoo	tutaenakatta desyoo
Conditional	**INFORMAL**		tutaetara	tutaenakattara
	FORMAL		tutaemasitara	tutaemaseñ desitara
Alternative	**INFORMAL**		tutaetari	tutaenakattari
	FORMAL		tutaemasitari	tutaemaseñ desitari

	INFORMAL AFFIRMATIVE INDICATIVE
Passive	tutaerareru
Potential	tutaerareru
Causative	tutaesaseru
Causative Pass.	tutaesaserareru

Honorific	**I**	otutae ni naru
	II	otutae nasaru
Humble	**I**	otutae suru
	II	otutae itasu

to be employed, to exert oneself

		AFFIRMATIVE	NEGATIVE
Indicative	**INFORMAL**	tutomeru	tutomenai
	FORMAL	tutomemasu	tutomemaseñ
Imperative	**INFORMAL I**	tutomero	tutomeru na
	II	tutomenasai	tutomenasaru na
	III	tutomete kudasai	tutomenai de kudasai
	FORMAL	otutome nasaimase	otutome nasaimasu na
Presumptive	**INFORMAL I**	tutomeyoo	tutomemai
	II	tutomeru daroo	tutomenai daroo
	FORMAL I	tutomemasyoo	tutomemasumai
	II	tutomeru desyoo	tutomenai desyoo
Provisional	**INFORMAL**	tutomereba	tutomenakereba
	FORMAL	tutomemaseba	tutomemaseñ nara
		tutomemasureba	
Gerund	**INFORMAL I**	tutomete	tutomenai de
	II		tutomenakute
	FORMAL	tutomemasite	tutomemaseñ de
Past Ind.	**INFORMAL**	tutometa	tutomenakatta
	FORMAL	tutomemasita	tutomemaseñ desita
Past Presump.	**INFORMAL**	tutometaroo	tutomenakattaroo
		tutometa daroo	tutomenakatta daroo
	FORMAL	tutomemasitaroo	tutomemaseñ desitaroo
		tutometa desyoo	tutomenakatta desyoo
Conditional	**INFORMAL**	tutometara	tutomenakattara
	FORMAL	tutomemasitara	tutomemaseñ desitara
Alternative	**INFORMAL**	tutometari	tutomenakattari
	FORMAL	tutomemasitari	tutomemaseñ desitari

	INFORMAL AFFIRMATIVE INDICATIVE
Passive	tutomerareru
Potential	tutomerareru
Causative	tutomesaseru
Causative Pass.	tutomesaserareru

Honorific	**I**	otutome ni naru
	II	otutome nasaru
Humble	**I**	otutome suru
	II	otutome itasu

tutum.u
to wrap up   TRANSITIVE

			AFFIRMATIVE	NEGATIVE
Indicative	INFORMAL		tutumu	tutumanai
	FORMAL		tutumimasu	tutumimaseñ
Imperative	INFORMAL	I	tutume	tutumu na
		II	tutuminasai	tutuminasaru na
		III	tutuñde kudasai	tutumanai de kudasai
	FORMAL		otutumi nasaimase	otutumi nasaimasu na
Presumptive	INFORMAL	I	tutumoo	tutumumai
		II	tutumu daroo	tutumanai daroo
	FORMAL	I	tutumimasyoo	tutumimasumai
		II	tutumu desyoo	tutumanai desyoo
Provisional	INFORMAL		tutumeba	tutumanakereba
	FORMAL		tutumimaseba	tutumimaseñ nara
			tutumimasureba	
Gerund	INFORMAL	I	tutuñde	tutumanai de
		II		tutumanakute
	FORMAL		tutumimasite	tutumimaseñ de
Past Ind.	INFORMAL		tutuñda	tutumanakatta
	FORMAL		tutumimasita	tutumimaseñ desita
Past Presump.	INFORMAL		tutuñdaroo	tutumanakattaroo
			tutuñda daroo	tutumanakatta daroo
	FORMAL		tutumimasitaroo	tutumimaseñ desitaroo
			tutuñda desyoo	tutumanakatta desyoo
Conditional	INFORMAL		tutuñdara	tutumanakattara
	FORMAL		tutumimasitara	tutumimaseñ desitara
Alternative	INFORMAL		tutuñdari	tutumanakattari
	FORMAL		tutumimasitari	tutumimaseñ desitari

	INFORMAL AFFIRMATIVE INDICATIVE
Passive	tutumareru
Potential	tutumeru
Causative	tutumaseru
Causative Pass.	tutumaserareru

Honorific	I	otutumi ni naru
	II	otutumi nasaru
Humble	I	otutumi suru
	II	otutumi itasu

			AFFIRMATIVE	NEGATIVE
Indicative	**INFORMAL**		tuzukeru	tuzukenai
	FORMAL		tuzukemasu	tuzukemaseñ
Imperative	**INFORMAL**	I	tuzukero	tuzukeru na
		II	tuzukenasai	tuzukenasaru na
		III	tuzukete kudasai	tuzukenai de kudasai
	FORMAL		otuzuke nasaimase	otuzuke nasaimasu na
Presumptive	**INFORMAL**	I	tuzukeyoo	tuzukemai
		II	tuzukeru daroo	tuzukenai daroo
	FORMAL	I	tuzukemasyoo	tuzukemasumai
		II	tuzukeru desyoo	tuzukenai desyoo
Provisional	**INFORMAL**		tuzukereba	tuzukenakereba
	FORMAL		tuzukemaseba	tuzukemaseñ nara
			tuzukemasureba	
Gerund	**INFORMAL**	I	tuzukete	tuzukenai de
		II		tuzukenakute
	FORMAL		tuzukemasite	tuzukemaseñ de
Past Ind.	**INFORMAL**		tuzuketa	tuzukenakatta
	FORMAL		tuzukemasita	tuzukemaseñ desita
Past Presump.	**INFORMAL**		tuzuketaroo	tuzukenakattaroo
			tuzuketa daroo	tuzukenakatta daroo
	FORMAL		tuzukemasitaroo	tuzukemaseñ desitaroo
			tuzuketa desyoo	tuzukenakatta desyoo
Conditional	**INFORMAL**		tuzuketara	tuzukenakattara
	FORMAL		tuzukemasitara	tuzukemaseñ desitara
Alternative	**INFORMAL**		tuzuketari	tuzukenakattari
	FORMAL		tuzukemasitari	tuzukemaseñ desitari

	INFORMAL AFFIRMATIVE INDICATIVE
Passive	tuzukerareru
Potential	tuzukerareru
Causative	tuzukesaseru
Causative Pass.	tuzukesaserareru

Honorific	I	otuzuke ni naru
	II	otuzuke nasaru
Humble	I	otuzuke suru
	II	otuzuke itasu

			AFFIRMATIVE	NEGATIVE
Indicative	INFORMAL		ueru	uenai
	FORMAL		uemasu	uemaseñ
Imperative	INFORMAL	I	uero	ueru na
		II	uenasai	uenasaru na
		III	uete kudasai	uenai de kudasai
	FORMAL		oue nasaimase	oue nasaimasu na
Presumptive	INFORMAL	I	ueyoo	uemai
		II	ueru daroo	uenai daroo
	FORMAL	I	uemasyoo	uemasumai
		II	ueru desyoo	uenai desyoo
Provisional	INFORMAL		uereba	uenakereba
	FORMAL		uemaseba	uemaseñ nara
			uemasureba	
Gerund	INFORMAL	I	uete	uenai de
		II		uenakute
	FORMAL		uemasite	uemaseñ de
Past Ind.	INFORMAL		ueta	uenakatta
	FORMAL		uemasita	uemaseñ desita
Past Presump.	INFORMAL		uetaroo	uenakattaroo
			ueta daroo	uenakatta daroo
	FORMAL		uemasitaroo	uemaseñ desitaroo
			ueta desyoo	uenakatta desyoo
Conditional	INFORMAL		uetara	uenakattara
	FORMAL		uemasitara	uemaseñ desitara
Alternative	INFORMAL		uetari	uenakattari
	FORMAL		uemasitari	uemaseñ desitari

	INFORMAL AFFIRMATIVE INDICATIVE
Passive	uerareru
Potential	uerareru
Causative	uesaseru
Causative Pass.	uesaserareru

Honorific	I	oue ni naru
	II	oue nasaru
Humble	I	oue suru
	II	oue itasu

		AFFIRMATIVE	NEGATIVE
Indicative	**INFORMAL**	ugoku	ugokanai
	FORMAL	ugokimasu	ugokimaseñ
Imperative	**INFORMAL** I	ugoke	ugoku na
	II	ugokinasai	ugokinasaru na
	III	ugoite kudasai	ugokanai de kudasai
	FORMAL	ougoki nasaimase	ougoki nasaimasu na
Presumptive	**INFORMAL** I	ugokoo	ugokumai
	II	ugoku daroo	ugokanai daroo
	FORMAL I	ugokimasyoo	ugokimasumai
	II	ugoku desyoo	ugokanai desyoo
Provisional	**INFORMAL**	ugokeba	ugokanakereba
	FORMAL	ugokimaseba	ugokimaseñ nara
		ugokimasureba	
Gerund	**INFORMAL** I	ugoite	ugokanai de
	II		ugokanakute
	FORMAL	ugokimasite	ugokimaseñ de
Past Ind.	**INFORMAL**	ugoita	ugokanakatta
	FORMAL	ugokimasita	ugokimaseñ desita
Past Presump.	**INFORMAL**	ugoitaroo	ugokanakattaroo
		ugoita daroo	ugokanakatta daroo
	FORMAL	ugokimasitaroo	ugokimaseñ desitaroo
		ugoita desyoo	ugokanakatta desyoo
Conditional	**INFORMAL**	ugoitara	ugokanakattara
	FORMAL	ugokimasitara	ugokimaseñ desitara
Alternative	**INFORMAL**	ugoitari	ugokanakattari
	FORMAL	ugokimasitari	ugokimaseñ desitari

INFORMAL AFFIRMATIVE INDICATIVE

Passive	ugokareru
Potential	ugokeru
Causative	ugokaseru
Causative Pass.	ugokaserareru

Honorific	I	ougoki ni naru
	II	ougoki nasaru
Humble		

		AFFIRMATIVE	NEGATIVE
Indicative	INFORMAL	ukabu	ukabanai
	FORMAL	ukabimasu	ukabimaseñ
Imperative	INFORMAL I	ukabe	ukabu na
	II		
	III		
	FORMAL		
Presumptive	INFORMAL I	ukaboo	ukabumai
	II	ukabu daroo	ukabanai daroo
	FORMAL I	ukabimasyoo	ukabimasumai
	II	ukabu desyoo	ukabanai desyoo
Provisional	INFORMAL	ukabeba	ukabanakereba
	FORMAL	ukabimaseba	ukabimaseñ nara
		ukabimasureba	
Gerund	INFORMAL I	ukañde	ukabanai de
	II		ukabanakute
	FORMAL	ukabimasite	ukabimaseñ de
Past Ind.	INFORMAL	ukañda	ukabanakatta
	FORMAL	ukabimasita	ukabimaseñ desita
Past Presump.	INFORMAL	ukañdaroo	ukabanakattaroo
		ukañda daroo	ukabanakatta daroo
	FORMAL	ukabimasitaroo	ukabimaseñ desitaroo
		ukañda desyoo	ukabanakatta desyoo
Conditional	INFORMAL	ukañdara	ukabanakattara
	FORMAL	ukabimasitara	ukabimaseñ desitara
Alternative	INFORMAL	ukañdari	ukabanakattari
	FORMAL	ukabimasitari	ukabimaseñ desitari

	INFORMAL AFFIRMATIVE INDICATIVE
Passive	ukabareru
Potential	ukaberu
Causative	ukabaseru
Causative Pass.	ukabaserareru

Honorific	I	oukabi ni naru
	II	oukabi nasaru
Humble		

to be born

		AFFIRMATIVE	NEGATIVE
Indicative	**INFORMAL**	umareru	umarenai
	FORMAL	umaremasu	umaremaseñ
Imperative	**INFORMAL I**	umarero	umareru na
	II		
	III		
	FORMAL		
Presumptive	**INFORMAL I**	umareyoo	umaremai
	II	umareru daroo	umarenai daroo
	FORMAL I	umaremasyoo	umaremasumai
	II	umareru desyoo	umarenai desyoo
Provisional	**INFORMAL**	umarereba	umarenakereba
	FORMAL	umaremaseba	umaremaseñ nara
		umaremasureba	
Gerund	**INFORMAL I**	umarete	umarenai de
	II		umarenakute
	FORMAL	umaremasite	umaremaseñ de
Past Ind.	**INFORMAL**	umareta	umarenakatta
	FORMAL	umaremasita	umaremaseñ desita
Past Presump.	**INFORMAL**	umaretaroo	umarenakattaroo
		umareta daroo	umarenakatta daroo
	FORMAL	umaremasitaroo	umaremaseñ desitaroo
		umareta desyoo	umarenakatta desyoo
Conditional	**INFORMAL**	umaretara	umarenakattara
	FORMAL	umaremasitara	umaremaseñ desitara
Alternative	**INFORMAL**	umaretari	umarenakattari
	FORMAL	umaremasitari	umaremaseñ desitari

INFORMAL AFFIRMATIVE INDICATIVE

Passive	
Potential	
Causative	umaresaseru
Causative Pass.	umaresaserareru

Honorific	**I**	oumare ni naru
	II	oumare nasaru
Humble		

*This corresponds to the passive derived form of *um.u* 'to give birth.'

			AFFIRMATIVE	NEGATIVE
Indicative	INFORMAL		uru	uranai
	FORMAL		urimasu	urimaseñ
Imperative	INFORMAL	I	ure	uru na
		II	urinasai	urinasaru na
		III	utte kudasai	uranai de kudasai
	FORMAL		ouri nasaimase	ouri nasaimasu na
Presumptive	INFORMAL	I	uroo	urumai
		II	uru daroo	uranai daroo
	FORMAL	I	urimasyoo	urimasumai
		II	uru desyoo	uranai desyoo
Provisional	INFORMAL		ureba	uranakereba
	FORMAL		urimaseba	urimaseñ nara
			urimasureba	
Gerund	INFORMAL	I	utte	uranai de
		II		uranakute
	FORMAL		urimasite	urimaseñ de
Past Ind.	INFORMAL		utta	uranakatta
	FORMAL		urimasita	urimaseñ desita
Past Presump.	INFORMAL		uttaroo	uranakattaroo
			utta daroo	uranakatta daroo
	FORMAL		urimasitaroo	urimaseñ desitaroo
			utta desyoo	uranakatta desyoo
Conditional	INFORMAL		uttara	uranakattara
	FORMAL		urimasitara	urimaseñ desitara
Alternative	INFORMAL		uttari	uranakattari
	FORMAL		urimasitari	urimaseñ desitari

	INFORMAL AFFIRMATIVE INDICATIVE
Passive	urareru
Potential	ureru
Causative	uraseru
Causative Pass.	uraserareru

Honorific	I	ouri ni naru
	II	ouri nasaru
Humble	I	ouri suru
	II	ouri itasu

		AFFIRMATIVE	NEGATIVE
Indicative	**INFORMAL**	utau	utawanai
	FORMAL	utaimasu	utaimaseñ
Imperative	**INFORMAL I**	utae	utau na
	II	utainasai	utainasaru na
	III	utatte kudasai	utawanai de kudasai
	FORMAL	outai nasaimase	outai nasaimasu na
Presumptive	**INFORMAL I**	utaoo	utaumai
	II	utau daroo	utawanai daroo
	FORMAL I	utaimasyoo	utaimasumai
	II	utau desyoo	utawanai desyoo
Provisional	**INFORMAL**	utaeba	utawanakereba
	FORMAL	utaimaseba	utaimaseñ nara
		utaimasureba	
Gerund	**INFORMAL I**	utatte	utawanai de
	II		utawanakute
	FORMAL	utaimasite	utaimaseñ de
Past Ind.	**INFORMAL**	utatta	utawanakatta
	FORMAL	utaimasita	utaimaseñ desita
Past Presump.	**INFORMAL**	utattaroo	utawanakattaroo
		utatta daroo	utawanakatta daroo
	FORMAL	utaimasitaroo	utaimaseñ desitaroo
		utatta desyoo	utawanakatta desyoo
Conditional	**INFORMAL**	utattara	utawanakattara
	FORMAL	utaimasitara	utaimaseñ desitara
Alternative	**INFORMAL**	utattari	utawanakattari
	FORMAL	utaimasitari	utaimaseñ desitari

	INFORMAL AFFIRMATIVE INDICATIVE
Passive	utawareru
Potential	utaeru
Causative	utawaseru
Causative Pass.	utawaserareru

Honorific	**I**	outai ni naru
	II	outai nasaru
Humble	**I**	outai suru
	II	outai itasu

189

		AFFIRMATIVE	**NEGATIVE**
Indicative	**INFORMAL**	utu	utanai
	FORMAL	utimasu	utimaseñ
Imperative	**INFORMAL I**	ute	utu na
	II	utinasai	utinasaru na
	III	utte kudasai	utanai de kudasai
	FORMAL	outi nasaimase	outi nasaimasu na
Presumptive	**INFORMAL I**	utoo	utumai
	II	utu daroo	utanai daroo
	FORMAL I	utimasyoo	utimasumai
	II	utu desyoo	utanai desyoo
Provisional	**INFORMAL**	uteba	utanakereba
	FORMAL	utimaseba	utimaseñ nara
		utimasureba	
Gerund	**INFORMAL I**	utte	utanai de
	II		utanakute
	FORMAL	utimasite	utimaseñ de
Past Ind.	**INFORMAL**	utta	utanakatta
	FORMAL	utimasita	utimaseñ desita
Past Presump.	**INFORMAL**	uttaroo	utanakattaroo
		utta daroo	utanakatta daroo
	FORMAL	utimasitaroo	utimaseñ desitaroo
		utta desyoo	utanakatta desyoo
Conditional	**INFORMAL**	uttara	utanakattara
	FORMAL	utimasitara	utimaseñ desitara
Alternative	**INFORMAL**	uttari	utanakattari
	FORMAL	utimasitari	utimaseñ desitari

		INFORMAL AFFIRMATIVE INDICATIVE
Passive		utareru
Potential		uteru
Causative		utaseru
Causative Pass.		utaserareru

Honorific	**I**	outi ni naru
	II	outi nasaru
Humble	**I**	outi suru
	II	outi itasu

		AFFIRMATIVE	NEGATIVE
Indicative	**INFORMAL**	wakaru	wakaranai
	FORMAL	wakarimasu	wakarimaseñ
Imperative	**INFORMAL I**	wakare	
	II		
	III	wakatte kudasai	
	FORMAL		
Presumptive	**INFORMAL I**	wakaroo	wakarumai
	II	wakaru daroo	wakaranai daroo
	FORMAL I	wakarimasyoo	wakarimasumai
	II	wakaru desyoo	wakaranai desyoo
Provisional	**INFORMAL**	wakareba	wakaranakereba
	FORMAL	wakarimaseba	wakarimaseñ nara
		wakarimasureba	
Gerund	**INFORMAL I**	wakatte	wakaranai de
	II		wakaranakute
	FORMAL	wakarimasite	wakarimaseñ de
Past Ind.	**INFORMAL**	wakatta	wakaranakatta
	FORMAL	wakarimasita	wakarimaseñ desita
Past Presump.	**INFORMAL**	wakattaroo	wakaranakattaroo
		wakatta daroo	wakaranakatta daroo
	FORMAL	wakarimasitaroo	wakarimaseñ desitaroo
		wakatta desyoo	wakaranakatta desyoo
Conditional	**INFORMAL**	wakattara	wakaranakattara
	FORMAL	wakarimasitara	wakarimaseñ desitara
Alternative	**INFORMAL**	wakattari	wakaranakattari
	FORMAL	wakarimasitari	wakarimaseñ desitari

INFORMAL AFFIRMATIVE INDICATIVE

Passive	
Potential	
Causative	wakaraseru
Causative Pass.	wakaraserareru

Honorific	**I**	owakari ni naru
	II	owakari nasaru
Humble		

wara.u
to laugh TRANSITIVE

warai

		AFFIRMATIVE	NEGATIVE
Indicative	**INFORMAL**	warau	warawanai
	FORMAL	waraimasu	waraimaseñ
Imperative	**INFORMAL I**	warae	warau na
	II	warainasai	warainasaru na
	III	waratte kudasai	warawanai de kudasai
	FORMAL	owarai nasaimase	owarai nasaimasu na
Presumptive	**INFORMAL I**	waraoo	waraumai
	II	warau daroo	warawanai daroo
	FORMAL I	waraimasyoo	waraimasumai
	II	warau desyoo	warawanai desyoo
Provisional	**INFORMAL**	waraeba	warawanakereba
	FORMAL	waraimaseba	waraimaseñ nara
		waraimasureba	
Gerund	**INFORMAL I**	waratte	warawanai de
	II		warawanakute
	FORMAL	waraimasite	waraimaseñ de
Past Ind.	**INFORMAL**	waratta	warawanakatta
	FORMAL	waraimasita	waraimaseñ desita
Past Presump.	**INFORMAL**	warattaroo	warawanakattaroo
		waratta daroo	warawanakatta daroo
	FORMAL	waraimasitaroo	waraimaseñ desitaroo
		waratta desyoo	warawanakatta desyoo
Conditional	**INFORMAL**	warattara	warawanakattara
	FORMAL	waraimasitara	waraimaseñ desitara
Alternative	**INFORMAL**	warattari	warawanakattari
	FORMAL	waraimasitari	waraimaseñ desitari

	INFORMAL AFFIRMATIVE INDICATIVE
Passive	warawareru
Potential	waraeru
Causative	warawaseru
Causative Pass.	warawaserareru

Honorific	**I**	owarai ni naru
	II	owarai nasaru
Humble		

			AFFIRMATIVE	NEGATIVE
Indicative	**INFORMAL**		wasureru	wasurenai
	FORMAL		wasuremasu	wasuremaseñ
Imperative	**INFORMAL**	**I**	wasurero	wasureru na
		II	wasurenasai	wasurenasaru na
		III	wasurete kudasai	wasurenai de kudasai
	FORMAL		owasure nasaimase	owasure nasaimasu na
Presumptive	**INFORMAL**	**I**	wasureyoo	wasuremai
		II	wasureru daroo	wasurenai daroo
	FORMAL	**I**	wasuremasyoo	wasuremasumai
		II	wasureru desyoo	wasurenai desyoo
Provisional	**INFORMAL**		wasurereba	wasurenakereba
	FORMAL		wasuremaseba	wasuremaseñ nara
			wasuremasureba	
Gerund	**INFORMAL**	**I**	wasurete	wasurenai de
		II		wasurenakute
	FORMAL		wasuremasite	wasuremaseñ de
Past Ind.	**INFORMAL**		wasureta	wasurenakatta
	FORMAL		wasuremasita	wasuremaseñ desita
Past Presump.	**INFORMAL**		wasuretaroo	wasurenakattaroo
			wasureta daroo	wasurenakatta daroo
	FORMAL		wasuremasitaroo	wasuremaseñ desitaroo
			wasureta desyoo	wasurenakatta desyoo
Conditional	**INFORMAL**		wasuretara	wasurenakattara
	FORMAL		wasuremasitara	wasuremaseñ desitara
Alternative	**INFORMAL**		wasuretari	wasurenakattari
	FORMAL		wasuremasitari	wasuremaseñ desitari

		INFORMAL AFFIRMATIVE INDICATIVE
Passive		wasurerareru
Potential		wasurerareru
Causative		wasuresaseru
Causative Pass.		wasuresaserareru

Honorific	**I**	owasure ni naru
	II	owasure nasaru
Humble	**I**	owasure suru
	II	owasure itasu

yak.u   yaki
to burn   TRANSITIVE

		AFFIRMATIVE	NEGATIVE
Indicative	**INFORMAL**	yaku	yakanai
	FORMAL	yakimasu	yakimaseñ
Imperative	**INFORMAL I**	yake	yaku na
	II	yakinasai	yakinasaru na
	III	yaite kudasai	yakanai de kudasai
	FORMAL	oyaki nasaimase	oyaki nasaimasu na
Presumptive	**INFORMAL I**	yakoo	yakumai
	II	yaku daroo	yakanai daroo
	FORMAL I	yakimasyoo	yakimasumai
	II	yaku desyoo	yakanai desyoo
Provisional	**INFORMAL**	yakeba	yakanakereba
	FORMAL	yakimaseba	yakimaseñ nara
		yakimasureba	
Gerund	**INFORMAL I**	yaite	yakanai de
	II		yakanakute
	FORMAL	yakimasite	yakimaseñ de
Past Ind.	**INFORMAL**	yaita	yakanakatta
	FORMAL	yakimasita	yakimaseñ desita
Past Presump.	**INFORMAL**	yaitaroo	yakanakattaroo
		yaita daroo	yakanakatta daroo
	FORMAL	yakimasitaroo	yakimaseñ desitaroo
		yaita desyoo	yakanakatta desyoo
Conditional	**INFORMAL**	yaitara	yakanakattara
	FORMAL	yakimasitara	yakimaseñ desitara
Alternative	**INFORMAL**	yaitari	yakanakattari
	FORMAL	yakimasitari	yakimaseñ desitari

		INFORMAL AFFIRMATIVE INDICATIVE
Passive		yakareru
Potential		yakeru
Causative		yakaseru
Causative Pass.		yakaserareru

Honorific	**I**	oyaki ni naru
	II	oyaki nasaru
Humble	**I**	oyaki suru
	II	oyaki itasu

TRANSITIVE   *to stop, to give up* (doing something)

			AFFIRMATIVE	NEGATIVE
Indicative	**INFORMAL**		yameru	yamenai
	FORMAL		yamemasu	yamemaseñ
Imperative	**INFORMAL**	I	yamero	yameru na
		II	yamenasai	yamenasaru na
		III	yamete kudasai	yamenai de kudasai
	FORMAL		oyame nasaimase	oyame nasaimasu na
Presumptive	**INFORMAL**	I	yameyoo	yamemai
		II	yameru daroo	yamenai daroo
	FORMAL	I	yamemasyoo	yamemasumai
		II	yameru desyoo	yamenai desyoo
Provisional	**INFORMAL**		yamereba	yamenakereba
	FORMAL		yamemaseba	yamemaseñ nara
			yamemasureba	
Gerund	**INFORMAL**	I	yamete	yamenai de
		II		yamenakute
	FORMAL		yamemasite	yamemaseñ de
Past Ind.	**INFORMAL**		yameta	yamenakatta
	FORMAL		yamemasita	yamemaseñ desita
Past Presump.	**INFORMAL**		yametaroo	yamenakattaroo
			yameta daroo	yamenakatta daroo
	FORMAL		yamemasitaroo	yamemaseñ desitaroo
			yameta desyoo	yamenakatta desyoo
Conditional	**INFORMAL**		yametara	yamenakattara
	FORMAL		yamemasitara	yamemaseñ desitara
Alternative	**INFORMAL**		yametari	yamenakattari
	FORMAL		yamesmasitari	yamemaseñ desitari

INFORMAL AFFIRMATIVE INDICATIVE

Passive	yamerareru
Potential	yamerareru
Causative	yamesaseru
Causative Pass.	yamesaserareru

Honorific	I	oyame ni naru
	II	oyame nasaru
Humble	I	oyame suru
	II	oyame itasu

			AFFIRMATIVE	NEGATIVE
Indicative	INFORMAL		yaru	yaranai
	FORMAL		yarimasu	yarimaseñ
Imperative	INFORMAL	I	yare	yaru na
		II	yarinasai	yarinasaru na
		III	yatte kudasai	yaranai de kudasai
	FORMAL		oyari nasaimase	oyari nasaimasu na
Presumptive	INFORMAL	I	yaroo	yarumai
		II	yaru daroo	yaranai daroo
	FORMAL	I	yarimasyoo	yarimasumai
		II	yaru desyoo	yaranai desyoo
Provisional	INFORMAL		yareba	yaranakereba
	FORMAL		yarimaseba	yarimaseñ nara
			yarimasureba	
Gerund	INFORMAL	I	yatte	yaranai de
		II		yaranakute
	FORMAL		yarimasite	yarimaseñ de
Past Ind.	INFORMAL		yatta	yaranakatta
	FORMAL		yarimasita	yarimaseñ desita
Past Presump.	INFORMAL		yattaroo	yaranakattaroo
			yatta daroo	yaranakatta daroo
	FORMAL		yarimasitaroo	yarimaseñ desitaroo
			yatta desyoo	yaranakatta desyoo
Conditional	INFORMAL		yattara	yaranakattara
	FORMAL		yarimasitara	yarimaseñ desitara
Alternative	INFORMAL		yattari	yaranakattari
	FORMAL		yarimasitari	yarimaseñ desitari

		INFORMAL AFFIRMATIVE INDICATIVE
Passive		yarareru
Potential		yareru
Causative		yaraseru
Causative Pass.		yaraserareru

Honorific	I	oyari ni naru
	II	oyari nasaru
Humble		

			AFFIRMATIVE	NEGATIVE
Indicative	**INFORMAL**		yaseru	yasenai
	FORMAL		yasemasu	yasemaseñ
Imperative	**INFORMAL**	I	yasero	yaseru na
		II	yasenasai	yasenasaru na
		III	yasete kudasai	yasenai de kudasai
	FORMAL		oyase nasaimase	oyase nasaimasu na
Presumptive	**INFORMAL**	I	yaseyoo	yasemai
		II	yaseru daroo	yasenai daroo
	FORMAL	I	yasemasyoo	yasemasumai
		II	yaseru desyoo	yasenai desyoo
Provisional	**INFORMAL**		yasereba	yasenakereba
	FORMAL		yasemaseba	yasemaseñ nara
			yasemasureba	
Gerund	**INFORMAL**	I	yasete	yasenai de
		II		yasenakute
	FORMAL		yasemasite	yasemaseñ de
Past Ind.	**INFORMAL**		yaseta	yasenakatta
	FORMAL		yasemasita	yasemaseñ desita
Past Presump.	**INFORMAL**		yasetaroo	yasenakattaroo
			yaseta daroo	yasenakatta daroo
	FORMAL		yasemasitaroo	yasemaseñ desitaroo
			yaseta desyoo	yasenakatta desyoo
Conditional	**INFORMAL**		yasetara	yasenakattara
	FORMAL		yasemasitara	yasemaseñ desitara
Alternative	**INFORMAL**		yasetari	yasenakattari
	FORMAL		yasemasitari	yasemaseñ desitari

		INFORMAL AFFIRMATIVE INDICATIVE
Passive		yaserareru
Potential		yaserareru
Causative		yasesaseru
Causative Pass.		yasesaserareru
Honorific	I	oyase ni naru
	II	oyase nasaru
Humble		

			AFFIRMATIVE	NEGATIVE
Indicative	INFORMAL		yasumu	yasumanai
	FORMAL		yasumimasu	yasumimaseñ
Imperative	INFORMAL	I	yasume	yasumu na
		II	yasuminasai	yasuminasaru na
		III	yasuñde kudasai	yasumanai de kudasai
	FORMAL		oyasumi nasaimase	oyasumi nasaimasu na
Presumptive	INFORMAL	I	yasumoo	yasumumai
		II	yasumu daroo	yasumanai daroo
	FORMAL	I	yasumimasyoo	yasumimasumai
		II	yasumu desyoo	yasumanai desyoo
Provisional	INFORMAL		yasumeba	yasumanakereba
	FORMAL		yasumimaseba	yasumimaseñ nara
			yasumimasureba	
Gerund	INFORMAL	I	yasuñde	yasumanai de
		II		yasumanakute
	FORMAL		yasumimasite	yasumimaseñ de
Past Ind.	INFORMAL		yasuñda	yasumanakatta
	FORMAL		yasumimasita	yasumimaseñ desita
Past Presump.	INFORMAL		yasuñdaroo	yasumanakattaroo
			yasuñda daroo	yasumanakatta daroo
	FORMAL		yasumimasitaroo	yasumimaseñ desitaroo
			yasuñda desyoo	yasumanakatta desyoo
Conditional	INFORMAL		yasuñdara	yasumanakattara
	FORMAL		yasumimasitara	yasumimaseñ desitara
Alternative	INFORMAL		yasuñdari	yasumimasitari
	FORMAL		yasumimasitaroo	yasumimaseñ desitaroo

	INFORMAL AFFIRMATIVE INDICATIVE
Passive	yasumareru
Potential	yasumeru
Causative	yasumaseru
Causative Pass.	yasumaserareru

Honorific	I	oyasumi ni naru
	II	oyasumi nasaru
Humble		

			AFFIRMATIVE	NEGATIVE
Indicative	INFORMAL		yobu	yobanai
	FORMAL		yobimasu	yobimaseñ
Imperative	INFORMAL	I	yobe	yobu na
		II	yobinasai	yobinasaru na
		III	yoñde kudasai	yobanai de kudasai
	FORMAL		oyobi nasaimase	oyobi nasaimasu na
Presumptive	INFORMAL	I	yoboo	yobumai
		II	yobu daroo	yobanai daroo
	FORMAL	I	yobimasyoo	yobimasumai
		II	yobu desyoo	yobanai desyoo
Provisional	INFORMAL		yobeba	yobanakereba
	FORMAL		yobimaseba	yobimaseñ nara
			yobimasureba	
Gerund	INFORMAL	I	yoñde	yobanai de
		II		yobanakute
	FORMAL		yobimasite	yobimaseñ de
Past Ind.	INFORMAL		yoñda	yobanakatta
	FORMAL		yobimasita	yobimaseñ desita
Past Presump.	INFORMAL		yoñdaroo	yobanakattaroo
			yoñda daroo	yobanakatta daroo
	FORMAL		yobimasitaroo	yobimaseñ desitaroo
			yoñda desyoo	yobanakatta desyoo
Conditional	INFORMAL		yoñdara	yobanakattara
	FORMAL		yobimasitara	yobimaseñ desitara
Alternative	INFORMAL		yoñdari	yobanakattari
	FORMAL		yobimasitari	yobimaseñ desitari

		INFORMAL AFFIRMATIVE INDICATIVE
Passive		yobareru
Potential		yoberu
Causative		yobaseru
Causative Pass.		yobaserareru

Honorific	I	oyobi ni naru
	II	oyobi nasaru
Humble	I	oyobi suru
	II	oyobi itasu

		AFFIRMATIVE	NEGATIVE
Indicative	INFORMAL	yomu	yomanai
	FORMAL	yomimasu	yomimaseñ
Imperative	INFORMAL I	yome	yomu na
	II	yominasai	yominasaru na
	III	yoñde kudasai	yomanai de kudasai
	FORMAL	oyomi nasaimase	oyomi nasaimasu na
Presumptive	INFORMAL I	yomoo	yomumai
	II	yomu daroo	yomanai daroo
	FORMAL I	yomimasyoo	yomimasumai
	II	yomu desyoo	yomanai desyoo
Provisional	INFORMAL	yomeba	yomanakereba
	FORMAL	yomimaseba	yomimaseñ nara
		yomimasureba	
Gerund	INFORMAL I	yoñde	yomanai de
	II		yomanakute
	FORMAL	yomimasite	yomimaseñ de
Past Ind.	INFORMAL	yoñda	yomanakatta
	FORMAL	yomimasita	yomimaseñ desita
Past Presump.	INFORMAL	yoñdaroo	yomanakattaroo
		yoñda daroo	yomanakatta daroo
	FORMAL	yomimasitaroo	yomimaseñ desitaroo
		yoñda desyoo	yomanakatta desyoo
Conditional	INFORMAL	yoñdara	yomanakattara
	FORMAL	yomimasitara	yomimaseñ desitara
Alternative	INFORMAL	yoñdari	yomanakattari
	FORMAL	yomimasitari	yomimaseñ desitari

	INFORMAL AFFIRMATIVE INDICATIVE
Passive	yomareru
Potential	yomeru
Causative	yomaseru
Causative Pass.	yomaserareru

Honorific	I	oyomi ni naru
	II	oyomi nasaru
Humble	I	oyomi suru
	II	oyomi itasu

yorokobi

TRANSITIVE

yorokob.u
to be happy, to rejoice

		AFFIRMATIVE	NEGATIVE
Indicative	**INFORMAL**	yorokobu	yorokobanai
	FORMAL	yorokobimasu	yorokobimaseñ
Imperative	**INFORMAL** I	yorokobe	yorokobu na
	II	yorokobinasai	yorokobinasaru na
	III	yorokoñde kudasai	yorokobanai de kudasai
	FORMAL	oyorokobi nasaimase	oyorokobi nasaimasu na
Presumptive	**INFORMAL** I	yorokoboo	yorokobumai
	II	yorokobu daroo	yorokobanai daroo
	FORMAL I	yorokobimasyoo	yorokobimasumai
	II	yorokobu desyoo	yorokobanai desyoo
Provisional	**INFORMAL**	yorokobeba	yorokobanakereba
	FORMAL	yorokobimaseba	yorokobimaseñ nara
		yorokobimasureba	
Gerund	**INFORMAL** I	yorokoñde	yorokobanai de
	II		yorokobanakute
	FORMAL	yorokobimasite	yorokobimaseñ de
Past Ind.	**INFORMAL**	yorokoñda	yorokobanakatta
	FORMAL	yorokobimasita	yorokobimaseñ desita
Past Presump.	**INFORMAL**	yorokoñdaroo	yorokobanakattaroo
		yorokoñda daroo	yorokobanakatta daroo
	FORMAL	yorokobimasitaroo	yorokobimaseñ desitaroo
		yorokoñda desyoo	yorokobanakatta desyoo
Conditional	**INFORMAL**	yorokoñdara	yorokobanakattara
	FORMAL	yorokobimasitara	yorokobimaseñ desitara
Alternative	**INFORMAL**	yorokoñdari	yorokobanakattari
	FORMAL	yorokobimasitari	yorokobimaseñ desitari

	INFORMAL AFFIRMATIVE INDICATIVE
Passive	yorokobareru
Potential	yorokoberu
Causative	yorokobaseru
Causative Pass.	yorokobaserareru

Honorific	I	oyorokobi ni naru
	II	oyorokobi nasaru
Humble	I	oyorokobi suru
	II	oyorokobi itasu

201

English — Japanese Index

This index includes all of the verbs found in the foregoing tables. Transitive verbs are followed by *T*.

Index of Informal Affirmative Gerunds Identified by Citation Form

n the early stages of learning Japanese, students often have trouble in identifying verb on the basis of its informal affirmative gerund. The following index should be of some help in this respect. It lists alphabetically all the informal affirmative gerunds found in the text and gives the citation form of the verb or verbs which correspond to each gerund.

The sound changes which occur when forming the gerund also take place when any suffix beginning with -t is added to the verb stem. Therefore, this index will also help in identifying a verb by its (informal affirmative) past indicative, conditional, or alternative forms. For example: the gerund of a verb whose past indicative is *todoketa* will be *todokete*; that of a verb whose past indicative is *totta* will be *totte*. Consulting our list of gerunds we find that these belong to *todokeru* (p. 166) and *toru* (p. 172), and if we consult the tables for these verbs we will find that, indeed, their past indicative forms are *todoketa* and *totta* respectively.

A

agatte **agaru**
agete **ageru**
akete **akeru**
aratte **arau**
arawarete **arawareru**
arawasite **arawasu**
aruite **aruku**
asoñde **asobu**
atte **aru, au**
azukete **azukeru**

D

damasite **damasu**
dasite **dasu**
dekite **dekiru**
dete **deru**

H

haite **haku**
haitte **hairu**
hakatte **hakaru**
hanasite **hanasu**
haratte **harau**
harete **hareru**
hataraite **hataraku**
hayatte **hayaru**
hazimatte **hazimaru**
hazimete **hazimeru**

hiite **hiku**
hirotte **hirou**
huite **huku**
hutotte **hutoru**
hutte **huru**

I

irasite **irassyaru**
irassyatte **irassyaru**
irete **ireru**
isoide **isogu**
itadaite **itadaku**
itañde **itamu**
itasite **itasu**
ite **iru (to exist)**
itte **iku, iru (to be necessary), iu**

K

kaesite **kaesu**
kaete **kaeru (to change)**
kaette **kaeru (to return)**
kaite **kaku**
kakete **kakeru**
kamatte **kamau**
kañgaete **kañgaeru**
karite **kariru**
kasite **kasu**
katazukete **katazukeru**
katte **katu, kau**

207

kawaite kawaku
kawatte kawaru
kayotte kayou
kazoete kazoeru
kesite kesu
kiete kieru
kiite kiku
kikaete kikaeru
kikoete kikoeru
kimete kimeru
kite kiru (to wear), kuru
kitte kiru (to cut)
koborete koboreru
kobosite kobosu
komatte komaru
koñde komu
konoñde konomu
kootte kooru
korosite korosu
kotaete kotaeru
kotowatte kotowaru
kowarete kowareru
kowasite kowasu
kudasatte kudasaru
kumotte kumoru
kurabete kuraberu
kurete kureru

M

magatte magaru
magete mageru
maitte mairu
makasite makasu
makete makeru
matigatte matigau
matte matu
mazete mazeru
miete mieru
migaite migaku
misete miseru
mite miru
mitomete mitomeru
mitukatte mitukaru
mitukete mitukeru
mookete mookeru
moratte morau
motte motu

N

naite naku
naosite naosu
naotte naoru
narabete naraberu
naratte narau
nasatte nasaru
natte naru
nete neru
nigete nigeru
nigitte nigiru
nobotte noboru
nokotte nokoru
noñde nomu
nosete noseru
notte noru
nurete nureru
nusuñde nusumu
nutte nuru

O

oboete oboeru
odoroite odoroku
odotte odoru
oite oku
okite okiru
okosite okosu
okutte okuru
omotte omou
orite oriru
osiete osieru
ossyatte ossyaru
otite otiru
otosite otosu
owatte owaru
oyoide oyogu

S

sagasite sagasu
saite saku
sawaide sawagu
sibatte sibaru
siite siku
sikatte sikaru

simatte **simaru**
simete **simeru**
siñde **sinu**
sirabete **siraberu**
site **suru**
sitte **siru**
sizuñde **sizumu**
sodatete **sodateru**
sugite **sugiru**
suite **suku**
sumasete **sumaseru**
suñde **sumu**
sutete **suteru**
suwatte **suwaru**

T

tabete **taberu**
-tagatte **-tagaru**
tanoñde **tanomu**
taorete **taoreru**
taosite **taosu**
tarite **tariru**
tasukete **tasukeru**
tatete **tateru**
tatte **tatu**
tetudatte **tetudau**
tigatte **tigau**
todoite **todoku**
todokete **todokeru**
tokete **tokeru**
tomatte **tomaru**
tomete **tomeru**
toñde **tobu**
tootte **tooru**
totte **toru**

tuite **tuku**
tukamaete **tukamaeru**
tukarete **tukareru**
tukatte **tukau**
tukiatte **tukiau**
tukutte **tukuru**
tumotte **tumoru**
tutaete **tutaeru**
tutomete **tutomeru**
tutuñde **tutumu**
tuzukete **tuzukeru**

U

uete **ueru**
ugoite **ugoku**
ukañde **ukabu**
umarete **umareru**
utatte **utau**
utte **uru, utu**

W

wakatte **wakaru**
waratte **warau**
wasurete **wasureru**

Y

yaite **yaku**
yamete **yameru**
yasete **yaseru**
yasuñde **yasumu**
yatte **yaru**
yoñde **yobu, yomu**
yorokoñde **yorokobu**

JAPANESE FOR BEGINNERS   Developed from Japanese courses offered at the Osaka University of Foreign Studies

Here is a simplified text designed especially for people with no background in Japanese that teaches basic conversational skills in a practical, efficient manner. The thirty-lesson format emphasizes natural Japanese—the everyday language of the people. All explanations and grammar rules are given in easy-to-understand English and conversational Japanese is presented in Romanized script. Suitable for self-study or classroom. $19.95 May be used in conjunction with two sixty-minute pre-recorded cassette tapes. Please see order form on next page to order both items.

BARRON'S EDUCATIONAL SERIES, INC. / WOODBURY, N.Y.

JAPANESE FOR TODAY   **Developed from Japanese courses offered at the Osaka University of Foreign Studies**

This companion to *Japanese for Beginners* helps students lay the foundation for active participation in Japanese life. Its comprehensive approach uses *kanji* and *kana* to introduce conversational Japanese. Each of the thirty lessons contain presentations, grammar explanations, practice exercises, conversations, and readings that may be adapted to individual needs. Students who master this text are sure to have a firm grasp of contemporary written and spoken Japanese. $29.95 Eight cassette tapes have been designed to accompany the text. Please see order form on next page to order both items.

BARRON'S EDUCATIONAL SERIES, INC. / WOODBURY, N.Y.

How to Write
Better Résumés
By Adele Lewis Pres., Career Blazers Agency, Inc.

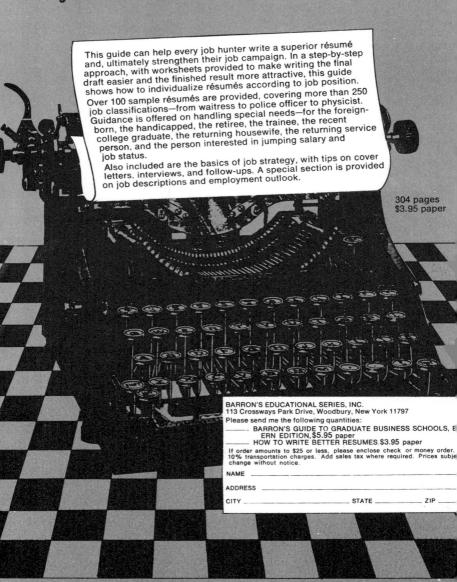

This guide can help every job hunter write a superior résumé and, ultimately strengthen their job campaign. In a step-by-step approach, with worksheets provided to make writing the final draft easier and the finished result more attractive, this guide shows how to individualize résumés according to job position.

Over 100 sample résumés are provided, covering more than 250 job classifications—from waitress to police officer to physicist. Guidance is offered on handling special needs—for the foreign-born, the handicapped, the retiree, the trainee, the recent college graduate, the returning housewife, the returning service person, and the person interested in jumping salary and job status.

Also included are the basics of job strategy, with tips on cover letters, interviews, and follow-ups. A special section is provided on job descriptions and employment outlook.

304 pages
$3.95 paper